INDIGENOUS PEOPLES
and
INTERNATIONAL ORGANISATIONS

Compiled and edited by
Lydia van de Fliert

SPOKESMAN

Lydia van de Fliert is a cultural anthropologist and parliamentary research assistant to Ken Coates MEP, the president of the European Parliament's Sub Committee on Human Rights.

First published in Great Britain in 1994 by
Spokesman
Bertrand Russell House
Gamble Street
Nottingham, England
Tel. 0602 708318
Fax 0602 420433

Copyright © Spokesman, 1994

All rights reserved.
Enquiries should be addressed to the publishers.

British Library Cataloguing in Publication Data available on request.
ISBN 0-85124-566-8 cloth
ISBN 0-85124-567-6 paper

Printed by the Russell Press Ltd, Nottingham
(Tel. 0602 784505)

Contents

Foreword by *Ken Coates* MEP — v

Acknowledgements — vi

Introduction by *Lydia van de Fliert* — 1

PART 1 — SUPRANATIONAL AND INTERGOVERNMENTAL ORGANISATIONS

I. Supranational: — 11
   The Institutions of the European Union and Indigenous Peoples
   Lydia van de Fliert
   1. The European Parliament — 15
   2. The Council of Ministers — 30
   3. The Commission — 34

II. Intergovernmental: — 54
    The United Nations System and Indigenous Peoples
    1. International Labour Organisation and Convention 169
       a. The ILO and Indigenous and Tribal Peoples, — 56
          Lee Swepston and Manuela Tomei
       b. Convention 169 concerning Indigenous and Tribal Peoples — 64
          in Independent Countries
    2. The World Bank and Operational Directive 4.20
       a. The World Bank and Indigenous Peoples, *Shelton Davis* — 75
       b. Operational Directive 4.20 on Indigenous Peoples — 83
    3. United Nations Working Group on Indigenous Populations
       a. The United Nations and Indigenous Peoples, *Julian Burger* — 90
       b. The UNWGIP final Draft Declaration on Indigenous Peoples, — 96
          1993
    4. United Nations Development Programme (UNDP)
       a. UNDP and the International Year of the World's Indigenous — 104
          Peoples, *Marcel Viergever*
       b. The International Year for the World's Indigenous Peoples, — 108
          Report of the Administrator
    5. United Nations Educational, Scientific and Cultural — 111
       Organisation (UNESCO), *Barbara Ischinger*
    6. United Nations High Commission for Refugees (UNHCR), — 113
       Kate Jastram Balian

	7. International Fund for Agriculture and Development (IFAD), *Roberto Haudry de Soucy*	115
	8. 1993, Year of the World's Indigenous People — A New Partnership, *Helen McLaughlin*	119
III.	Regional Intergovernmental Organisations: The Inter American System	
	1. a. Human Rights Protection for Indigenous Peoples in the Inter-American System, *Felipe Sanchez Rodriguez and Denise Gilman*	125
	b. Presenting Cases before the Inter-American System: The Example of CEJIL, a Consortium of NGOs *Jose Miguel Vivanco*	131
	2. The Indigenous Peoples Fund (IPF)	137

PART 2 — NON-GOVERNMENTAL ORGANISATIONS

Indigenous Peoples and Protected Areas

I.	The World Wildlife Fund, *Elizabeth Kempf*	143
II.	Amnesty International, *Tracy Ulltveit-Moe*	153

ANNEXES

I.	Resolutions on indigenous peoples adopted by the European Parliament	163
II.	European Commission Involvement in Indigenous Peoples' Projects	174
III.	United Nations Conference on Environment and Development (UNCED)	181
	1. a. The Kari-Oca Conference in Rio, *Marcos Terena* b. The Kari-Oca Declaration	
	2. Statement of Principles on Forests	
	3. Convention on Biological Diversity	
	4. Rio-Declaration on Environment and Development	
	5. Agenda 21: Chapter 11 and Chapter 26	
IV.	B'okob' Declaration of the First World Summit of Indigenous Peoples	194
V.	Declaration of the World Conference on Human Rights and the role of indigenous people	196

Foreword
by Ken Coates MEP

Over time, there has been a steady growth in the awareness among peoples of the countries which call themselves "advanced", that indigenous people throughout the world are suffering deep discrimination. Harrowing reports demonstrate such suffering to be very much alive, and continuous.

More than fifteen years ago, a dedicated, but largely isolated, group of European activists joined forces to create a Russell Tribunal on the Rights of the Indians of the Americas. This, the fourth Russell Tribunal, gathered in Rotterdam, long ago in 1980. How amateur we all were! And how few! Today the conferences gather under the flag of the United Nations and express concerns which are truly world-wide.

In retrospect, it is easy to see that the growth of environmental concern, in a world which has been choking in the poisons it has itself created, was itself bound to alert men and women to the plight of indigenous peoples. Had such peoples not developed, over many centuries, complex cultures and intricately balanced eco-systems? The contrast was surely apparent to anyone who cared to think about it. Modern industrial civilisation has created overpowering ecological problems, within the limited space of a couple of hundred years. Today it takes only months to destroy an evolution which took millions of years to develop.

These recent years have been dominated by the ethos of conflict with nature, in which men and women have sought to "subjugate" natural forces, "harness" natural laws, "tame" the wild. But the uncountable earlier centuries had developed very differently, and throughout much of their evolution, with notions of greater or lesser harmony with the planet's life-sustaining systems. Civilised people frequently invoke the idea of nature as "red in tooth and claw". It is easy to understand why, and the perception is not without force. But redder by far in claw and tooth has been the advance of civilisation.

Within a few millennia, technologies have evolved which have multiplied a million-fold the damage that people can do to one another, and to their natural environment.

The later eighties became aware of a watershed as preparations were made to mark the five hundredth anniversary of the arrival of Christopher Columbus in the Americas. While there were many conventional accounts of the valour of those European explorers, there were also more and louder voices ready to speak of the suffering of the peoples who were "discovered", usually to their very great cost. That debate peaked in 1992, because there is magic in numbers, even in the sophisticated modern world. International organisations, in particular, go forward from anniversary to anniversary, as if the future had never been discovered. As a result, 1993 was designated, by the United Nations, as the Year of the Indigenous Peoples. Perhaps because consciences had already been touched, the thought arose that a year might not be quite enough to encompass all the necessary repentence, and so it came about that the Decade of the Indigenous Peoples was also named.

The European Parliament has constantly been reminded of the problems of indigenous peoples, as their pressure groups have discovered how to lobby in Europe, and a wide variety of human and civil rights groupings have agreed to joint action with them.

The Sub-committee on Human Rights has been the target for many lobbyists, and as its Chairman I have received countless deputations, petitions and memoranda. I could never have coped with this extraordinary workload, if it were not for the tireless work of Lydia van de Fliert, who has now devoted her talents to preparing this book, as a guide to the policies and programmes of international organisations on the indigenes. It is a labour of love, and I am sure that it will be extremely useful. Unfortunately, this record maps only something of what has been done. What remains to be done will fill many, many more volumes. Alas!

* * *

Acknowledgements

I am grateful to all contributors to this book, without whose support and enthusiasm this project would never have worked. Hopefully fruitful working relations and coordination will develop and improve between all these different international organisations. But most of all, in the light of the International Decade of the World's Indigenous People, I hope a genuine partnership results between international organisations and indigenous peoples.

I am particularly indebted to Manuela Tomei, Sian Petman and Maire McCormack, and also want to thank Tracy Ulltveit Moe, Julian Burger, Barry Waters, Kenny Bell, Peter Asman, Richard Corbett, Sabine Luning, Tiemo Oostenbrink, Matthew Cowey, Ken Fleet and Tony Simpson for their advice and support. I am most grateful to Ken Coates for all his encouragement. We also gratefully acknowledge Broederlijk Delen's financial contribution to the publication of this book.

Lydia van de Fliert
June 1994

Introduction
by Lydia van de Fliert

This book is divided into two parts.

Part I seeks to explain the policies and programmes of supranational and intergovernmental organisations with regard to indigenous peoples. It presents a series of recent and relevant resolutions, declarations, policy directives and conventions concerning Indigenous Peoples drawn up by the UN system (the ILO, the World Bank, etc.), the Organisation of American States and the European Community. The potential value and shortcomings of these instruments are considered and analyzed in contribution by experts, some of whom are directly involved in their implementation.

Part II looks at the policies of two international Non-Governmental Organisations (NGOs), one, Amnesty International, dealing with global human rights issues, and the other, the World Wildlife Fund and IUCN (World Conservation Union), concentrating on environmental matters, but both, from their different perspectives, concerned with the situation of indigenous peoples. Amnesty International initiated an 'Indigenous Peoples of the Americas Programme' in 1992. WWF and IUCN (World Conservation Union) have recently reshaped their policy on the role of indigenous peoples and protected areas.

The *Annex* contains the resolutions adopted by the European Parliament, the projects supported by the European Commission, declarations, statements and resolutions adopted at United Nations Conference on Environment and Development (UNCED), the final Declaration of the Vienna World Conference on Human Rights (June 1993) and the B'okob' Declaration of the First World Summit of Indigenous Peoples in Guatemala (May 1993). It also contains a short list of addresses of international indigenous peoples organisations and support groups.

The purpose of the book

In recent years, various bodies of the European Parliament, individual Members and their assistants have met with representatives of Indigenous Peoples who have been visiting Brussels or Strasbourg in increasing numbers. At such meetings, the indigenous representatives repeatedly sought a comprehensive overview of the activities of the European Community and other international organisations in the field of indigenous peoples, development and human rights. The number of international organisations adopting resolutions concerning indigenous peoples, drafting policy guidelines, or creating special funds has been growing rapidly. As 1992 marked the quincentenary of Columbus' arrival in the Americas, 1993 has been designated by the UN as the year of the World's

Indigenous People and as the General Assembly has proclaimed the International Decade of the Worlds' Indigenous People, commencing on 10 December 1994, there could not be a more appropriate time to respond to this request.

The purpose of this book is not to provide a philosophical description of the important role which indigenous peoples play in our world. Nor is it to offer an account of the wrongs that are still being committed against indigenous peoples. Rather the purpose is to present an overview of official policies on indigenous peoples and funds established to support them. The book is more about international organisations, than about indigenous peoples and will hopefully serve to facilitate access to such organisations which too often appear complex and remote. It attempts to bring the "Culture of International Organisations" closer to the people affected by its decisions. It thus aims to provide a tool to all those concerned with the situation of indigenous peoples, in particular indigenous representatives, seeking to improve the design and implementation of international standards, policies and funds. The reinforcement of international legal instruments should contribute to improving the situation of indigenous peoples if efforts are pursued to secure its application at national level. States and international organisations must be held accountable for the implementation of their policies and allocation of funding. It is in the interest of us all that sophisticated international declarations touch the real life of indigenous communities and will be more than "paper tigers".

Growing awareness

In recent years the World's Indigenous Peoples have become the focus of international attention and have stepped into the limelight — not in the shadow of the disappearing tropical forest or of rare animals — but in their own capacity. There has been a remarkable growth of interest in indigenous peoples — their plight, their cultures and their highly refined knowledge and understanding of complex ecosystems in which many of them live. Western advertising agencies are now searching for indigenous models in order to portray them as stereotypes belonging to a "disappearing world of exotic wilderness". No longer is it merely anthropologists, romantic idealists or support groups which take an interest in indigenous cultures but also governments, UN agencies, the European Community, and the Nobel Peace Prize Committee.

To a large extent, this rise in awareness can be attributed to the ceaseless endeavours of indigenous peoples themselves to draw attention to their plight, prompting an awakening consciousness and curiosity about their cause and cultures in the industrialised countries. It is worth trying to understand why after so many years of practically ignoring their existence, the West is becoming more receptive and wishes to learn about the cultures and survival of indigenous peoples. A growing concern about human rights, environmental protection and inter-ethnic conflicts are important reasons, but not the only ones. Could it be that the state of economic depression in the world has led to further alienation between the individual and the industrialised society and has inspired a renewed search for different value systems?

Numerous statements and several international legal instruments concerning indigenous peoples have come into being since 1989. The important role of NGOs providing checks and balances against abuse of organisations, states and groups of states should, however, not be neglected (for examples of their work, see Part 1, IIIb, Part 2 and Annex 3). As an example of Inter Governmental (IGO) initiatives, it is important to cite the new instrument of international law adopted by the International Labour Organisation (ILO) in 1989, the Indigenous and Tribal Peoples Convention (No.169). In September 1991, the World Bank took a remarkable step by adopting Operational Directive 4.20 on Indigenous Peoples to ensure that they are not adversely affected by Bank projects and that the social and economic benefits they receive are in harmony with their cultural preferences. The Asian Development Bank in 1991 adopted guidelines for Social Analysis of Bank projects which place special emphasis on projects affecting "ethnic minorities". In 1992, the Conference on Security and Cooperation in Europe (CSCE), at the Helsinki II meeting, included provision 29 regarding Indigenous People in the chapter on Human Development. Thereby it opened the possibility for indigenous peoples to make use of CSCE mechanisms. That same year, Pope John Paul II made a statement publicly "calling on the descendants of the Indigenous Peoples of the Americas to forgive the Spanish conquerors for abuses committed when colonising the continent". The president of Bolivia launched an initiative to establish the Indigenous Peoples Fund. Also in 1992, the Inter-American Commission began the preparation of a new instrument on indigenous rights. In 1993, the European Community considerably increased its funds for indigenous peoples' projects and many UN Agencies appointed "focal points" for all questions related to indigenous peoples. The Dutch government adopted a government policy in 1993 with respect to the issue of indigenous peoples in the context of foreign policy and development cooperation. Under the new Dutch policy on indigenous peoples, legal protection, human rights, reinforcement of indigenous cultures and increased participation and representation in national and international fora are considered the pillars of its policy.[1] In December 1993, the Australian Parliament adopted a new law recognising native title rights if Aboriginals had maintained a close association with a piece of land. With that ruling, the doctrine of *terra nullius* was overturned. Having declared 1993 the year of the World Indigenous People, the UN General Assembly went further deciding to declare the next 10 years its 'Decade of Indigenous People'.

In view of all these new developments, it is becoming increasingly difficult to find a way through the thicket of initiatives that are emerging. In light of the chosen theme for 1993: "Indigenous People, a new partnership", we hope that this compilation of international policies and instruments will help to show a route through the jungle.

Some clarifications

For the purpose of clarification, some basic concepts used throughout the book are introduced below.

The concept of Indigenous Peoples

According to the United Nations there are approximately 300 million Indigenous People worldwide. Indigenous societies are very heterogeneous. There are considerable differences in the lifestyles, cultures and political demands of the North American Indians, the Wanniya-Laeto from Shri Lanka or the Pygmies from Cameroon. Persons educated in indigenous societies will probably be as diverse as people brought up in industrialised circles or in any of the various sub-cultures which make up modern society. At the same time, the problems that indigenous peoples experience as a group are often remarkably similar: lack of statehood, economic and political marginalisation from mainstream society, cultural and racial discrimination and close attachment to the land.

It is also important to realise that the concept of indigenous peoples has been variously interpreted. While some anthropologists are increasingly critical of the term and reluctant to use it,[2] indigenous representatives are becoming more forthright in their wish that international fora adopt it and more convinced that their plight is unique and that they share a common destiny. The Kari-oca Declaration (see Annex 3), for instance, drafted and adopted at the Indigenous Peoples Conference in Rio during the UNCED, calls for the promotion of the term **Indigenous Peoples** in article 8.

These differences of opinion over the use of the term 'Indigenous Peoples' suggest that some caution should be applied when using it. It is by no means a clear term. Taken in isolation, it does not do sufficient justice to the complexity and dynamics of intercultural relations between "indigenous and other peoples". It is nonetheless an important notion. Some academic circles may find it controversial and ambiguous but in the political arena it has helped to focus the increasing interest in indigenous societies which could even be said to represent a new dimension in Western thinking about the meaning of culture, human rights and development.

In any event, a wide variety of international organisations have adopted the term and work with indigenous peoples all over the world. A frequently quoted definition is that given by the special UN rapporteur for the study on the problem of discrimination against Indigenous Peoples in 1984, Mr Martínez Cobo:

> "Indigenous communities, peoples and nations are those which, having a historical continuity with pre-invasion and pre-colonial societies that developed on their territories, consider themselves distinct from the other sectors of the societies now prevailing in those territories, or parts of them. They form at present non-dominant sectors of society and are determined to preserve, develop and transmit to future generations their ancestral territories, and their ethnic identity as the basis of their continued existence as peoples, in accordance with their own cultural patterns, social institutions and legal systems. In short, Indigenous Peoples are the descendants of the original inhabitants of a territory overcome by conquest or settlement by aliens."

The Martínez Cobo definition applies only to the indigenous peoples of the Americas, Australasia and the Pacific. The description of ILO Convention 169 (1989) is broader and applies to both tribal peoples "whose social, cultural and economic conditions distinguish them from other sections of the national community and whose status is regulated wholly or partially by their own customs or traditions or by special laws or regulations", and to peoples "who are regarded as indigenous on account of their descent from the populations which inhabited the country at the time of conquest or colonisation . . ." The most recent description of Indigenous Peoples is given by the World Bank (operational directive 4.20, 1991): "Indigenous Peoples can be identified in particular geographical areas by the presence in varying degrees of the following characteristics: (a) close attachment to ancestral territories and to the natural resources in these areas; (b) self-identification and identification by others as members of a distinct cultural group; (c) an indigenous language, often different from the national language; (d) presence of customary social and political institutions; and (e) primarily subsistence-oriented production."

The rights of peoples
It is considered of crucial importance by indigenous and some international organisations that the term *"peoples"* or "nations" is used and not 'populations', 'people' or 'minorities'. The Chairwoman of the UN Working Group on Indigenous Populations (Mrs E. Daes) calls the title of her own Working Group a 'relic of racism and racial discrimination'. The ILO abandoned the term Populations by adopting Convention 169 (on Indigenous and Tribal Peoples) which revised ILO Convention 107 (on Indigenous and Tribal Populations).[3] In international law, peoples have more rights than populations and people and indigenous peoples are not always minorities (in Guatemala some estimates suggest they may constitute as much as 65% of the population, other sources give even higher estimates). Peoples not only have the rights of an individual — e.g. civil, political, economic, social and cultural rights — but also those of collective entities, in particular the right to self-determination. "The Indigenous Peoples ask to be accorded the same rights which the UN accords to the other peoples of the world" said Chief Ten Moses of the Grand Council of the Crees at the Human Rights Conference in Vienna.[4]

Over the centuries, the notion of individual rights and freedoms has assumed a dominant position in Western political thinking and legal systems. This is generally considered an important accomplishment, particularly in Europe where ideologies placing the group above the individual and one race above all others have been a feature of times of great suffering, e.g. the upsurge of tribalism and bloodshed in Ex-Yugoslavia.

The rights of some peoples can not be considered superior to those of others. Indigenous Peoples are calling upon states to adopt pluralistic policies and recognise their right to be different, not superior. For Indigenous Peoples' respect for individual rights is inextricably linked to respect for *collective rights*. Rigoberta Menchú, who won the Nobel Peace Prize for 1992, refutes the argument that demands for collective rights generate nationalist or separatist conflicts: "Cultural diversity is not a danger to anyone. Ethnic multiplicity strengthens nations, it does not divide them. There would be a risk if the right to participation in the nation and the rights to be different are denied."[5] Collective rights in this sense are a supplement to individual rights and necessary to protect non-dominant groups in our societies. Inadequate grass-root participation in national decision making structures in many countries make it important that both individual and collective rights of Indigenous Peoples are defended. They also need to protect themselves against different forms of discrimination. Total misconception of the meaning of "culture" has caused racial discrimination against indigenous peoples for many centuries. Such discrimination has often been based on erroneous notions about the superiority of "western culture" over "primitive cultures". Future violations of indigenous peoples rights and discrimination against them must be prevented by improving the means of redress and enhancing the duties and accountability of States and international organisations towards indigenous peoples.

Self-determination; a key issue

Indigenous claims to *self-determination* are generally strongly opposed by States because they are interpreted as "claims to secession".[6] Self-determination, however, can take a variety of different forms. For example: In Nicaragua[7] two Autonomous Indigenous Regions were established in the Costa Atlantica. In Canada[8] the new northern territory of Nunavut for the Inuit is being created and will have the form of a public government complete with a legislative assembly. Another example from Canada is the model of regional government of the Naskapi and Cree Indians, where the indigenous peoples are responsible for the maintenance of public order, collecting certain taxes, issuing business permits, regulating land use and managing public health. In certain other circumstances, indigenous peoples enjoy limited rights of self-government, for example in the case of Greenland Home Rule and in Colombia ("resguardos").

During the Vienna Conference on Human Rights, the Chairperson of the UN Working Group on Indigenous Populations explained the issue of self-determination very clearly: "Since [some] indigenous peoples have an alternative vision of democracy, they should be given the opportunity to continue to provide us with a source of inspiration in our struggle for democracy and effective protection of human rights and freedoms worldwide. But they can only do this if their own distinct systems of government survive. It is essential that they be empowered to exercise political, legal and economic autonomy, including the control of their own environment and process of sustainable development. In this context, indigenous peoples should have the opportunity, in the free exercise of their right to self-determination, to negotiate new constitutional and other legislative arrangements with the governments and the legislative authorities in the States in which they live. These arrangements can guarantee indigenous peoples rights and strengthen national unity at the same time."[9]

The right to "Development"

The concept of development is of great significance to indigenous peoples. The 11th and final Draft Declaration prepared by the United Nations Working Group on Indigenous Populations (UNWGIP, see II-3) states that indigenous peoples have a right to development in accordance with their own needs and interests. Paragraph 66 of the Kari-Oca Declaration rejects "the current definition of development as being useful to our peoples".

However, doctrinaire beliefs in some models of economic development have made certain well-intentioned Western donors more preoccupied with bringing "development" to the "developing world" than with respecting the variety of needs of different peoples. "The economic viewpoint is notoriously colour blind" writes Wolfgang Sachs: it recognises the cost-yield relationship with extreme clarity, but it is hardly able to perceive other dimensions of reality; neither land nor work are for indigenous peoples mere production factors waiting to be optimally combined.[10] By way of illustration, in many indigenous languages, no words exist for terms such as "development" or "progress". In some African languages, development is sometimes described as "the creation of chaos". In Cameroon, the word for "project" is translated with "raising funds". The French concept of "planification" has even on occasions bee interpreted as: "la rêve du blanc" (the dream of the white man)!

Development has been described as: "a comfortably ethnocentric term, resting on assumptions of progress and inevitability, but it might better be replaced by a more accurate and less ethnocentric term such as 'transformation'. The social advantages of progress, as defined in terms of increased incomes, higher standards of living, greater security and better health, are thought to be positive, universal goods, to be obtained at virtually any price. While it may often be acknowledged that tribal peoples must sacrifice their traditional cultures to obtain these benefits, it is generally felt by government planners that this is a small price to pay for such obvious advantages."[11]

Indigenous Peoples themselves will determine the price they wish to pay for development. "We are not myths of the past, ruins in the jungle, or zoos", says Rigoberta Menchú, "we are people and we want to be respected, not to be victims of intolerance and racism." Both intolerant and patronising development programmes, reflecting a contempt for indigenous peoples lifestyles or the opposite, an ingenious idealisation of the same lifestyle, will stand in the way of indigenous peoples' development. Today, the term 'sustainable development' is used to describe an indigenous way of relating to and using the environment. The "Charter of the Indigenous-tribal peoples of the tropical forests" (see Annex 6) proposes the following: National or international agencies considering funding development projects which may affect us, must set up tripartite commissions — including the funding agency, government representatives and our own communities as represented through our representative organisations — to carry through the planning implementation, monitoring and evaluation of the projects. Or, in the words of Marcos Terena, spokesman of the Indigenous Peoples at UNCED: *"Our great fear is to be developed without being consulted."*

The need for self-identification of peoples as "indigenous peoples" has been made all too evident by a long historic experience of injustices inflicted upon them by dominant states. Indigenous Peoples, by emphasising a common struggle for more justice, the need for better division of power and a quest for survival, contribute to the creation of a pluralistic world, more diverse than two mutually exclusive groups. Some indigenous peoples may wish to become assimilated into mainstream society, others will prefer to live according to their own cultural traditions. They must be free to choose, with their rights being respected and without the threat of extinction. The role of supranational and intergovernmental organisations is crucial. They are taking on the responsibility for the promotion of advanced policies to respect the rights of indigenous peoples which are often at odds with national policies and practices. The good intentions of international organisations have, however, to be converted into good deeds to make this happen.

References

1. On 29 March 1993, the Netherlands Minister for Foreign Affairs, and the Minister for Development Cooperation sent a memorandum to the Dutch Parliament, to inform it about the Netherlands Government Policy with respect to the issue of indigenous peoples in the context of foreign policy and development cooperation. In this memorandum, the Ministers also respond to the advisory reports submitted by the Advisory Committee on Human Rights and Foreign Policy and the National Advisory Council on Development Cooperation. *Indigenous Peoples in the Netherlands Foreign Policy and Development Cooperation*, 14 May, 1993, INFORMATIE, Voorlichtingsdienst Ontwikkelingssamenwerkingvan het Ministerie van Buitenlandse Zaken, 's Gravenhage.
2. "In the postmodern condition it has been claimed that there are no 'natives' left, meaning that there are no cultural isolates of which one can claim to be indigenous. We all live in a global village, where the speed of communication and the range of possibilities open to anyone makes all talk about cultures meaningless" in: Hastrup, Kirsten, *The native voice — and the anthropological vision*, Social Anthropology, the Journal of the European Association of Social Anthropologists, Cambridge University Press 1993.
3. Article I, subsection 3, of ILO Convention 169, however, reads: "The use of the term 'peoples' in this Convention shall not be construed as having any implications as regards the rights which may attach to the term under international law."
4. As stated in paragraph 1, Part II of the Declaration of the World Conference on Human Rights in Vienna, June 1993, "All peoples have the right of self-determination. By virtue of that right they freely determine their political status, and freely pursue their economic, social and cultural development." At the conference, some governments were persistent in rejecting any movement towards recognition of the word "peoples" for "indigenous peoples". The original Vienna Conference draft referred to peoples, as did the Bangkok and San Jose regional declarations. This was changed at the Fourth (and final) Prepcom (Preparatory Committee to the Vienna Conference) to "People", because of fear that indigenous peoples will interpret the right to self-determination as a right to secede from the nation-state within which they reside. Most governments of countries with indigenous peoples have made it clear that the right of indigenous peoples to determine freely their relations with States (see the first article of the Draft Declaration on Indigenous Peoples) can not imply any secession or separatism. The Chairwoman of the UN Working Group on Indigenous Populations told the Plenary in Vienna: "I share the pain and disappointment of the indigenous peoples at the use of the term 'people'."
5. *Terra Viva*, the independent daily of the World Conference on Human Rights in Vienna, Saturday, 19 June, 1993.
6. For a more detailed discussion of this concept than is given here, see the chapter of Julian Burger on the question of self-determination.
7. In 1987, after a long and, in the end, bitter confrontation between the Indigenous peoples of Nicaragua and the ruling Sandinista government, the latter recognised that their efforts to integrate the indigenous peoples into mainstream society had adverse effects and had created a lot of resistance. The Treaty of Autonomy of the Costa Atlantica was signed to guarantee self government for Nicaragua's Indigenous Peoples. This Treaty is unique in the context of the entire American continent, for it has made the establishment of a regional parliament and government possible. Two autonomous regions were created (RAAN and RAAS) that have judicial personality under public law. Each region has a Council of 45 elected members.
8. According to an official Canadian Government brochure, *Information*, "Beyond the referendum on aboriginal self-government", Indian and Northern Affairs, Canada, 1993, the right to self-government means First Nations having the right to make decisions on issues that directly affect their people. The Nunavut Final Land Claim Agreement, signed on May 15, 1993, finalises the settlement of the largest land claim agreement in Canada comprising 1.9 million square kilometres, one fifth of the land mass of Canada and gives the Inuit title to 350,000 square kilometres of Nunavut. Inuit will be full partners in the future economic and political development of their homeland.
9. Address at the World Conference on Human Rights, Austria Centre, 18 June 1993 by Professor Erica-Irene Daes, Chairperson-Rapporteur of the UN Working Group on Indigenous Populations.
10. "The Economist's prejudice", Essay no.4 of "The Archaeology of the Development Idea, Six Essays", Wolfgang Sachs, in: *Cultures and Development*, liaison bulletin of the South-North Network Cultures and Development, Brussels.
11. J.H. Bodley, *Victims of Progress*, 1982.

Part 1

Supranational and Intergovernmental Organisations

I. The Institutions of the European Union and Indigenous Peoples
by Lydia van de Fliert

The European Union[1] is a supranational organisation and presently has 12 Member States. The six founding countries — Belgium, France, Germany, Italy, Luxembourg and the Netherlands were later joined by Denmark, Ireland, the United Kingdom and Greece and finally in 1986 by Spain and Portugal. Despite difficulties and periodic crises, such as in recent years with the elaboration and ratification of the new treaty on European Union, the so-called "Maastricht treaty", the process of European integration and enlargement has steadily continued. In December 1991, forty years after the birth of the European Community in 1951, the twelve Member States agreed on the texts of a new Treaty on European Union including Economic and Monetary Union and associated protocols. This agreement, which came into force on 1 November 1993, extends Community action into areas not previously covered by the EC Treaties. A common foreign and security policy has become a new pillar of European Union. The Treaty gives the European Community additional powers, particularly those of the Parliament are extended and the democratic deficit is reduced, although definitely not sufficiently. Another important new principle of the Maastricht Treaty is the notion that political, economic and monetary union can only be achieved if the wealthy regions show solidarity with the less developed ones to help gradually reduce economic disparities. Finally, the Maastricht Treaty creates a "European Union" which incorporates the already existing Community, and the term "Union" is gradually replacing the term "Community" in popular usage.

The twelve Member States of the European Community have transferred some of their sovereign powers to the Union. The Community's decision-making process involves: *the European Commission, the European Parliament* and the *Council of Ministers*. The roles of the institutions are summarised below.

The European Commission, the Community's executive branch, has 17 Commissioners (two from each large Member State, and one from the smaller ones) who are responsible for different policy areas and 23 Directorate Generals (DGs). Relevant areas are: President of the Commission (Mr Jacques Delors), External Economic Relations (Sir Leon Brittan); External Political Relations (Mr Hans van den Broek) and Development Cooperation (Mr Manuel Marin). The corresponding Directorate Generals are DG I and DG VIII. The principle tasks of the Commission are:

(i) **To propose** to the Council of Ministers and the European Parliament measures for the development of Community policies.

(ii) **To implement Community policies** on the basis of Council Decisions or following directly from Treaty provisions.

(iii) **To manage the funds** and common policies which account for most of the Community budget. Cooperation programmes with non-member countries are financed from the Community budget or by the separate European Development Fund, financed by national contributions. The Commission carries responsibility for the actual expenditure of the budget of the Community, 69 billion ECUS.[2] The Community budget is divided in two parts, compulsory expenditure (mainly agriculture and expenditure fixed in international agreements) and non-compulsory expenditures (most other expenditure). The European Parliament has the final say in the adoption of the budget and in finalising the non-obligatory expenditure, within the ceilings jointly agreed by Parliament and Council.

(iv) **To ensure** that Community rules and the principles of the common market are observed.

The Commission's role in negotiating agreements with third countries, the most important of which have to be approved by both the European Parliament and the Council of Ministers, is increasing, although Member States still have sovereign control over their own foreign policies. The European Parliament has the right to veto the accession of any state to the EC and also to reject some categories of Trade and Cooperation Agreements with third states. It sometimes does this on the basis of, for instance, violations of human rights.

The Council of Ministers is the principle legislative and decision-making institution. It is composed of Ministers from the twelve Member States (for example: ministers for development, or ministers for agriculture) and has the power to adopt legislation submitted to it by the Commission. Each Member State acts as President of the Council for a six month period. The Ministers of Foreign Affairs are responsible for the Community's external relations and for political cooperation on international problems and general affairs. The governments of the EC Member States have committed themselves to jointly attempt to formulate and implement a European foreign policy. The *European Political Cooperation* (EPC) has been the framework used for many years. The country holding the six month presidency of the EC Council also presided over the EPC. Under the recent treaty changes agreed in Maastricht, foreign policy becomes the responsibility of the Council.

The European Parliament is the second legislative body, after the Council of Ministers and is the only elected international parliament in the world. Parliament has been directly elected by roughly as many European citizens as there are Indigenous Peoples in the world, 318 million. It has 518 members, elected every five years. Since the unification of Germany the Community has 342 million inhabitants and 17 additional observers. In June 1994, a new European Parliament is elected and the overall number of members will increase.

The European Parliament is a dynamic meeting place of 12 European cultures and 9 languages. It contains eight political groups, 19 committees, 3 sub-committees and Interparliamentary Delegations for Relations with specific countries and regions. The Committees of most relevance to Indigenous Peoples are: the Foreign Affairs Committee, the External Relations Committee, the

Development Committee, the Environment Committee and the Sub-Committee on Human Rights. Each committee has a chairperson, vice-chairs, full members and substitute members and reflects the overall composition of the Parliament in terms political grouping. Members of the European Parliament also meet in Interparliamentary Delegations for Relations with Third Countries, such as the Delegations for Relations with North, Central and South America, ASEAN countries, Australia, New Zealand etc. Members of Interparliamentary Delegations meet annually with their counterparts of Parliaments in third countries to discuss a wide variety of issues. A very special Interparliamentary Delegation is the ACP/EEC Joint Assembly that brings together 69 Members of the European Parliament and representatives of 69 ACP countries (mainly Europe's former colonies in Africa, the Caribbean and Pacific). The Assembly meets twice a year and adopts resolutions relating to current issues, also in the field of human rights. In 1992 it passed one on Indigenous peoples.

The Parliament meets in plenary in Strasbourg (France) for one week each month, except in August. The remaining three weeks are spent primarily in committee work (two weeks) and meetings of the political groups (one week) in Brussels. The Parliament has the following functions;

(i) **A legislative role**: Parliament participates in the formulation of directives, regulations and Community decisions by giving its opinion on and amending proposals from the European Commission, eg. Parliament receives the proposal for the Council Regulation on Operations to Promote Tropical Forests, appoints a rapporteur and drafts amendments. In some cases Parliament can reject or veto draft legislation.

(ii) **A budgetary role**: Parliament can amend the Community budget within certain ceilings and has the final say on its adoption.

(iii) **An oversight role**: Parliament, through its committees, hearings, access to documents and rights to table parliamentary questions to the Commission and to Council, can monitor and scrutinize policy implementation. It may dismiss the Commission by a vote of censure.

(iv) **A role as a political force**: Parliament is a forum for European opinion.

The European Parliament only has the right to amend legislation, not to initiate or draft it, which is the exclusive right of the Commission. Parliament's amendments are not always adopted by the Council of Ministers, but if they are not, Parliament can, in some areas, reject the legislation. As regards foreign policy, its resolutions are not always implemented. but its views have been taken into account by the foreign ministers. The influence of the Parliament and the Commission remains limited in this respect, due to the fact that EC foreign policy is still not supranational but intergovernmental. Nevertheless, the Parliament has gained international recognition for its work in the field of human rights. Its human rights initiatives are a response to the concerns of the electorate and its resolutions on indigenous peoples can therefore be seen as a testimony of the growing interest of the European people in their plight. The Parliament has great institutional freedom and little bilateral interests and therefore an important role to play in helping the European Community to develop an active human rights policy. "Parliament is at times accused of being too belligerent an advocate of human rights. But it is clear from the many and various approaches to Parliament that citizens expect this of the institution. It is in large measure because of the work of NGOs and individuals in recent decades that governments have begun to look more seriously at the human rights aspects of foreign policy. For Parliament regular contact and inter-action with major human rights NGOs and individual groups, is essential."[3]

The European Investment Bank is the Community's financial institution and helps implement the Community's policy by providing loans for infrastructure, industrial and agricultural projects to third countries.

The European Court of Justice is the Community's equivalent of a supreme court. It is the final arbiter of Community law.

Across the world there are several examples of international organisations which bring together countries that develop common policies. The European Union is more than that. It is not an intergovernmental organisation but a supranational structure. Its institutions have powers in their own right and can adopt legal instruments which have the force of law and directly apply to Community citizens. These legal instruments are: (i) *regulations*, which apply directly; (ii) *Directives*, which lay down compulsory objectives which have to be transposed into national legislation; (iii) *decisions*, which are binding only on the Member States, firms or individuals to whom they are addressed; (iv) *recommendations* and opinions, which are not binding. For example, the Council Regulation on Operations to promote Tropical Forests was submitted in the form of a proposal by the Commission to the Parliament and the Council. The Parliament formulates an opinion about the Regulation and amends it where necessary. The Council takes the final decision about the content of the regulation.

Within the territory of the European Community, there are indigenous peoples — from French Guyana and French Polynesia — for example, and one of the Members of the European Parliament is an indigenous person, Mr Ukeiwe, a Kanak born in Lifou, New Caledonia. During the April 1994 part-session, the Presidents of the Saami parliaments of Finland, Sweden and Norway visited the European Parliament in Strasbourg. Enlargement of the European Union will actively involve more indigenous representatives in the European institutions. But there are other considerations that not only justify but also make it necessary for the Community to focus attention and develop policies on indigenous peoples. EC foreign policy, trade and cooperation agreements, development and environment programmes and projects are affecting indigenous peoples around the world. And respect for the human rights of indigenous peoples should be a matter of concern to the European Community and all its citizens.

References
1. For an introduction to the workings of the European Community see; *The European Community Fact Book*, Alex Roney, Kogan Page Limited, 1991; or: *The European Parliament*, Jacobs, Corbett and Shackelton, 1992.
2. An ECU is a European Currency Unit and equals about 1.14 US Dollar (July 1993).
3. European Parliament *Annual report on human rights in the world and Community human rights policy, for the years 1991-1992*, adopted in March 1993.

1. The European Parliament

This chapter is divided in two. The first part discusses a variety of resolutions adopted by the European Parliament concerning indigenous peoples in the world. The second lists a number of written and oral parliamentary questions to the "executive" European institutions on the same subject.

The European Parliament, particularly after 1990, adopted an increasing number of resolutions on human rights violations in the world and in particular on the situation of indigenous peoples. What were almost hesitant declarations at the outset, have gradually developed into much more forceful and clear positions. This reflects a growing awareness of the plight, not only of the "indians" in the Americas, but also of indigenous peoples in Africa and Asia. During the period 1988-1993, the European Parliament drew up over 28 reports and resolutions in which indigenous peoples are specifically mentioned or in which situations are addressed which directly affect them. **These resolutions are presented in Annex I in chronological order (Resolution a, b, c etc)..** Relevant recitals (A,B,C etc) and Paragraphs (1,2,3 etc.) are quoted in full (see Annex I).

Resolutions of the European Parliament include the situation of many different indigenous peoples in the world: Penan, Kelabit and Kayan in Sarawak (Malaysia), Yanomami and Awa Guaja from Brazil, Mohawks and Inuit in Canada, Tuareg people in Mali and Niger, the Siona, Secoya, Cofan, Quiscuah, Huaorani, Quischua, Shiwiar and Achuar people from Ecuador, indigenous peoples in India, like the Nagas, the Karen of Myanmar, the Paez indians of Colombia, the peoples of the Chittagong Hill Tracts in Bangladesh and the Nuba people of Sudan.

In addition to these specific resolutions, the Parliament has twice appointed rapporteurs to study and monitor the overall situation of indigenous peoples in the world and make recommendations for European Community policy. In addition, resolutions have been adopted, for example Resolution (m): 1992, *Indigenous peoples and the Quincentenary*. This resolution expresses concern at reports from Amnesty and Survival International of human rights violations against indigenous peoples (recital F). In it, governments of countries with indigenous peoples are requested to settle disputes over land before engaging in economic activities in those areas where indigenous people claim to have title to the land and where the activities are not supported by the majority of the indigenous population. The European Commission is urged to comply with Parliament's wish to allocate funding for special projects with indigenous peoples, developed by and for native communities. The 'Human Rights Unit' of the European Parliament is instructed to provide a background document on the situation of indigenous peoples and its competent committee is asked to appoint a rapporteur to investigate the human, territorial and cultural rights of the indigenous peoples of the Americas. Following this resolution, a study on the situation of indigenous peoples in the Americas was completed on the basis of a questionnaire forwarded to Governments concerned.

It was in 1987 that the Parliament appointed a rapporteur to study the situation of indigenous peoples for the first time, leading to the adoption of resolution (e) *on the position of the world's Indians* the following year. In March 1992, further to Resolution (m) on the Quincentenary and several motions for a resolution, a Parliamentary rapporteur was nominated for the second time by the Committee on Foreign Affairs and Security to study the issue of: *the Implementation of International Legislation on the Environment and the Rights of Indigenous Peoples*. When a Parliamentary rapporteur is nominated, draft reports are written, submitted and debated at Committee level. After Members of the Committee amend and adopt a text, a resolution is subsequently put on the agenda of the Plenary Session in Strasbourg and is voted upon by all members of the European Parliament. Indigenous representatives and European environmental and human rights groups are in contact with rapporteurs, presenting documents and lobbying in support of their ideas. The draft report on the implementation of International Legislation makes an interesting suggestion in its operative paragraphs, namely that during the next European Parliamentary electoral period, 1994-1999, "an inter-parliamentary delegation should be established comprising of Members of the European Parliament and Representatives of indigenous peoples". (See resolution (ac) on: Action required internationally to provide effective protection for indigenous peoples).

Another resolution (y) which mentions the general situation of indigenous peoples in the world was adopted in May 1993 on: *the United Nations World Conference in Vienna in June 1993*. It makes a number of recommendations about human rights policy and refers to the role of indigenous peoples at the World Conference (for example, it requests that the mandate of the UN Working Group on Indigenous Populations be continued, even after adoption of the Declaration).

The **impact of such European Parliament resolutions** is often difficult to evaluate. Basically, resolutions can have two important consequences:

(i) Inter-institutional
Almost every resolution calls on the European Commission, the Council of Ministers or on the Twelve Foreign Affairs Ministers (EPC) to take certain actions. At each plenary session of the European Parliament in Strasbourg and at most meetings of parliamentary committees, representatives of the Commission and the Council are present to respond to resolutions debated by Parliament, to answer Members' questions and to explain past and future policies;

(ii) Political
Parliamentary resolutions express the political will of the EP and often reflect concerns of citizens of the European Community or of representatives of human rights organisations (such as indigenous peoples) from outside the Community who often visit Brussels or Strasbourg. Once adopted, resolutions can have a significant political effect (this will be illustrated in case studies).

Of particular importance is Parliament's power to accept or reject some categories of Cooperation Agreements with third States, for example the Lomé

Convention with 69 countries from Africa, the Pacific and the Caribbean, the ALA Agreement — (EC cooperation with Asia and Latin America), or in the future the TACIS Agreement (EC cooperation with the countries of the former Soviet Union). On 29 June 1992, the Framework Agreement for cooperation between the EC and the Federative Republic of Brazil was signed in Brasilia. This Agreement provides in the first instance "that cooperation ties between the Community and Brazil and the Agreement in its entirety are to be based on respect for the democratic principles and human rights which inform the domestic and external policies of both the Community and Brazil" (art. 3). Parliament approved the conclusion and entry into force of the Framework Agreement in Legislative Resolution (A3-0311/92). In resolution (v) *on economic and commercial relations between the EC and Brazil*, however, paragraph 1 "expresses concern at the fact that, despite Brazil's declared efforts towards democractic development, there are still unacceptable violations of human rights, the characteristics of Indigenous Peoples are not respected and there is corruption in the institution". Non-legislative resolutions such as these are there to be a marker, a reconciliation with reality which requires that attention is drawn to violations of human rights in spite of the fact that approval is given to an EC Framework Cooperation Agreement. The Commission has noted the wishes expressed by Parliament in this resolution, and intends to act on them on the basis of the new agreement, while stepping up and consolidating existing cooperation.

The last paragraph of each Parliamentary resolution is customarily a request to its President to forward the resolution to the relevant European Institutions, the Governments of the countries that are cited in the resolution and sometimes to intergovernmental organisations or agencies such as the World Bank and other UN bodies. An adopted resolution can lead to or guide exchanges of views and negotiations with third country governments. Complaints or recommendations may be acted upon by the Commission or Council or taken into account by third governments.

Case study on the follow-up to an EP resolution
In order to illustrate the political impact which a parliamentary resolution can have, the follow-up of resolution (e) *on the situation of indigenous peoples in Canada* adopted in September 1990, can be taken as an example. This resolution is concerned with the Oka/Kahnawake crisis which developed after the municipality of Oka, Quebec decided to expand its golf course to eighteen holes from the current nine by annexing grounds the Mohawk claimed as their traditional burial grounds. The Oka crisis received worldwide attention in the media. In addition, Members of the EP were given detailed reports on the day to day situation by both Mohawk and European human rights groups. Paragraph 1 of resolution (e) states that, "parties are urged to cease hostilities and commit themselves to the use of judicious and prudent measures to secure a peaceful and just resolution to the current situation". Paragraph 5 "calls on its delegation for relations with Canada to send observers to Quebec and to enter the Mohawk question on the agenda for the next inter-parliamentary meeting".

Visit of Indigenous Peoples from Canada to the EP

On the 24th of October 1990, shortly before a parliamentary mission set off for Canada, and following the adoption of resolution (e), the Inter-parliamentary Delegation for Relations with Canada agreed to receive nine indigenous representatives from Canada at their meeting in Strasbourg. The purpose of this meeting was to better understand the particular events surrounding the Oka Crisis and the general situation of the indigenous peoples in Canada. The Delegation included Mohawk, Métis, Inuit, Haudenosaunee and Native Council of Canada representatives and Chief Elijah Harper (who became widely known for playing a crucial role in stopping the Meech Lake Accord). They met not only with the Delegation but also spoke to the President of the European Parliament and the Chairman of its Subcommittee on Human Rights. Following this visit to Strasbourg, some of the indigenous delegates presented a paper called: "Possible actions/resolutions by the European Parliament" with regards the situation of indigenous peoples in Canada. This paper states in paragraph 1 that the Mohawk crisis is the latest in a series of confrontations between indigenous peoples and national governments in both Canada and the US which go back a long time. "The Iroquois peoples have historic rights in both countries. The failure to accommodate these rights, *is a proper subject for continuing concern by the European Parliament, especially given the source in European historical doctrines and laws"*. The paper further encourages the Parliament in paragraph 3 *"to establish a sub-delegation for relations with indigenous peoples which would enable liaison efforts with international indigenous organisations and with first nations which are difficult within the current structure"*. In light of the emerging recognition in international law that standards are required for the relations of states and incorporated indigenous peoples (the ILO Convention 169 and the UNWGIP), "there is certainly adequate cause to open up a more permanent basis for the EP to address itself on a regular basis to indigenous issues of relevance to its members". Paragraph 4 observes that the European Parliament can further assist matters by *"encouraging the Canadian government in implementing its state policy of support for constitutionally entrenching self government regimes for aboriginal peoples"*.

The EP Delegation visits Canada

As a result of paragraph 5 of the Resolution, Members of the EP Inter-parliamentary Delegation for Relations with Canada carried out a fact-finding mission from 13 to 18 January 1991 to Montreal, Ottawa and to Kahnawake and Kanehsatake (both Mohawk communities). They met with representatives of the Mohawk and other indigenous peoples in Canada, NGOs, human rights organisations, the Quebec Provincial Authorities and the Canadian Federal Authorities. The mission was given substantial press coverage in Quebec. On their return, a report on the fact-finding mission was drawn up and discussed at the next meeting of the Delegation and of the EP Subcommittee on Human Rights. Additionally, the chairman of the Delegation, submitted a paper on the situation of the aboriginal peoples of Canada called: "Broken promises: Canada and its Aboriginal Peoples". The conclusions of the paper argue that "the rights of aboriginal people in Canada to an adequate standard of living and to a fair trial have been infringed. The Federal Government's policy of requiring aboriginals to give up their title to the land as part of a claims settlement, is in breach of the Canadian constitution. Aboriginals cannot be denied the inherent right to self-government. They have, after all, been living in what is now Canada long before Europeans arrived to impose their laws on them. Only a paradigmatic shift in Canada's policy toward its indigenous people would appear capable of eliciting the degree of trust necessary to establish just and stable relations. *What is needed is a new social contract between aboriginals and non aboriginals, based first and foremost on respect for differing cultural identities".*

The adoption of the resolution caused a lively exchange of letters between Canadian Government officials and European Parliamentarians. On the 14 of September, the day after the adoption of the Resolution, the Quebec Minister for International and Aboriginal Affairs, wrote a letter to the President of the European Parliament, saying: "C'est avec consternation que les citoyens du Québec ont pris connaissance de la teneur de la résolution que le Parlement Européen a jugé bon d'adopter hier. Le Secrétaire d'Etat aux Affaires extérieures du Canada, le très Honorable Joe Clark, a déja eu l'occasion de vous souligner que la résolution était fondée sur une interprétation des faits qui ne correspond pas à la réalité . . ." A month later, however, the Minister of Indian Affairs and Northern Development of the Canadian Government, in a letter to the Human Rights Sub-Committee Chairman (Oct. 31, 1990) stated that: "the Government has heard the earnest and sincere call from chiefs and elders for changes in our policies. We are now determined to act and in the process create a new relationship between aboriginal and non aboriginal Canadians based on dignity, trust and respect".

Since September 1990, both indigenous representatives and Canadian Government officials have continued to visit the European Parliament and ceaselessly drawn the attention of Members, their Assistants and Officials, their Committees and Delegations to the issue of the situation of the indigenous peoples in Canada. Chief Ominayak of the Lubicons, for example, visited the European Parliament in March 1993 to inform Members about Lubicon land claims and the "lack of effective legal redress within Canada" of indigenous claims. That same month the Deputy Minister of Indian and Northern Affairs, a Mohawk from Kahnawake visited Brussels to outline "positive developments that have occurred in ensuring that Canadian indigenous people are better able to safeguard their way of life and enhance their standard of living". In July, the president of the National Assembly of Quebec met with the President of the Parliament and the Sub Committee on Human Rights, again to discuss the situation of indigenous peoples. A great number of study documents have been distributed among members on a wide variety of issues relating to the situation of Aboriginal Peoples in Canada since the adoption of the Resolution. Also many written and oral parliamentary questions have been submitted by members on the subject.

"There is much that the European Parliament can do regarding indigenous peoples" according to Rick Ponting, Professor of the Department of Sociology of the University of Calgary. He met with the Parliamentary Delegation in

Canada and as a result, wrote a paper called: "Internationalisation; perspectives on an Emerging Direction in Aboriginal Affairs". The paper proposes that "in their future meetings with Canadian Parliamentarians, European Parliamentarians could discuss the constructive potential of re-structuring sovereignty, that is, of power-sharing. In informal interaction they could draw the many parallels between the European and the Canadian experience and try to convince Canadian legislators of the need for bold initiatives rather than mere incremental tinkering with the status quo . . . the European Parliament could urge its Member States to take an interest in Canadian aboriginal affairs and in Canadian human rights abuses, such as by providing seed money for the educational programmes of European groups supporting Canadian aboriginals. Also the European Parliament could urge Canadian legislators to establish targets and target dates for the attainment of improved conditions . . ."

After the European Parliament adopted resolution (e):
– The issue of indigenous peoples in Canada has been raised at almost every meeting of the EP Delegation for Relations with Canada in Brussels or Strasbourg and with Canadian parliamentarians;
– Members of the European Parliament have become more aware of the position of indigenous peoples in the world and in Canada in particular;
– It could be said that relations between NGOs and support groups concerned with indigenous peoples rights on the one hand and the European Parliament on the other have since improved;
– Politicians, the public and the media in Canada have taken the issue very seriously, demonstrating a keen interest in the follow-up of this resolution and possible European action on other indigenous matters.

In 1992, the year of the Quincentenary of Columbus' arrival in the Americas, a meeting took place at the European Parliament in Brussels between representatives of 24 indigenous peoples from all corners of the world and Members of the EP. Two indigenous representatives and two Members of Parliament co-chaired this meeting and at the end of the discussions, the following common statement was presented by the indigenous delegation:

Conclusions from the delegates of the "symbolic discovery"[1]
We, the Indigenous delegates participating in the "Symbolic Discovery of Europe", having contacted a variety of different institutions, recognise that there exists discrimination when the term "indigenous" is used. This discrimination is a direct result of the division of Indigenous Peoples rights into smaller, disconnected categories.

As Indigenous Peoples, we see this as an attempt to decentralise Indigenous Rights into various categories (for example: developed and underdeveloped regions, languages, protection of the environment, etc.), instead of supporting the struggle of Indigenous Peoples which encompass all of the aforementioned issues and many others, since time immemorial.

Considering
The good intentions European Institutions have shown in supporting our cause,
Believing
That it is imperative for Indigenous Peoples to be consulted and closely involved in the preparation, decision making and implementation of programmes that directly

affect Indigenous Peoples.
We demand:
1. The solidarity of the European Parliament with Indigenous Peoples, manifested through political pressure applied towards our respective Governments as well as the political recognition of our own existing representative organisations.
2. The creation of an efficient means of communication and information with Indigenous Peoples about those specific clauses that involve them in all Agreements and Conventions signed between the E.C. and our respective governments.
3. Concerning the "International Year of the World's Indigenous Peoples", in 1993, we suggest that the European Parliament should support us in obtaining financial support to set up an International indigenous Foundation in Europe.
4. That these intentions become a reality and not just more empty promises never realising their full potential, as they would be an important step in our struggle for self-administration, self-determination, self-development and sovereignty.[2]

In October 1993, inspired by the theme of the UN Year of the World's Indigenous Peoples, an "Intergroup for Indigenous Peoples" was set up at the European Parliament. The members of this Parliamentary Intergroup represent different political parties and meet on a regular basis, at least once a month. Its agenda aims to cover current affairs related to the situation of indigenous peoples and the role of the European Union. With the Subcommittee on Human Rights, the Intergroup serves as a focal point at the European Parliament for indigenous issues. It liases with other international organisations, indigenous and support groups on relevant matters.[3]

Human rights, development and environment

The European Parliament, through its work in committees and delegations and by means of its resolutions has, despite the limitation of its competences, endeavoured to play an active role in drawing public attention to the situation of indigenous peoples. Generally, Members of Parliament table resolutions concerning indigenous peoples in the context of: (i) violation of Human Rights, (ii) Development programmes and projects or (iii) the protection of the Environment.

Sometimes a resolution on indigenous peoples is submitted following a concern for the *violation of human rights* of indigenous peoples.

In such cases, human rights organisations, both from the Community and from other countries in the world, write letters to the President of the Parliament, to officials or the President of the Subcommittee on Human Rights or they may visit the premises of the Parliament to draw attention to a certain situation of human rights abuse in the world. When such complaints coincide with some newspaper coverage on the subject, it helps stimulate a Parliamentary debate. For instance, resolutions have been adopted: on the threat to the existence of the *Yanomami people in Brazil* (d and aa) "shocked and dismayed by the brutal murder of 18 Yanomami men women and children . . ."; on *human rights in Colombia* (p): "Strongly protests against the massacre of Paez Indians in Coloto on 16 December 1991"; on the massacres and inhuman treatment of *Tuareg people in Mali and Niger* (r): "If the killing, uprisings and bloody repressions continue, an entire people will be threatened with annihilation".

In October 1992 Parliament adopted resolution (t) on *the award of the Nobel Peace Prize to Rigoberta Menchu*. It "warmly welcomes the award of the 1992 Nobel Peace Prize to the indigenous human rights activist from Guatemala, Rigoberta Menchu". Continuing human rights violations against indigenous peoples, NGOs and lawyers who support them, however, are deplored. Resolution (t) also *calls upon all Governments of countries with Indigenous People to ratify ILO Convention 169*.

Occasionally, it is the effect which *development programmes* may have on the lives of indigenous peoples which inspires the European Parliament to draft resolutions, for example l (1991) and q (1992) on the *Narmada project in India*. Resolution l on the disastrous consequences of the Narmada project notes that: "resettlement arrangements, necessary for the construction of the Sardar Sarovar Dam have been unsatisfactory and that the resettled people complain about poor quality land, poor irrigation and lack of employment opportunities in their new homes". Another resolution (o) on the Community's policy in relation to the developing countries adopted in May 1992 calls on the Commission to give an undertaking that by 1995 the import of tropical hardwoods that are not produced using sustainable methods will be prohibited. It underlines the need for drawing up an environmental and social impact assessment prior to implementation of EC development projects.

A concern for continuing *deforestation and the state of the environment* and the threat this causes to indigenous peoples is often a motivating factor for the Parliament to table a motion for a resolution or appoint a rapporteur, to monitor and debate the situation of indigenous peoples as forest dwellers and symbols of nature conservation. Both in 1988 and in 1993, for example, Parliament passed resolutions on *deforestation in Sarawak, Malaysia* (a and z). Resolution (a), on the catastrophic environmental impact of large-scale deforestation in Sarawak, considers that: "large scale logging in Sarawak constitutes a serious threat to the environment and to the indigenous people who live in and from the tropical rain forest. When logging concessions are granted, insufficient attention is paid to such threats and the traditional land rights of indigenous peoples are ignored". Parliament therefore calls on the Community and its Member States to suspend imports of timber from Sarawak until it can be established that these imports are from concessions which do not cause unacceptable ecological damage and do not threaten the way of life of the Indigenous People. Resolution (z) adopted five years later, recalls that in its resolution of 1988 a moratorium on the imports of tropical hardwoods from Sarawak was called for. It stresses that the way of life of the indigenous peoples of Sarawak continues to be destroyed by logging and states that Parliament is aware that the EC Council and Commission have never agreed to implement its appeal. It again "calls on the Commission to implement an import ban of non-sustainable exploited hardwood at the beginning of 1995".

The Commissioner's response in Strasbourg to the complaints and recommendations voiced in resolution (a) demonstrates a clear difference of opinion between the two European institutions: "While the European Commission agrees with Parliament that tropical forests should not only be sustainably managed but also exploited with the objective of financing the development of the producer countries, it has repeatedly expressed its opposition to restrict the export of tropical timber from certain countries. I must tell Parliament that the Commission does not regard that as an appropriate step, amongst other reasons because the European Community is not the party primarily responsible for the destruction of forests in the world, but only one of them. Irrespective of what would be a measure difficult to implement on an international scale, the Commission lacks the technical means to bring it about". In 1993, when Resolution (z) was adopted the Commission said that "in its dialogue with the Malaysian authorities, concern was expressed about the intensive exploitation of the rain forest in Sarawak and the situation of the indigenous peoples".

In 1989 and 1990, the Parliament adopted a series of resolutions based on reports prepared by the Environment Committee and the Development Committee regarding deforestation and the negative effects of financing from the European Community and various international organisations on the environment of the Amazon region. The Commission is requested "to make the conservation of the Amazon region a major priority in Community cooperation with Latin America and not to cooperate in projects which are a threat to indigenous peoples or to the environment", resolution (b). In November 1990, three more Parliamentary reports on tropical forests were adopted in Strasbourg (g, h and i). Resolution (g) on *the environmental problems in the Amazon region* criticises the role played by the World Bank in promoting and financing the Carajas iron mining project without taking adequate account of the consequences for the indigenous peoples and the natural environment. The Commission is urged to put together a clear package of instruments and procedures and to publicise them with a view to preventing undesirable consequences for the environment and the indigenous and local people from EC aided projects located outside the Community. Resolution (h) on *measures to protect the ecology of the tropical forests*, requests the Commission "in the context of EC development programmes to give priority to legal support for indigenous peoples and local NGOs, institutions and training establishments committed to the objectives of forestry conservation and regeneration". Resolution (i) on *the conservation of tropical forests* "calls on the Twelve to take account of the long term conservation and management of tropical forests by Indigenous Peoples and forest and rural population". In particular, it is suggested that "an embassy of Indigenous Nations to the Community be established to strengthen the systematic consultation of the people of the forests each time an action concerning tropical forests is undertaken". It is stressed that "the conservation and sustained management of tropical forests for the livelihood and survival of Indigenous Peoples and other local communities and the problem of poverty is exacerbated by forest destruction". The Commission should refuse, according to Parliament, "all financial or technical assistance to any project which endangers the environment or the indigenous population or adversely affects the cultural freedom of the forest people".

During the debates in Strasbourg on October 12, 1990, the Commissioner responsible who replied to questions by Members on the reports on tropical forests:

"In 1982, after receiving a request for financial help from Brazil, the Commission in effect decided to contribute under the ECSC (European Coal and Steel Community) to the financing of a scheme to work the iron ore mines, aimed at securing supplies for the European iron and steel industry. That scheme, known as the small Carajas, concerned only the extraction of iron ore. As far as the Grande Carajas project is concerned, the Commission was not involved in the financing of that project which is having extremely worrying effects at environmental level, given the substantial areas of forest that are being destroyed, seriously threatening the living conditions of the Indigenous Peoples. In connection with the establishment of a pilot programme to protect Brazil's tropical forests, the Parliaments' proposals inviting the Commission to look at alternatives to the use of charcoal come at a particularly opportune moment. The Commissioner points out that *the rights of the Indigenous Peoples have not so far been protected as they should be*; they appear seriously at risk and in many cases close to extinction. The contributing factors, in addition to deforestation, are the violent encroachment of huge livestock ranches, the presence of groups of gold prospectors, of "diamanteros" and, finally, the extension of the military zones in the north of the Amazon. The Commission, like the Parliament, attaches great importance to exploiting and marketing in a practical and sustainable fashion the many products of the tropical forests in such a way as to preserve natural resources and ensure the survival of the Indigenous Peoples. The Commission supports the objective of the ITTO (International Tropical Timber Organisation) that by the year 2000, only sustainably processed wood can be commercialised. It supports the implementation of positive measures to protect the forests of Sarawak. *As far as aid to the people of Sarawak is concerned, the Commission is favourably disposed to this*. As far as the Tropical Forest Action Plan is concerned, the Commission broadly shares the views of the Council in its resolution on tropical forests. It seems appropriate to support firmly the envisaged reforms which must be directed towards strengthening that aspect relating to forest conservation, bringing to the fore the rights of the Indigenous Peoples, encouraging the participation of non-governmental organisations and effecting a genuine multi-sectoral approach".

Several of Parliament's recommendations have, meanwhile been implemented by the Community. In 1992, for example, on the basis of the above EP resolutions, the Commission Communication 'a common platform: guidelines for the Community for the UNCED', 1992 (SEC(91)1693) and Council conclusions of December 1991 on guidelines for the Community for UNCED, a new budget line was created on Tropical Forests. This budgetline gives priority to projects where the local population, being the most suitable persons for conservation of tropical forests, are fully involved (see the next chapters).

In yet another resolution (k) on *the human and ecological disaster in the Pastaza region in Ecuador*, adopted in 1991, the Parliament expresses "concern about the increase of oil exploitation over the last 20 years in the Ecuadorian rainforest by Conoco, Arco, Unocal, Occidental, City, British Gas, Parker Constructore and Texaco" (recital A). "Continued exploration and extraction along existing exploitation methods by oil companies is not contributing to sustainable development and can do serious damage to the region", according to Recital C. The resolution "calls upon the Ecuadorian government to recognise the rights of their indigenous peoples". It is "concerned at the difficulties which have arisen with regard to finding a negotiated settlement to the conflict". It requests the Ecuadorian authorities and the Indigenous Federations "to resume negotiations, implement the Sarayacu agreements and resolve the conflicts by peaceful means". It also requests the Ecuadorian government "to recognise the inherited rights of their Indigenous Peoples to land they have lived on for centuries and to impose a moratorium on oil prospecting and exploitation until this has been achieved".

This resolution was widely discussed in Ecuador and also commented upon in the newspapers. The "Comercio" of 22.08.91, for example, states that the European Parliament rightly calls for a recognition of the inherited rights of the indigenous peoples to their land and a moratorium on oil exploration and exploitation until indigenous rights are guaranteed. The president of the OPIP (the Organisation of the Indigenous Peoples of the Pastaza), Antonio Vargas, giving his reaction to the resolution, declares in the newspaper that the national Government should take seriously these proposals supported by an exhaustive analysis of the situation of the Amazon indians in Ecuador. Another indigenous leader, Marcello Aragon, commented that it was really satisfying to see that institutions of international importance such as the European Parliament are concerned with the lives of the indigenous peoples in the Amazon . . ."[4]

During the Parliamentary debates in July, the response of the Commissioner for Environment to this resolution was as follows: "The Commission is aware of the troubles of the peoples covered by the Sarayacu Agreement and entirely shares the concern expressed by Members. It intends to work to improve the lot of the Indigenous Peoples of Ecuador and other Latin American countries, and that is why, in its development aid or other schemes of economic cooperation, it has never supported projects which might adversely affect the local population, and nor will it do so in the future. In terms of the programme of aid for Ecuador for the financial year 1992, it might be possible to agree to a special project to improve the situation of the Sarayacu peoples, in close cooperation with the Ecuadorian Government, if all the necessary conditions are met."

Finally, Parliament has adopted several resolutions that do not directly mention indigenous peoples but are indeed of relevance to them. For example in March 1990, resolution (j) was adopted on the right of nations to information concerning their history and the return of national archives. The Parliament demands that Member States, acting in a spirit of mutual understanding and solidarity, should grant all requests from the ACP countries for the return of cultural artefacts and archives, where these are, within the criteria established by UNESCO of fundamental spiritual and cultural value. It further believes that in principle, developing countries have a legitimate right to the return of their archives but considers there is a need for appropriate guarantees of the conservation of archives and cultural artefacts, including those of minority groups.

During the plenary debates, the Commission promised that in accordance with Parliament's proposal and in liaison with the Council and the Member States, a register would be drawn up of cultural agreements and treaties of independence signed by the Members States with the developing countries which would make reference to the issue of the return of archives.[5]

Apart from resolutions, another instrument used by the European Parliament to monitor the situation of indigenous peoples in the world and the activities of the European Commission and the Council in this field, is that of written and oral questions, with or without debate. A number of such questions are presented below. This list is not exhaustive, but the selection of questions seems relevant and the answers illustrative of the Community's actions regarding particular situations of indigenous peoples somwhere in the world.

PARLIAMENTARY WRITTEN AND ORAL QUESTIONS to the Council, Commission or European Political Cooperation

Written Question No.80188 on *Yuqui Indians* in Bolivia. What measures does the Commission intend to take in respect of development aid to Bolivia to safeguard the life of the Yuquis and prevent their total extinction as a result of intensive exploitation of the forests?,

The Commission shares the Member's concern about the danger of total extinction of the Yuqui Indians in Bolivia. It believes they have a right to live in their native lands, which can ensure their survival as a group and preserve their social and cultural identity. *The Commission is prepared to examine any project to help the Yuqui Indians* submitted by the Bolivian authorities or by a non-governmental organisation. The Commission has not as yet received any request on these lines.

Question (H-48788) asks the Commission whether it is aware that there are special laws in Australia governing the lives of *Aboriginals* and that an unduly large number of Aboriginals are in police custody. Knowing Australia's abhorrence of apartheid in South Africa, how does it tolerate this at home?

The Commission is aware that a large number of Aboriginals are in police custody and that the imprisonment rate of this section of the population is much higher than the one for non-aboriginal Australians (between 10 and 23 times higher). This sad reality is indeed proof of the fact that a problem does exist. The Australian authorities have acknowledged this and have set in motion initiatives to redress the situation. In 1975 as a result of the enactment of the Racial Discrimination Act, all discriminatory State law has been repealed and in 1986 the Australian Law Reform Commission submitted a number of recommendations whose implementation is under way. The existence of an aboriginal issue can certainly not be denied, however, its existence is not the result of discriminatory legislation, a comparison with South Africa is definitely unfounded and out of place.

Written question No.70088 on *Surinam Indians* requests information from the Commission on the proportion of Community aid to Surinam that has been allocated to the Lokono, Kalinja, Trio, Wayana and Akoerio indigenous peoples. Answer: Under European Development Fund 3 and 4, one project for medical infrastructure in the interior totalling 0,81 million ECU was funded to help this group of the Surinamese population. Furthermore, in the first half of 1987, the EC funded 0,91 million ECU towards the Dutch "medecins sans frontieres" to operate in Maengo and Brokopondo areas. This team, however, was expelled by the army in mid 1987.

Oral question (H-37/89) on the destruction of the Amazonian biotope threatening the survival of the *Guayaquil* Indians to the EC Ministers of Foreign Affairs. The President in Office answered that the Community and its Member States are aware of the fate of the Guayaquil Indians and hope that the government of Brazil, in the exercise of its sovereignty and having regard to the country's legitimate development needs, will not overlook the social and ecological aspects of the issue.

Written question No.201190 on diplomatic initiatives concerning violent incursions by garimpeiros into *Yanomami* native territory.
According to the Commission, "worldwide awareness of the seriousness of the tropical forests question should help in the search for solutions to related matters. The question of the future of the indians is very directly related to the fate of the Amazon forest. Nevertheless, given the nature of the problem, it must be clear that, whilst the many criticisms and excessive applications of pressure help publicise the situation, they profoundly irritate the authorities concerned and that, if we are to achieve our goal and put an end to present developments and their disastrous side-effects, more diplomatic initiatives are necessary".

Written question No.13390 expresses concern about the threat to the existence of the *Yanomami indians* in Brazil by the development in particular by gold prospectors in the region. Are Community development projects carried out in the indigenous settlements?
The Commission is kept informed about the situation of the Yanomami indians and shares the concern expressed by Parliament in its resolution of 18 January 1990. It notes that their plight is closely linked to the serious problems threatening tropical forests. It is the Commission's hope that the Brazilian authorities will join in its endeavour to seek solutions. At the same time, the Community *must not infringe the principle of national sovereignty* to avoid reactions which might jeopardise its effort. The Community is trying to use its geopolitical capacity to bring its contribution to the quest for a satisfactory solution to the problems posed by the exploitation of the resources of the Amazon river. At the human level, the same principles guide its effort to preserve indigenous cultures.

Oral question (H-073092) asks the Commission to clarify whether the 1992 Technical Assistance Programme to develop oil and gas exploitation in Siberia takes account of the presence of Indigenous minorities, including the *Nenets* and *Khants* people and their dependence on the fragile Arctic environment.
"The Commission is aware of the presence of Indigenous People in the arctic regions of the Russian Federation, including the Tyumen region and the Yamal peninsula. It is also a well-known fact that most of those people prefer to continue their traditional lifestyle, including hunting and fishing. On measures to prevent damage to the environment it should be pointed out that the Commission has no authority in the Russian Federation, including the above mentioned areas. However, the efforts of the Commission in its Tyumen Task Force project will be aimed at among other objectives, a reduction of oilspills and other losses. Furthermore, the project foresees support to integrated rural development, also

in the Northern areas. The position of the indigenous people will be part of this development plan."

In the answer to oral question (H-045392) on the destruction of the French Guyana Rain forest and the land rights of the *Galibi* Indigenous People, the Commission explains that several measures have been taken to strengthen environmental protection in the Guyanese tropical rain forest. Action taken under the Integrated Operational Programme, is designed to ensure a satisfactory level of development for the population, which is concentrated in the coastal area, without endangering the survival and the biodiversity of the tropical forest's flora and fauna. The forest of French Guyana is the sole example of tropical rain forest on the territory of a Community Member State, and, as such, all Community laws and policies apply to it.

Written question No.849/92 to the Commission on imports of wood from areas with ill-defined rights of use. (i)Is the Commission aware that in British Colombia (Canada) forest clearance operations are carried out even in instances where the land rights, rights of use and ownership of the indian nations, the government and the timber industry have not been defined? (i)Is the Commission aware that the UN Human Rights Commission has found Canada guilty of infringing Art. 27 of the ICCPR because of illegal extraction of raw materials from the territory of the *Lubicon Cree* and the destruction of their subsistence economy? (iii) And, what consequences does this have for the Community's policy on wood imports?
(i) The Commission is aware that land use rights in BC are currently defined by the Canadian constitution, by provincial laws and regulations, and by existing treaties between the government and aboriginal groups. It is also aware that the government of BC has expressed its intention to negotiate modern treaties reflecting the full range of aboriginal title to parts of British Colombia. All forestry companies in BC must comply with the existing system of forest and tree farm licensing, which takes into account, the interests and concerns of those aboriginal groups claiming title to such lands. In future, such firms will also be compelled to comply with the provisions of the modern treaties to be negotiated between the province and all aboriginal groups in BC. (ii) The Human Rights Commission has confirmed that an obligation to the Lubicon Cree exists, an obligation which the Government of Canada acknowledges. It also found that the offer which Canada made was fair, that it would meet Canada's obligations under the ICCPR, and that it constituted an appropriate remedy. The Lubicon leadership has so far refused to accept the Canadian offer. (iii) The Commission draws no conclusions from the above facts pertaining to the Community's policy on wood imports.

The European Parliament's role as a political driving force is crucial, if less well-defined than its legislative, budgetary or supervisory responsibilities. In the future, the European Parliament will certainly continue to raise the situation of indigenous peoples in its resolutions, written and oral questions and monitor the issue through its official relations with other parliaments in third countries. Indigenous peoples' representatives will, without a doubt, continue their visits to the European institutions in Brussels and Strasbourg. Combined efforts should eventually lead to the improvement of European policy and perhaps even contribute to a better application of international standards.

The European Parliament
Rue Belliard 97-113
B-1047 Brussels
Tel: 32.2.2841111

References
1. Support groups for Indigenous Peoples in Belgium, Holland, Italy and Switzerland launched a campaign with indigenous representatives from all over the world to mark the Symbolic discovery of Europe by Indigenous Peoples. The European Commission, national charities and private gifts helped the support groups to finance this project. Around 75 Indigenous Peoples representatives arrived by ship to Amsterdam harbour on the 16th of May. The delegation also visited France, Switzerland, Italy, Germany and Belgium.
2. This resolution was signed by: Doreen Eatts (Aborigenee/Kalkadoon), National Committee to Defend Black Rights (NCDBR),5/10-16 Glebe, St.Glebe N.S.W., Sydney 2037, Nakoa B. Prejean (Kanaka Maoli), International Indian Treaty Council, 710 Clayton St. X 1, San Francisco, 94117 California; Alejandro Lopez (Guarani), San Martin 1961, 3300 Posadas Missiones, Argentina; Segundina Cumapa R. (Shipibo), Feconau — casilla 426, Pucallpa, Peru; Juliana Ulcuango (Quichua), Pichincha Riccharimui Runacunapac, Apartado 17-19-00-76-B, Avenida los Grandos 6 Diciembre 2553, Quito, Ecuador; Andrea Flores Tonconi (Aymara), Organizacion de Mujeres Aymaras del Kollasuyo (OMAK), Casilla postal 13195, La Paz, Bolivia; Murphy Almendarez R. (Sumu), Oficina Sukawala, Organizacion Nacional de las Comunidades Sumus, Villa Rafaela Herrera A-25, Managua, Nicaragua; Mauricia Castro Garmendia (Jicaque), Federacion de tribus Xicaques de yoro (Fetrixy), B. las Delicias yoro, Honduras; Pablo Santos (Aeta), National Federation of Indigenous Peoples of the Phillipines, Rm. 701 Web-Jet Bldg., 64 Quezon Ave, Quezon city, Phillipines; Moana Kohu (Maori), Maori Womens Center, P O. Box 1560 Hamilton, Aotearoa (New Zealand); Ramona Quiroga (Mapuche), Comite Exterior Mapuche, Faktory 53-1825-HB Alkmaar, Holland; Enrique Ruben Morales (Diaquita), Comunidad India Calchaqui, 4137-Amoicha del Valle, Tucuman, Argentina.
3. The contact address of the European Parliamentary Intergroup for Indigenous Peoples is: MAE 411, Rue Belliard 97-113, B-1047 Brussels.
4. Free translation from newspaper clipping.
5. In this connection, it is interesting to refer to the first international conference on the cultural and intellectual property rights of indigenous peoples, the *Mataatua Declaration on Cultural and Intellectual Property Rights of Indigenous Peoples* of June 1993 (E/CN.4/Sub.2/AC.4/1993/CRP.5). Over 150 Delegates from 14 countries attended, including indigenous representatives from Ainu (Japan), Australia, Cook Islands, Fiji, India, Panama, Peru, Philippines, Surinam, USA and Aotearoa. Article 2.13 reads: "Museums and other institutions must provide to the country and indigenous peoples concerned, an inventory of any indigenous cultural objects still held in their possession".

2. The Council of the European Union

Following Commission proposals and resolutions of the European Parliament, the Council of the European Union adopted a number of resolutions, guidelines, regulations and statements in the field of human rights, development and environment in which the situation of indigenous peoples is specifically mentioned.

On May 29, 1990, the Council adopted a *Resolution*[1] *on Tropical Forests: development aspects* as a follow-up to the Commission Communication Doc. 6723/90 of September 1990. In this resolution, the Council attaches great importance to the preservation, rehabilitation and sustainable management supported by reforestation of tropical forest resources. It notes the estimated need to double the present level of donor resources devoted to forestry and associated activities and therefore considers that a major increase in funding is needed by all donors. The Council welcomes the increased priority given to tropical forestry in the Lome IV Convention and in its future consideration of cooperation with developing countries in Asia and Latin America. It also considers that greater emphasis must be placed on the conservation of tropical forests. The Community and its Member States recognise the necessity of a worldwide co-ordinated strategy for tropical forest resources and endorse i.e. the following principles and activities;

- Responsibility for tropical forest lies with the countries concerned. Donors should concentrate on supporting action taken by the developing countries themselves;
- The Tropical Forest Action Plan should be the basic framework for coordinated funding and action in the support of forest activities;
- Countries actively supporting the conservation of their remaining natural resources through legal, fiscal and institutional measures, and the revision of land use policies should merit special attention. Action to correct policies which encourage forest destruction should also be fostered and supported.
- Particular importance has to be attached to the *social dimension of forestry*. The traditions and experience of *Indigenous forest dwellers* should be respected and drawn upon while at the same time the needs and problems of new settlers and those living on the periphery of the forest should be addressed. Active steps should be taken to involve local populations in planning and implementation of projects.
- Special emphasis must be given to the involvement of international and national NGO's in the TFAP process, particularly at local level.
- The total exports of tropical timber products should come from sustainably managed resources by the year 2000.
- Reinforcement of the research capacities of the developing countries themselves should be a priority. Particular emphasis should be placed on improving sustainable productivity of forests, identifying non-timber resources and key areas of biodiversity and evaluating the environmental services provided by trees and forests.

On 4 February 1991, the Council adopted the *Final Conclusions on Guidelines for Cooperation with the Asian and Latin American Developing Countries* for the 1990s. These guidelines clarify the principles and the framework for granting aid to ALA countries. Community aid will, as a general rule, take the form of grants. The Guidelines state that the potential recipients of Community aid should include not only States or regions but *also local and traditional communities, institutes and private operators as well as NGOs*. According to Article 2 of the Guidelines, development policy and cooperation should take into account respect for human rights, fundamental freedom and democratic principles. Increased Community support will thus be earmarked for the countries most committed to these principles, particularly for positive initiatives by those countries to put them into practice. In those cases where human rights are violated and democratic principles infringed, the Community should amend the implementation of cooperation by confining cooperation to directly benefit those sectors of the population in need. The Council believes that Community action in Asia and Latin America should concentrate on seven major areas:

(i) Support for the rural sector in the broad sense, (ii) environment, (iii) the fight against drugs, (iv) the human dimension of development. "Aboriginal ethnic groups must continue to receive special attention in all the ALA developing countries with a view to both integration and respect for specific cultural characteristics in order to prevent the situation from worsening", (v) the structural dimension of development, (vi) regional cooperation, (vii) natural disasters. The overall financial requirements for five years could total ECU 2,750 thousand million ECU, of which 10% would be allocated to the environment and in particular to the protection of tropical forests, with 1,742 earmarked for 1993-1995.

In February 1992, the Council adopted regulation (No. 443/92) on *financial and technical assistance to, and economic cooperation with the developing countries of Latin America and Asia*, in which it is foreseen that indigenous peoples (referred to in the text as 'Ethnic minorities') *warrant special attention through measures designed to improve their living conditions while respecting their cultural identity*. Protection of the environment and natural resources and sustainable development, shall be long-term priorities. Art. 5 of the Regulation further states that the human dimension of development shall be present in all areas of action, the cultural dimension of development must remain a constant objective and aid should accordingly be allocated, inter alia, to specific projects for the spread of democracy, good governance and human rights. Aware that respect for, and the exercise of, human rights and fundamental freedoms and democratic principles are preconditions for real and lasting economic and social development, the Community shall give increased support to those countries most committed to these principles, particularly where positive initiatives are put into practice (Art. 2). *In the case of fundamental and persistent violations of human rights and democratic principles, the Community could amend or even suspend the implementation of cooperation with the States concerned* by confining cooperation to activities of direct benefit to those sections of the population in need. The recipients of aid (Art. 3) and partners in cooperation may include not only States and regions but decentralised authorities, regional organisations, public agencies, local or traditional communities, private institutes and operators, including cooperatives and NGOs.

On the 25th of May 1993, the Council of the EC, under the presidency of Denmark, adopted a *resolution on Human Rights, Democracy and Development*. Paragraph 10 states that 'one of the central objectives pursued by the Community and its Member States is to provide for a strengthening of the positive support for human rights and democracy by providing technical assistance in key areas, such as institution building within the public sector, strengthening of a pluralistic civil society and the protection of vulnerable groups. Paragragh 13 specifically refers to the situation of indigenous peoples and reads: The recognition [of the importance of the principle of full participation by the people in the democratic and pluralistic processes, as well as full observance of human rights, political and civil liberties, the rule of law, the subordination of military and security forces to civil authority, separation of powers and the independence and impartiality of the judiciary . . .] by the EC and its development partners should be reflected in the Final Document of the World Conference which should provide for a strengthening of development cooperation in areas such as: (x) strategies for the protection of the rights of indigenous people, taking into account their needs and wishes in development processes.'

The Council's *Annual Memorandum to the European Parliament* (PE 205.574, 11 June 1993) on the activities of the Community and its Member States in the field of human rights, recalls that indigenous people in many parts of the world are particularly vulnerable to human rights abuses. The Council believes that the International Year will contribute to the better protection of the human rights of indigenous people, the strengthening of their identity and culture, the enhancement of their participation in national decision-making processes as well as the larger focus in international fora on their plight. All the activities of the European Community and its Member States reflect the refusal of the Community "to accept that state sovereignty can be used as a shield for any country to carry out violations of human rights".

On the occasion of the fourth session of the Preparatory Committee of the World Conference on Human Rights, the European Community and its Member States submitted a *Position Paper* on Consideration of the final outcome of the World Conference, taking into consideration the preparatory work and the conclusions of the regional meetings. In Part Two (concrete measures, human rights, democracy and development) the Community and its Member States recommend that the final document of the World Conference should include the following elements on human rights, democracy and development, i.e. support to and follow-up on action and activities within the objectives of the International Year of the World's Indigenous Peoples with a view to furthering, i.e. the current work on rights of indigenous peoples. The European Community and its Member States consider that the World Conference should take action on the rights of indigenous peoples, taking into account the recommendations made by UN bodies and NGOs in formulating specific proposals.

The Minister of Foreign Affairs of Denmark, on behalf of the EC and its Member States presented a statement in Vienna on the 15th of June. The statement acknowledges that "the State is the principal custodian of human rights;

its role is to respect and enforce these rights. But the State has in too many cases been transformed into an instrument of direct oppression of its own people . . .".
And: "Among the many other areas of particular concern [the Community] believes that action should be taken to further the implementation of the rights of persons with disabilities, the rights of the elderly and the rights of indigenous peoples".

Lastly, the "Development Council" agreed on 18 November 1992 to release an initial tranche of 600 MECU in 1993 in the framework of the implementation of the financial initiative announced at Rio by the Union and its Member States. A commitment had been given to place the sum of 3000 MECU at the disposal of the developing countries to promote the application of Agenda 21. However, the Council has yet to make a pronouncement on the tangible measures to be adopted for the execution of this initiative, notably with regard to the percentage of new and additional resources.

The Council of the European Community
Rue de la Loi 170
B-1048 Brussels
Tel: 32.2.2346111

References
1. Contrary to European Parliament own initiative resolutions which have a primarily political importance but are not binding, resolutions of the European Council lay the basis for Communautarian policy. Council resolutions adopted on the basis of the Commission Communications are the most appropriate framework for laying down guidelines, fixing procedures and determining what lines of action the Member States should take in their bilateral policies.

3. The European Commission

This chapter discusses Commission strategies affecting indigenous peoples, seeks to explain the Commission's involvement in developing projects with indigenous peoples and gives a digest of Community resources available for financing indigenous peoples programmes. Some conclusions and recommendations will be presented at the end of this chapter regarding the need to develop a coherent Union policy on indigenous peoples.

Within the European Commission, the Unit that is directly responsible for the coordination of departmental activities concerning human rights, including issues of interest to indigenous peoples, is the Human Rights Unit of the Directorate-General for External Political Relations.[1] However, at this stage, no Directorate General has been provided with clear policy guidelines on indigenous peoples. As a result, consideration of their interests in the elaboration and implementation of development assistant projects is left to the responsibility of the different Directorates and takes place on a relatively ad hoc basis.

COMMISSION STRATEGIES in the field of Human Rights, Development, Tropical Forests and Indigenous Peoples

The Commission has submitted to Parliament and Council a number of relevant proposals of interest to indigenous peoples concerning human rights, development and tropical forests. Recent developments on the international scene and in many developing countries have thrust the issues of human rights and democracy to the forefront, especially where Community development cooperation policies are concerned. Growing European Commission concern for the situation of indigenous peoples is the result of increasing appreciation of: (i) the universality of human rights and the plight of indigenous peoples in particular (ii) the effect which development programmes and EC trade and cooperation agreements may have on indigenous peoples, and: (iii) the need for environmental protection.

The debate in the European institutions on the relationship between *human rights* and development originated with the submission of a Communication on Human Rights, Democracy and Development Cooperation Policy to the Council and Parliament by the Commission in the beginning of 1991. "The time has come to feature human rights and democracy more prominently in cooperation policy guidelines and to ensure that political reactions to developments in both these areas take due account of the aims of development cooperation", reads the Communication. As a result, the Council and Parliament adopted resolutions on the same topic.[2] Human Rights have become one of the cornerstones of European cooperation and are an important aspect of relations between the EC and other countries. "The Community and its member States refuse to accept that State sovereignty can permit any country to carry out violations of human rights".[3]

The political, economic and social objectives which underpin *EU development policy* are: the prevention and solution of conflicts, respect for human rights, support for the process of democratisation and economic liberalisation, and regional integration or cooperation. The most important objective of the

Commission development Cooperation policy in the run-up to 2000, has become environmental protection. These new dimensions in EC policy are of tremendous importance to indigenous peoples because they show a European commitment to "improve political transparency and prevent government high handedness" and "a readiness to cooperate with non-governmental organisations".[4]

The EC and its Member States are the world's leading source of development assistance. Almost all Community aid consists of grants rather than loans. The European Community has contractual relations with States in different parts of the world with which it has signed conventions (Lomé) or protocols (Latin America, Asia). In this framework Community assistance is provided in agreement with the national authorities. The Council authorises the Commission to negotiate Trade and Framework Cooperation Agreements with Third countries. Increasingly, human rights clauses are inserted. Following the Council Resolution on "Human Rights, Democracy and Development", respect for democratic principles and human rights has become an essential part of all new Agreements. Articles referring to the need for the protection of the environment and sustainable development are also included. Article 1 of the Agreement with the Andean Pact countries, for example, concerns human rights. Articles: 19, 21 and 28 deal with environmental matters, development and culture respectively. Despite the fact that indigenous peoples continue to be among the most threatened and marginalised peoples on earth, however, there are no Trade and Cooperation Agreements yet, that specifically mention them or their contribution to society.

Finally, the Community has a keen interest in *tropical forest conservation* and the promotion of sustainable development because it is a major importer of tropical timber products and a user of environmental services provided by forests (climate regulation, biodiversity reserve, etc.)[5] The Commission endorses the main points raised by the Parliament in its three reports adopted in October 1990, on: "Environmental problems in the Amazon region", "Measures to protect the Ecology of the Tropical Forests" and on "The Conservation of Tropical Forests". In particular, the Commission supports:

The need to protect Indigenous Peoples
The life, culture and, occasionally the very existence of indigenous peoples are intimately bound up with the forest. This concern is one of the priorities which the Commission is endeavouring to advance in the context of a wide-ranging pilot programme to save the Amazon forest.

The need to increase the financial resources allocated to the conservation of tropical forests
The Council has decided an appropriation of 2.750 million ECU for cooperation with the countries of Latin America and Asia for the period 1991-1995. 10% will be set aside for the environment, in particular projects designed to protect tropical forests (see description below of the pilot programme for the conservation of the tropical forest in Brazil). LIFE, the financial instrument for environment of the Community, will make action possible to protect the environment outside the Community to contribute to projects specifically designed to conserve tropical forests. Several pilot actions were financed in 1989.

These actions were considerably extended in the following years thanks to appropriation 5041 for tropical forest actions, proposed by the European Parliament.

The need to assess the environmental impact of Community funded projects on forest ecosystems

The Commission is financing various studies and programmes designed to define the methods and analytical instruments best suited to the specific requirements. The principle of prior assessment is contained in the fourth Lomé Convention.

The need to act within the TFAP

In order to ensure that protection of tropical forests and indigenous peoples is considered in the framework of the priority objectives the Community is closely monitoring the work on reforming the TFAP. It has set out its priorities clearly at the FAO Council meeting in Rome from 19 to 30 November 1990, namely;
– a better definition of the aims and objectives of the TFAP
the need to concentrate on projects compatible with the capacities of the beneficiary countries
– the improvement of techniques and instruments for monitoring the advancement of work in progress.

The trade in tropical timber

The Commission has launched studies about the legal, technical and economical aspects of an import regime of tropical timber. The Commission supports the ITTO position according to which by the year 2000 all trade in tropical timber should be limited to wood originating in sustainably managed forests and is actively engaged in efforts to draw up an action plan and time planning for the period between now and the year 2000. It is of the view that unilateral import bans on the basis of environmental damage which does not impact on the territory of the importing country should be avoided and that global environmental issues, such as deforestation, are more equitably tackled through multilateral agreements. Rather than applying unilateral import bans, positive signals should be sent to countries with major forestry industries to encourage them in the direction of the sustainable management of their forestry resources. Apart from financial cooperation, these positive signals could, where developing countries are concerned, include more favourable GSP treatment for processed timber provided that assurances are given on the respect of international norms on sustainable forest management.

The importance of research on tropical forestry and conservation

The Community research and development programmes such as STEP, TREES and EPOCH and the STD programme (DG XII, Research), both cover research in the field of tropical forestry and conservation. The creation of a network of research institutes concerned with tropical forests is envisaged. The Commission also collaborates with the European Space Agency to develop the TREES programme, designed to use remote sensing to improve knowledge of forest ecosystems.

Concern regarding threats to the rainforests

The main sources of funds for forestry conservation and development were, until

1992, those in the context of the Lomé Convention and Financial and Technical Assistance to Latin America and Asia. In addition to these funds, a decision was taken on the initiative of the European Parliament on 1st April 1992, to allocate 52 MECU to the budget line B7-5041, "Actions in favour of tropical forests", in the context of a supplementary budget.

Within the framework of Council Regulation on Financial and Technical Aid and Economic Cooperation with Latin America and Asia, the Commission is financing a *Pilot programme for the conservation of tropical forests in Brazil* (11 MECU for a period of three years). It is taking care to ensure that the pilot programme will in the future avoid difficulties of the type encountered in the Carajás project and mentioned in the parliamentary resolutions.[6] The overall objective of the pilot programme is to maximise the environmental benefits of Brazil's rain forests consistent with Brazil's development goals, through the implementation of a sustainable development approach that will contribute to a continuing reduction of the rate of deforestation. One of the specific objectives of the programme is to stabilise and safeguard the indigenous reserves of the Amazon region through demarcation, infrastructure and some minor provision of health care. Together with the Brazilian authorities and the World Bank, the European Commission has begun work on the pilot programme. In order to ensure the involvement of local communities and NGOs on the pilot programme, the Brazilian government has made provisions for them to participate in the pilot programme's Coordination Commission and the working teams for preparation of other projects, whenever appropriate. Local communities and NGOs are potential executors of a number of activities proposed under the various projects of the pilot programme.

The Brazilian government realises that the objectives of the pilot programme cannot be achieved without the active participation of civil society in the Amazon region. In May 1991, NGOs working in the Amazon region created a working group to facilitate their input into the design and implementation of the pilot programme. This working group, whose membership is still limited, is called the GTA-G7. The GTA-G7, however, lack the funds to meet more frequently, coordinate consultation among its members, increase its own representation in the Amazon region and broaden its participation in the pilot programme.

The scope of Community activities in the field of Conservation of Tropical Forests is set out in the COMMUNICATION of the Commission of October 1989 regarding the **Conservation of Tropical Forests: the Role of the Community** (OJ C, 264/01, 16.10.1989). This Communication, which was submitted to Council and Parliament, sets out a number of policy guidelines for development aid, trade in timber, financial resources, debt and research. The measures envisaged for trade include the establishment of a set of standards within the International Tropical Timber Organisation (model contracts, concessions, exploitation licences), the drawing up of a code of conduct and proposals for monitoring or bans under the Washington Convention (CITES).

The implementation of the Community strategy for the conservation of tropical forests has to be the result of a dialogue between the Union and the countries or regions concerned. The European Commission will only support projects

...luding in the field of indigenous peoples) where it receives government backing to do so. Five areas for possible action are proposed; (i) development aid and cooperation, (ii) actions relating to the trade in timber, (iii) development of additional resources, (iv) debt and environment, (v) research. The Commission recognises the importance of the role of indigenous peoples and with regard to their situation, the Communication states that: "The most immediate and severe suffering caused by tropical deforestation is felt by the true forest dwellers, who have lived in and off tropical forests for many thousands of years, practising slash-and-burn agriculture without destroying the forest. These indigenous forest dwellers possess knowledge of the properties of forest species which have proved, and could continue to be, valuable to industrial societies. In many areas territorial rights of such people are challenged by their governments, and their treatment is the subject of international controversy. Forest peoples are not infrequently moved into reservations too restrictive for their extensive forest conservation practices. Also the basic human rights of these people, as well as the knowledge and experience which they have of living in harmony with their environment have sometimes been ignored. The indigenous people's presence is challenged also by colonising forest farmers who seek to emulate their slash-and-burn agriculture but lack knowledge of, and respect for, the forest habitat. The numbers of these colonists also render impossible any notion of long fallows between periods of forest cultivation. Also to be considered is the social and humanitarian situation of the forest colonisers themselves, who enter the forest people's domain. As the colonisers misuse and destroy the forest they destroy the basis of their livelihood. While further forest remains they may hope to move on. However, when forest lands are cleared and become desertified, the landless become forestless as well, facing the prospect of worsening hunger or even mass starvation paralleling the plight of the former dwellers of Sahelian savanna lands".

In September 1992, the Commission transmitted to the European Council a **COMMUNICATION on the follow-up to UNCED** (SEC(92) 1631 final). This Communication proposes an initial, prompt response by the Community to the results of UNCED to re-assess its strategy towards sustainable development and make a proposal for Community participation in the Global Environment Facility. In the area of cooperation projects the Commission has provided financial and technical assistance to developing countries in the field of environment with particular emphasis on tropical forests. In addition, procedures for the environmental impact evaluation of all cooperation projects likely to have an impact on the environment, have been introduced in the project selection cycle. These take account primarily of the EEC's internal Directive 85EEC337, the World Bank Operational Directives on Environmental Assessment and the OECD Good Practices on Environment Assessment adopted in December 1991.

The seriousness of the threat to tropical forests and the need for coordinated international action within a perspective linking environment and development has called for action at Community level, complementing actions of the EC Member States. In February 1993, the Commission submitted a proposal for a **COUNCIL REGULATION on operations to promote tropical forests** (COM (93) 53 final). This draft regulation lays down objectives and modalities of such action that will promote the conservation and sustainable management of tropical forests. The European Parliament appointed a rapporteur to amend the regulation and the Council will take the final decision about the text.

Under this Regulation, Article 3 (1) "the Community shall provide financial support or technical expertise for actions which support and encourage the efforts of developing countries and their regional organisations to conserve their tropical forests, in the context of the sustainable development of those countries and regions". (2) The financing shall be directed to both public and private organisations, including NGOs and *representative associations of indigenous peoples* and of other forest dwellers, which include the conservation of tropical forests among their stated objectives or regular activities. Particular consideration shall be given to actions that promote e.g. the "involvement of local populations, including forest dwellers, in the planning and implementation of actions that are to be financed and of national and local forest utilisation plans [Art. 4(c]". The aim of the operation is to "conserve tropical forest resources through: (i) protection of forest resources by analyzing the causes of deforestation and introducing policies and measures to slow it down; (b) sustainable management of forests designated for the production of wood and other products; (c) involvement of local and native peoples in the preparation and implementation of the measures to be financed; (d) creation of the structures required for training, research, legislation and upgrading institutions concerned with the protection of forest resources". The target population is the "populations of developing countries with large areas of tropical forest, particularly people living in or around them".

Commission involvement in indigenous peoples' PROJECTS

Given the lack of available data, it is not possible to present an exhaustive overview of EC projects affecting indigenous peoples. *The long list of projects given in Annex 2* provides an interesting picture of the variety of actions that have been supported over the past few years in the field of human rights, development cooperation and environment (mostly tropical forest programmes). From 1991 onwards, there has been a remarkable increase in Community projects and programmes for indigenous peoples. Following Parliament's resolutions, this reflects growing awareness of their existence and their plight.[7] NGO projects with indigenous peoples that have been co-financed by the Commission (generally up to 50%) under budget item B7-5010 are not included in this list. Some examples are, however, described. The funding of NGO activities is generally very modest compared to support given to government programmes. The Commission has, since 1991, introduced a facility for financially supporting the activities of grassroots organisations and their networks in developing countries within the framework of the General Conditions for co-financing NGDO development schemes.

Central and South America

In its approach to development aid to Latin America, the Commission takes due account of the need to improve human rights and the social, economic and political situation of indigenous peoples. Deforestation is another important concern of the Commission. Major causes are: increasing inequalities in the distribution of wealth, especially land, migration, colonisation and government programmes, particularly road building and incentives to settle, cultivate and develop forested areas. In this context the Commission has considered that it is particularly important to support policy reforms aimed at sustainability and conservation and to encourage actions aimed at stemming migratory movements.[8]

The Commission welcomed the Parliament's adoption of resolution B3-033492 on 1992, Indigenous Peoples and the Quincentenary. It has taken action on the issue of the situation of the Amerindians in a number of ways: (i) The Commission took part in the third technical meeting on setting up an "Indigenous Fund" in La Paz from 9 to 11 April 1992 (see Part III, 2 on the Indigenous Peoples Fund). Following the meeting, it decided to support the fund. (ii) As part of its financial and technical cooperation with developing countries in Asia and Latin America, the Commission is financing rural and agricultural development projects in peasant farming areas, which help Indigenous campesinos in the uplands, (iii) Lowland Indians, i.e. of the tropical forests of Amazonia and Central America benefit from Community financing under "environment cooperation". (iv) The Commission has recently been involved in promoting programmes which not only seek to improve the socio-economic situation of the target group, but also aim at directly supporting indigenous peoples in their struggle to improve their human rights situation and their participation in the national process of consolidation of democracy. The presence of the Commission in South America is most clearly felt in tropical forest programmes. Support has been given to projects with indigenous peoples in areas such as demarcation of territory and strengthening of indigenous organisations on local, national and regional level.

In 1993 the Commission launched a large programme entitled "Development aid to the indigenous peoples of Central America" (Guatemala, El Salvador, Honduras, Nicaragua, Costa Rica and Panama) for a five year period, earmarking 7,500,000 ECU. The objective of this programme is to defend the rights and collective survival of indigenous peoples in this area and favour their contribution to the economic, social, political, and cultural future of the national societies of which they form a part. It aims to (a) reaffirm and consolidate the collective identity of the indigenous peoples, (b) promote their presence and participation in public life at all levels and (c) stimulate their economy, demarcate their territory and consolidate their control over natural resources. The development of programme sub-projects will be undertaken with the active participation of the beneficiary communities and their organisations or representatives. Responsibility for the execution of the programme will be entrusted primarily to indigenous organisations representing the communities. The management of the project lies in the hands of an executive unit under the supervision of the Commission and is headed by two co-directors, a European and an indigenous person. The experience gained during project development, should enable the Commission to build up a theoretical and practical basis, at present almost non-existent, for future projects with indigenous peoples in the Americas and elsewhere in the world.

ACP Countries

The overall framework for development cooperation between the EC and ACP countries for the decade 1990-2000 is the Lomé IV Convention. The Convention's financial instrument is the European Development Fund (EDF). The Commission can only fund projects that are submitted by an ACP country government. Article 3 of the Convention clearly states that "the ACP States shall determine the development principles; strategies and models for their economies and societies in all sovereignty". Hence, the Commission does not have much room for manoeuvre. It can not draft project proposals that support the interests of minorities or indigenous peoples and will only agree to funding if: (i) an ACP central government submits such a proposal, (ii) a project is financed under the new human rights budgetline (B7 5053) for ACP countries, or (iii) when an NGO, through budget appropriation B7-5010 submits a project. In most cases, projects in the field of cultural cooperation concentrate on strengthening the national identity, the majority culture. In other cases, such as in Tanzania, it has been government policy not to favour or disfavour any specific ethnic group and prevent a single tribe from dominating national, provincial or disctrict politics.

Some EC projects, however, have had an impact on, or involve indigenous peoples in ACP countries. In view of the fact that the Commission considers that in Africa demographic expansion and the resultant increasing need for lands and fuelwood have been significant factors behind deforestation, actions to combat deforestation cover preservation structures, provision of fuel sources and actions to arrest land degradation. On the 28th of September 1990, the Commission decided to earmark *24 million ECU for a programme aimed at the Conservation and Rational Utilisation of Africa's Forest Resources*. Other projects affecting indigenous peoples have been funded by the Commission in e.g. Mali and Niger (Tuareg), Nigeria, Botswana and Kenya.

Asia

In Asia, and more specifically in South East Asia much deforestation has been caused by unsustainable logging and, to a lesser extent, shifting cultivation. Forest management and monitoring is therefore a central concern in Asian cooperation programmes for tropical forest conservation. The Commission considers that where forest concession policies have established private incentives which encourage rapid short-term forest exploitation, efforts to change management regimes should be supported. Due to the fact that, for instance in the Philippines, the overall objective of Community development policy has been poverty alleviation, many Community projects concern tribal peoples. The Commission further supports projects involving indigenous peoples in e.g. Malaysia, Indonesia and Laos (see Annex 2).

DIGEST of Community resources available for financing indigenous peoples programmes

In theory, the European Commission has always provided possibilities for indigenous peoples and governments or NGOs that operate on their behalf to apply for funding. Until 1993, however, indigenous peoples were not specifically mentioned in the Community Budget. As a result of amendments introduced by the European Parliament, two existing budget headings [see (2) and (9)] now include indigenous peoples.

The Community budget contains a number of funds for the environment, forest conservation, the promotion of human rights or pilot projects in the field of decentralised cooperation for all developing countries. The cofinancing of actions in developing countries by NGOs is carried out under a special budget line, the volume of which has greatly increased over the past years (B7-5010).

Some of the resolutions adopted by the European Parliament, decisions of the Council and Communications by the Commission that were discussed in the preceding pages have served as a legislative basis for the creation of budget items and are referred to in the "remarks" (explanatory specifications) of the Union budget.

The main resources are budget appropriations (i.e. the appropriations entered annually in the Commission's operating budget) and resources allocated to the European Development Fund (EDF) under the Lomé Convention. The overview given below is divided into two sections: community resources reserved for NGOs and those to which NGOs may have access. Indigenous organisations can in principle have direct access to those budget-headings which are marked with an *. All other appropriations are exclusively reserved for NGOs that have their headquarters in one of the Twelve Member States. In this case, an indigenous organisation can only submit a proposal through two or more registered EC NGOs. This provision is made in order to safeguard the allocation of funds and to promote cooperation between European NGOs and organisations in the rest of the world. In some cases, the European Commission still welcomes a direct application by an NGO in a third country and offers to help find a European partner that can present and coordinate the project. The Commission can also help directly by sending an expert or consultant to Africa, Asia or Latin America to assist in elaborating a project.[9] As budget headings can change from year to year, it should be noted that information concerning budget appropriations is valid for 1994, and can be subject to slight changes.

The European Commission is represented in every ACP State and in many other developing countries by a Delegation which comprises a Head of Delegation and several members of staff. In view of the fact that the significance and relevance of an action will be assessed in relation to the local situation, applications for financial assistance can be submitted to the local Commission Delegation. The Delegations will handle the project proposals and advise the applicant. Where appropriate, they may assist, in conjunction with headquarters, in seeking suitable partners. The Delegation can determine whether a project is compatible with other Community initiatives. It is therefore a good idea to make contact with the local Commission delegation before starting work on a project.

Selected description of relevant budget headings

A. Community Resources reserved for financing NGO activities

1) Subsidies for certain activities of NGOs pursuing humanitarian aims and promoting human rights

This appropriation is intended to cover the grant of aid to NGOs pursuing humanitarian aid and promoting human rights and also the *European Human Rights Foundation.*

The European Human Rights Foundation is funded largely by the European Community, but is independent of it. However, the Board and the Administrator work closely with the EC institutions by providing their collective and individual expertise to ensure that the resources made available for promoting human rights are put to best use. The Foundation is a charitable organisation registered in the Netherlands and distributes funds for the following objects;

(i) the promotion and protection throughout the world of civil, political, economic, social and cultural rights, collectively referred to as 'human rights', as they are at present laid down in international instruments, (ii) the furtherance of endeavours to realise aims of a humanitarian nature in general.

In accordance with the Foundation's statute, the Board is composed of a maximum of nine persons of acknowledged reputation in the field of human rights. The Board considers applications in the light of the following policy; (i) Action projects are preferred to research projects, There are no grants for educational courses, (ii) 'Seed' funding for innovative projects and/or organisations, (iii) Core-funding for organisations which find it difficult to raise funds, (iv) Development or social welfare projects are not funded unless these are directly linked to human rights, e.g. the rehabilitation of political detainees, (v) A geographic balance is maintained between the different regions of the world.

Grants seldom exceed 6,400 ECU and recipients have to report on the expenditure of the grant within 12 months of receiving it. Applicants for grants must apply only on the application forms supplied by the Foundation, which have been designed to give concisely and clearly the information required by the Board. Closing dates for receiving the completed application form are 15 April for the May meeting of the Board and 15 October for the November meeting.[10]

Aid under the item A-3030 of the EC budget is further granted to NGOs pursuing humanitarian aims and defending human rights in connection with projects to be undertaken in developing countries, Central and Eastern Europe and elsewhere, and in the Community itself, and NGOs aiming to combat racism and xenophobia, rehabilitate torture victims, offer practical help to victims of human rights abuses, train those called upon to teach others about human rights, reinforce respect for the rights of the child and help children who are victims of human rights abuses.

2. Community contribution towards schemes concerning developing countries carried out by NGOs

This appropriation is e.g. intended to cover: (i) financing, jointly with NGOs, of operations to benefit the poorest sections of the population in developing countries whether associated or not, and implementation of such joint financing, (ii) bearing in mind the results of the Earth Summit held in Rio de Janeiro in 1992, and the fact that the United Nations have declared 1993 as the Year of the World's Indigenous Peoples, this appropriation may finance through indigenous

Budget Heading/financing available	Type of Aid	Admin. Depart. respons.	Official in charge	Tel.	Address/Building/Floor/Office
1. B7-5240* 5 MECU	Subsidies for the defense of human rights	I/F/	D. Napoli	2957416	G-68 05/43
2. B7-5010* 145 MECU	Contribution towards schemes concerning dev. countries by NGOs	VIII/B/2	B. Ryelandt A. Brusasco	2999861 2992974	G-1 Astrid 1/18
3.* B7-5011 5 MECU	Purchase of food products by NGOs and int. org.	VIII/B/1	A. Reithinger M. Keyes	2999860 2993003	G-1 Astrid 2/130
4.* B7-5014 2 MECU	Aid to NGOs operating in Vietnam	VIII/B/2 I/J/2	B. Ryelandt I. Teufel	2999861 2993046	G-1 Astrid 1/18
5.* B7-5015 1 MECU	Aid to NGOs in Cambodia	VIII/8/2 I/J/2	B. Ryelandt E. Wilkinson	2999861 2992332	G-1 Astrid Science 14
6. B6-6224* 109,8 MECU	Science & Technology for development	XII/B/4	T. Hall (Agr.) M. De Bruycker (Medicine)	2952808 2959172	Square de Meeus 8
7. B6-8200	Research & development	XII/G/4	A. Herrero Molina	2954683	Square de Meeus 8
8.* B7-302 20 MECU	Aid to refugees in the ALA countries	1/1/12 1/J/3	C. Scano M. San Agustin	2992632 2990810	Science 14 Science 14
9.* B7-5040 20 MECU	Environment in dev. countries	VIII/A/1	T. Clarke A. De Villepin	2993205 2990708	G-12 Evere Green
10.* B7-5041	Tropical forests	VIII/D/5 1/K/2	E. Pironio K. Bell	2992576 2992321	Evere Green Science 14

11. B7-522 14 MECU	For operations promoting human rights	VIII/5	J. Freitha	2920/6	Evere Green
12. B7-5071 15 MECU	Rehabilitation programmes in Southern Africa	VIII/E/3	J. Houtman E. Pardon	2993267 2992743	Evere Green
13.* B7-5013 3,850 MECU	Aid to NGOs operating in Chile	VIII/B/2 VIII/B/2	B. Ryelandt F. Marion	2999861 2993014	Astrid Science 14
14.* B7-5077 5 MECU	Decentralised cooperation in dev. countries	VIII/B/2	B. Ryelandt B. Huchet	2999861 2992997	Astrid 1/18
15.* B7-523 11 MECU	Democratisation process in Latin America	I/i/1,2	C. De Domingo (CA) O. Lutz (SA)	2990851 2990944	Science 14
16.* B7-5080 10 MECU	Campaigns against drug abuse	III/B/2	E. Pallis (L. Am) P. Nielsen (As-Pac.) A. Cardoso Moto (Afr-Pr.Or)	2959485 2951470 2962544	Cortenberg 100
17. B7-510 41 MECU	Emergency Aid/Disasters	I/K/2d	G. Molinier	2993245	Geneve 1
18.* B7-516 13 MECU	Humanitarian Action in Third countries, ECHO		S. Gomez Reino	2954249	Geneve 1
19.* B7-631 5 MECU	Community participation in actions by NGOs benefiting C and E Europe and former USSR	I/L/5	S. Christian	2991900	Science 29 1/43
20.* LOME IV 255 100 MECU	Aid for refugees in ACP countries	VII/5	J.L. Houdart	2992802	Geneve 12 1/58

organisations, operations that will benefit indigenous peoples communities, (iii) supporting NGO activity at regional level for transnational projects, for example, in the environmental field, health and sanitation, (iv) missions for the control of project implementation.

Basically, two types of projects can be funded through this budgetline; 1. Development operations carried out by European NGOs in developing countries to help the poorest sections of the population, 2. Campaigns co-financed with the NGOs to promote public awareness in Europe of Third World development problems and to promote solidarity between people in Europe and people in developing countries. Cofinancing can be granted under the conditions set out in the General conditions for cofinancing.

B. Some Community Resources to which NGOs may have access

6. EEC Research and development programme in the field of life science and technologies for developing countries
Under this budget heading, indigenous research institutes or local universities, with partners in the European Community, could submit a request for cofinancing, for example in the field of traditional medicine. Some relevant objectives of the programme are: (i) further strengthening of research capacity in both the developing countries and in the Community Member States in areas defined as having priority for Third World development (agriculture, health, nutrition and the environment in tropical and subtropical areas), by means of joint research projects; (ii) significant progress on themes associated with development needs, including environmental protection and the rational management of natural resources to help improve living standards and health in the developing countries, particularly the poorest among them.

The programme budget is ECU 109.8 million over four years (1991-1994), divided between the agriculture sub-programme (reduction of food shortages, development of agricultural production of high economic value) and the Medicine/health/nutrition sub-programme. Projects under the programme are carried out through shared-cost contracts bringing together scientists from the EC and from developing countries. Proposals can be invited by research bodies in the Community or in developing countries (research centres, universities, NGOs involved in research).

7. Research and development
The aim of this budget heading is to establish scientific and technological cooperation links for implementing research projects and related activities in various fields of science and technology of mutual interest, between the EC and developing countries in e.g. Latin America and Asia. Proposals may be submitted by any organisation (research centres, universities, local suitably qualified NGOs etc.) from the ALA countries.

8. Aid towards self-sufficiency for refugees and displaced persons in Asian and Latin American developing countries

This budget article was created in 1984 on the initiative of the European Parliament. The aid is for Latin American and Asian developing countries, for refugees, displaced persons, returnees and other population groups which have left their country of origin or of residence. As a supplementary measure, it can also cover survival and repatriation operations. Such measures are designed to bring about self-sufficiency until lasting solutions can be found and include the provision of the means of production for crop farming, livestock production, fisheries and crafts, and also basic infrastructure and training in line with the immediate needs of the population groups concerned, including local population groups, without excluding longer term needs. Also expenditure on studies, meetings of experts, conferences, congresses, information and publications directly linked with the achievement of the objective of the measure of which they form an integral part can be financed. Requests for financing generally follow the same procedures as proposals for cofinancing with NGOs. As a general rule, projects will be implemented by NGOs and international bodies, though in some cases they may be implemented by the Commission, by the government of the host country, consultants or, in exceptional cases, by an indigenous organisation.[11] When the main purpose of cofinancing required for humanitarian aid to assist refugees, displaced persons and returnees in Asian and Latin American developing countries is not self-sufficiency, depending on the type of operation, NGOs may apply for other Commission budget instruments such as; emergency aid, food aid, financial and technical cooperation with Asian and Latin American developing countries.

9. Environment in developing countries

This aid is for operations to manage and protect the environment and natural resources in all developing countries (ACP, Latin America, Asia and Southern and Easter Mediterranean). It is intended to cover the achievement of sustainable development by contributing to a real integration of the environmental dimension in the development process. The creation of suitable instruments and the undertaking of seed projects will constitute the basic elements of such integration throughout the areas concerned, with particular attention to desertification control. It is also intended to finance projects for the conservation of endangered species, notably the rhinoceros, the elephant, etc. It covers expenditure on studies, meetings of experts, conferences, congresses, information and publication directly linked with the achievement of the objective of the measure of which they form an integral part.

The Commission decides on financing and implementing arrangements in agreement with the government concerned and with the body responsible for carrying out the operation. Operations are eligible for full financing, not excluding the possibility of cofinancing.

10. Operations to promote tropical forests

This appropriation is intended to cover the financing of operations for the protection and rational management of tropical rain forests, particularly forests of vital importance for blobal phenomena such as climatic change and cualtural and biological variety. Aid may take the form of sending experts, drawing up reports, funding sustainable development projects, etc. This appropriation is also used, pursuant to UNCED, to finance a number of pilot operations for th protection, regeneration and rational management of tropical forests. These projects must be developed in full cooperation with local communities, NGOs regions and specialists form the region, and of course in cooperation with governments. Indigenous People shall be involved in the preparation and implementation of projects. Priority will be given to projects where the local population, being the most suitable persons for conservation of tropical forests, are fully involved. Private and public institutions, both national and local, protected area authorities, and NGOs including indigenous associations and community groups could be recipients of aid under this heading.

11. Support for operations promoting human rights and democracy in the developing countries

This heading was created in 1992 following the Communication from the Commission to the Council and Parliament in April 1991 entitled "Human rights, democracy and development cooperation policy". It is stipulated that the funds are to be used in close connection with Community development policies and are made available for projects throughout the developing world, with exception of Latin America, which is covered by another budgetline. Purpose of the budget line is to strengthen the fabric of civil society: support for local human rights associations, boosting participation in grassroots associations in various development fields and to provide support for the transition to democracy and strengthen the rule of law. Any association specialised in the promotion of human rights will be eligible for funding. In this case, European based organisations may apply, but **priority will be given to local bodies**. Also cooperative movements linked to development programmes that help create and strengthen the fabric of democracy and press bodies are invited to submit proposals. Finally also government bodies whose role is to consolidate the rule of law (courts, parliaments, electoral operations) may receive financing from this budgetline.

14. Decentralised cooperation in the developing countries

Decentralised cooperation goes hand in hand with the Community's stated policy of supporting democratisation and promoting human rights in a developing context. It represents a new approach in development relations in seeking to establish direct links with local representative bodies e.g. local authorities, local associations and groupings representative of local interests or solidarity initiatives or organisations and networks from the productive sector, in particular freely established trade unions and cooperatives. The aim of decentralised cooperation is to promote local initiatives which reflect the whole gamut of specific situations and groups of population, it does not, however, take place outside the framework of official relations between the EC and developing countries. Given that the significance of an action will be assessed in relation to the local situation, applications for financial assistance should be sent to the local Commission Delegation.

15. Democratisation process in the Latin American region

This appropriation is intended to cover the financing of special activities to contribute to the process of democratisation in the Latin American region, including Haiti and Cuba, particularly in assisting the reintegration into civilian life of those who have fought in civil wars in Central America. It may also be used to support democratically elected authorities who have been the victims of coup attempts and who retain the confidence of the EC or cover expenditure on studies, meetings of experts, conferences, congresses, information and publications directly linked with the achievement of the objective of the measure of which they form an integral part. Furthermore, this budget heading reserves special attention for projects in favour of the most vulnerable groups of society, children, women and indigenous peoples. In 1993 there was a 50% increase of funds, 8 MECU for Central America and 7 MECU for South America.

16. Programme of North-South cooperation schemes in the context of the campaign against drug abuse

Under this budget item, local organisations are also invited to approach the Commission directly. In principle the possibility exists that an indigenous organisation submits a project proposal directly to the Commission requesting technical or financial support, for example, concerning changing the production of coca to another crop. This appropriation also covers the organisation of seminars, expert studies and research, the initiation of information, awareness-raising, education, treatment and rehabilitation schemes in the context of the campaign against drug abuse, and programmes to convert from illegal crops.

17. Emergency aid to disaster victims in developing and other third countries

Any information on emergency aid procedures is available from the body which coordinates NGO emergency aid at the following address; Disaster and Emergency Relief Group Secretariat, Postfach D-7800 Freibourg, Germany, Tel: 49.761.2000, Fax: 49.761.200583.

18. Humanitarian action in third countries

This appropriation in intended to cover support, in the form of Community cofinancing, for humanitarian initiatives of NGOs to help the disadvantaged sectors of the population in third countries. Such action is aimed principally at the undertaking of pilot projects by Community NGOs in conjunction with local NGOs. In particular it aims to improve the living and health conditions of people in specific difficult situations in order to help them to fend for themselves. The cost supplying equipment, training schemes and technical assistance may be financed. The appropriation is administered by ECHO, an independent Task Force financed by the Commission.

19. Community participation in actions by NGOs benefitting the countries of Central and Eastern Europe and the States of the former Soviet Union

This appropriation is intended to cover aid to NGOs benefiting the most disadvantaged groups in agriculture, health care and housing at local level. 3 MECU is reserved for the States of the former Soviet Union.

21. Lome IV, Articles 252 and 253, EDF Microprojects

As a practical response to the development needs of local communities, the European Development Fund (EDF) participates in the financing of microprojects at the ACP States' request. Programmes for microprojects cover small projects which are likely to have an economic and social impact on the life of the people and the local communities in the ACP States, both rural and urban areas. In order to be eligible for Community financing, microprojects must; (i) have a social and economic impact on the lives of local people, (ii) meet a real priority need expressed and observed at local level, (iii) be undertaken with the active participation of the local community.

Any operations for which Community aid is requested must be based on an initiative from the local community which is to receive the aid. As is the rule for all operations provided for in the Lomé Convention, the EDF contributes to the financing of microprojects at the request of the ACP States concerned.

Conclusions and recommendations

As has been indicated on repeated occasions the European Parliament has expressed interest and concern for the plight of indigenous peoples. The EC Council of Ministers has adopted various resolutions and regulations and the European Commission has made a number of proposals and also supported many projects concerning indigenous peoples. Directorates General I, VIII and XI, (External Relations, Development and Environment respectively) are active in developing programmes and projects and initiating studies on indigenous peoples. This activity, however, has tended to remain compartmentalised and the officials concerned do not have policy instruments to coordinate or guide their initiatives. In the International Year of the World's Indigenous People, the Commission increased both the number and quality of projects in defence of the rights of indigenous peoples. However, the Community has not yet developed a coherent policy framework for this field of activity.

It is difficult to determine the impact of Community projects on indigenous peoples. Indigenous peoples are only mentioned as a target group in a number of specific projects in Central and South America. On other continents, they are not even specifically identified or mentioned in proposals or project evaluations. For example the Community programme for the rational utilisation of Africa's Forest Resources mentions consultation of local populations but does not specifically refer to indigenous peoples.

Over the years, Community projects have undoubtedly had some effect on indigenous peoples all over the world. But since the notion of indigenous peoples (particularly in Asia and Africa) was practically unknown to policy makers until recently, this impact has not been systematically registered in Commission files. Indigenous groups have been variously classified as: "forest dwellers", "rural or urban poor" or as "peasants". As a result, the European Community has often given financial support to projects without proper consultation of the indigenous peoples living in the region. In some instances, indigenous representatives have brought this omission to the attention of the Community Institutions (see for example the study of the Montanosa Research and Development Centre in the Philippines on the EEC-CECAP project in the Cordilleras).[12]

Yet, when taking all this into account there is no doubt that all three Community institutions are demonstrating a growing concern for indigenous peoples and are recognising the need for appropriate and well-designed action. The Commission has developed proposals for *environmental impact evaluation* of all cooperation projects likely to have an effect on the environment. In addition it has stated: "environmental impact assessment procedures will cover the impact of projects on local populations, indigenous peoples included. In this context the Commission will examine the scope and content of the World Bank's directive on indigenous peoples and may well draw on it for the purposes of its own operations".[13]

According to Mrs Daes, chairwoman/rapporteur of the UN Working Group on Indigenous Populations: "Indigenous Peoples have told us that their human rights are part of a total quest for well-being. This holistic approach, which recognises the interconnection of development, peace, environment and human rights issues, is one which is increasingly recognised by the UN itself. We do not want the International Year to be a lot of empty words, we want there to be real advances".[14] In this spirit, the Decade of the World's Indigenous People should further encourage the development of new relationships between States, international organisations, including the EU, and indigenous peoples. It goes without saying that this partnership must be equitable and based on mutual respect and understanding.

To this end the following proposals are advanced:

(i) The Commission could draw up a proposal to the Council and Parliament on a **coherent Community policy** on indigenous peoples including specific guidelines for projects and programmes affecting indigenous communities in the field of human rights, development and environment;

(ii) The Commission could establish a specialised **Task Force on Indigenous Peoples** with a threefold remit:
- to coordinate all Community activities regarding indigenous peoples and improve expertise in this field,
- to provide technical advice and guidance concerning the specific needs and situation of indigenous peoples to desk officers, officials of Commission Delegations and technical units that are responsible for Community projects in countries where indigenous peoples live,
- to be a focal point of contact for any indigenous group, NGO or international organisation requesting information about Community policy, projects and programmes and provide assitance to groups soliciting financial support;

(iii) The Commission could create a **specific budget line** for indigenous peoples. Such funds should not be administered according to traditional European Community-designed development models but should develop new criteria for support on the basis of priorities set by indigenous communities;

(iv) The Parliament, Commission and Council could each **designate a focal point**: contact person, unit, task force, delegation, intergroup or committee, for the Decade of the World's Indigenous People;

(v) The Commission could **invite indigenous peoples** to participate in the planning, implementation and evaluation of programmes and projects affecting their living conditions and future. It could consult and request the consent of representatives of indigenous communities likely to be affected by Community projects at all stages of project implementation;

(vi) The Commission could **provide an annual report to the Council and Parliament** on the activities undertaken and the resources used involving indigenous communitities;

(vii) The Commission could establish a **network of contacts** with specialised international organisations and NGOs that can assist the Commission in its utilisation of resources and on issues requiring expert advice. It is worth noting in this connection that the UN General Assembly has recommended that the UN provides technical assistance to governments wishing to make provisions in their legislation for protecting the human rights of indigenous people, in particular on questions of land, environmental protection and strengthening cultural identity, and provide technical and financial assistance for implementing such legislation.

Commission of the European Communities
200 Rue de la Loi
B-1049 Brussels
Tel: 32.2.2991111

References

1. Mrs Daniela Napoli is the director of the Unit, Rue Belliard 68, 1st floor, Office 35, European Commission, Brussels, Tel: 32.2.2955501, Fax: 32.2.2957850).
2. Resolution of the Council and of the Member States meeting in the Council on "Human Rights, Democracy and Development", 28-11-1991; EP Resolution Doc. B3-1783/91, on Human Rights, Democracy and Development, November 1991.
3. Press Statement on the activity of the Community and its Member States in the field of human rights in 1992, Brussels, 11 December 1992.
4. SEC (92) 915 Final/2, Brussels 19 September 1992, Development Cooperation Policy in the Run-Up to 2000, the Community's relations with the developing countries viewed in the context of political union, the consequences of the Maastricht Treaty.
5. See also: Working document of the Commission Services on Tropical Forests Cooperation in 1992 under Budget Line B7-5041.
6. Annual report for 1990 on *action taken by the European Commission in response to Parliament's own-initiative resolutions.*
7. In view of the fact that the Commission does not keep a record or statistics of the impact its projects have on different sectors of the society, e.g. indigenous peoples, many different sources had to be used for the compilation of this list: answers to European Parliament written and oral questions, bi-annual reports of the Commission to own-initiative reports by the Parliament, letters to Members, assistance from desk officers, experts and civil servants of the Commission.
8. *Ibid* footnote 5.
9. Any additional information about NGOs in the European Community can be obtained from the Secretariat of the Liaison Committee of NGOs to the European Communities at the following address; 10, Square Ambiorix, B-1040 Brussels, Tel; 32.2.7364087, Fax; 32.2.7321934.
10. European Human Rights Foundation, Peter Ashman, Rue van Campenhout 13 B-1040 Brussels, Tel: 32.2.7349424, Fax: 32.2.7346831.

11. Under this budgetheading several projects have already been financed for indigenous peoples, although the peoples involved were not classified as such; in South East Asia, *Karen* refugees from Myanmar are considered to be displaced persons in Thailand, where a health programme financed by the Community is being carried out by an NGO. In Central America, *Guatemalan refugees* in the Mexican State of Campeche have been receiving aid via UNHCR since 1985 under a multi-annual programme. Among the various projects financed by the Community in Guatemala, is a project to resettle returnees and displaced persons implemented by the Ministry of Development since 1988 in Hueheutenango province.
12. *The EEC-CECAP and other ODA projects in the Cordillera*, Ma. Elena R. Regpala, Montanosa Research and development Centre (MRDC), Sagada, Mountain Province, Philippines, Rowena Reyes-Boquiren, University of the Philippines College Baguio, Baguio City, Center for Development Programmes in the Cordillera, Inc. Rm. 304 Hamada Bldg., Upper Mabini St., Baguio City. This investigation explains that indigenous peoples have suffered negative effects from not having participated in the planning stage of the programme. In the event, one of the recommendations of the study was included in the Financial Agreement for CECAP: "indigenous communities should be consulted at all stages of an EC project". Another indigenous study concerning a different project co-financed by the European Commission — the Aurora Integrated Area Development Project — demonstrates that lack of popular participation in the implementation of a project leads to discontent among indigenous peoples.

    In oral question (H-1139/93), however, the Commission states that it "is aware of the criticisms voiced by the Cordillera Peoples Alliance, and considers them to be entirely unfounded".
13. Quote from a letter of Commissioner van den Broek, responsible for Political Affairs to the President of the EP Sub-Committee on Human Rights, Ken Coates, May, 5, 1993. Recently, the Commission presented an *Environment Manuel* which lays down the new environmental provisions which will apply to all European Development Fund projects and programmes as from June 1993. These provisions provide procedural steps for ensuring that the environmental consequences of any action are adequately integrated into the project design. The manual is based on the Lome IV Convention, the OECD Good Practices for Environmental Impact Assessment of Development Projects, and the World Bank Operational Directive on Environmental Assessment. It presents procedures and a methodology for ensuring that development projects funded by the Community outside its borders follow broadly similar environmental procedures as those within (e.g. the EIA Council Directive 85/337/EEC on the Assessment of the Effects of Certain Public and Private Projects on the Environment).
14. *"Indigenous People, a new partnership, International Year 1993"*, published by the UN Department of Public Information, DPI1249-92710-July 1992-30M).

II. The United Nations System and Indigenous Peoples

The United Nations is an intergovernmental organisation with 184 member states (August 1993). It is an organisation of sovereign nations, not a world government. It provides the machinery to help find solutions to disputes or problems and deals with virtually any matter of concern to humanity. The UN does not legislate like a national parliament, but in meeting rooms representatives of almost all countries of the world have a voice and vote in shaping the policies of the international community. The main purpose of the UN is to preserve world peace and help resolve disputes between nations. One of the most important rights of the UN Charter is self-determination, or the right of peoples to govern themselves. In the first 15 years of the UN, most countries formerly under colonial rule attained self-government or independence. Another main function of the UN under the Charter is the promotion of higher standards of living, full employment and econmic and social progress.

1. It has been the main concern of the *ILO* (International Labour Organisation and specialised agency of the UN) to formulate international labour standards and to guarantee their effective implementation. Basically ILO seeks to improve working and living conditions through the adoption of international labour conventions and recommendations setting minimum standards in such fields as wages, hours of work, conditions of employment, and social security. It also conducts research and technical cooperation activities, including vocational training and management development. The ILO international legal standards concerning indigenous peoples are Convention 107 and 169 (see page 56). Unfortunately, only a limited number of countries have acceded to these Conventions (see page 72).

2. *The World Bank* and the IMF are the UN specialised agencies for international finance and money. The World Bank Group, with headquarters in Washington comprises: IBRD (International Bank for Reconstruction and Development), IDA (International Development Association) and IFC (International Finance Corporation). Formal relations between the Bank and the UN were approved in 1947. The common objective of these institutions is to help raise standards of living in the world by channeling financial resources from developed countries to developing countries. "While the World Bank has traditionally financed all kinds of infrastructure facilities such as roads, railways and power facilities, its present development strategy places increasing emphasis on investments which directly affect the poor by making them more productive and by including them as active participants in the developing process". The Bank works closely with UNDP and often serves as executing agency for UNDP

projects. It developed a special directive 4.20 concerning indigenous peoples (see page 83).

3. The United Nations Working Group on Indigenous Populations (*UNWGIP*) is one of the three Working Groups of the Subcommission on Prevention of Discrimination and Protection of Minorities. Its mandate is to review developments pertaining to the promotion and protection of human rights and fundamental freedoms of indigenous people and give special attention to the evolution of standards concerning the rights of indigenous people, taking into account both the similarities and the differences in the situations and aspirations of these people throughout the world. In 1988, the Subcommission abandoned the term "indigenous populations" in favour of "indigenous peoples". In 1993, the Working Group finalised the Draft Declaration on the Rights of Indigenous Peoples.

4. The purpose of the United Nations Educational, Scientific and Cultural Organisation (*UNESCO*) is to contribute to peace and security by promoting collaboration among the nations through education, science and culture in order to further universal respect for justice, the rule of law and for human rights and fundamental freedoms. UNESCO is a specialised UN agency that has prepared several conventions and recommendations relating to human rights.

5. In the forefront of efforts to bring about social and economic progress is *UNDP*, the UN Development Programme. It administers and coordinates the great majority of the technical assistance provided through the UN system. It works with the Governments of developing countries to carry out projects in various sectors, such as agriculture, industry and education. With an annual budget of 1,3 billion dollars, UNDP is the world's largest multilateral grant assistance organisation. Most of the projects funded by the Programme are executed by agencies and organisations within the UN system, including ILO and UNESCO.

6. The office of the UN High Commissioner for Refugees (*UNHCR*) provides international protection, material assistance and seeks durable solutions to the plight of millions of refugees all over the world. UNHCR is a related UN organ and has 43 members. Membership is on the widest possible geographical basis from those states (members of the UN and others) with a demonstrated interest in, and devotion to, the solution of the refugee problem.

7. The International Fund for Agricultural Development (*IFAD*), is a United Nations specialised agency for financing for agriculture. Its aim is to mobilise additional financial resources from donors to be made available on concessional terms for agricultural development in developing member states. To this end the fund provides financing primarily for projects and programmes specifically designed to introduce, expand, or improve food production systems, and to strengthen related policies and institutions within the framework of national priorities and strategies.

1. The International Labour Organisation and Convention 169

A. The ILO and Indigenous and Tribal Peoples

by Lee Swepston and Manuela Tomei

Introduction

Indigenous and tribal peoples are probably the largest identifiable disadvantaged group in the world, numbering 300 million people by some estimates. They are at the bottom of social indicators in almost every country where they live: with highest infant mortality rates, a large prison population and widespread poverty. They have the lowest levels of literacy and expenditure on education and health care. But despite all this they have received very little international attention until the last few years.

Why should this be so? In most countries, they have been victims rather than beneficiaries of economic development — a contradiction for those who have had high hopes of being able to create a stable and prosperous world through development. Their experience challenges, in many ways, the assumption that economic development brings benefit to everyone.

There is a growing momentum, however, to provide protection and assistance to indigenous and tribal peoples around the world. The major objective of the International Year of the World's Indigenous People has been to develop a partnership between the States and indigenous and tribal peoples. The International Labour Organisation has been at the forefront of this effort since its earliest days in two essential ways: standard-setting and technical assistance.

Globalisation and multi-ethnicity

During the past few years, dramatic changes have taken place on the national and international scene. Globalisation and regionalisation are weakening the ability of nation States to control economic events. The decline of economic power and influence of the nation State is accompanied by an increasing demand for decentralisation and participation.

Ethnicity is emerging as a political force worldwide replacing ideological differences. Ethnic identity, by evoking a universe of shared language, history and values, has become an important factor of aggregation and mobilisation for people. The concept of democracy has evolved from a situation characterised by the dominion of the majority to another based on the respect of the minorities. It has been said that wars do not explode any longer between States, but within States.[1] The human, social and economic costs entailed by inter-ethnic conflicts can no longer be denied or ignored.

Moreover, it is widely recognised that, even though economic growth can certainly facilitate an improvement in human development, it does not translate automatically into an improvement in the well-being of the people, namely their ability to conduct a long and healthy life, to cultivate their talents and to live with self-respect and dignity.[2]

This is particularly true in the case of indigenous and tribal peoples, who have far too often been the victims rather than the beneficiaries of progress and modernisation. Their diversity was once deemed to be the principal cause of their "backwardness" and "erasing" it was therefore the best and only solution possible. A process of forced and unsuccessful assimilation was launched which resulted in indigenous and tribal peoples remaining on the fringe of society, with no means or possibilities either to enter the mainstream economy on equal footing or to continue relying on their traditional economic systems. They were deprived of their dignity and self-esteem.

Drawing lessons from past experience and failures, the current development agenda places people and human capital development in the centre. Quality of life and secure livelihood have replaced income and consumption levels as the major targets of development programmes.

But this new orientation poses challenges, since it is anchored in concepts which are not easily quantifiable. They depend heavily on the system of values, perceptions and aspirations of each individual/social group within a given economic and political context. Uni-dimensional and pre-established models and patterns of development have shown their limitations.

> "True development is based on culture. . . . The systematic attempt to destroy the Quechua and Aymara cultures is the source of the nation's frustrations. . . . Carried away by a practical form of materialism, they have been led to believe that progress is based solely on the economic aspects of life. We peasants want economic development . . . We do not want to give up our noble inherited integrity in favour of a pseudo integrity. We are foreigners in our own country. . . . The lack of real participation in the economic, political and social life of the country is their biggest frustration. Without this it will be impossible to create national unity and achieve the dynamic, harmonious economic development which is appropriate to our needs and our reality".[3]

This new model of development requires a more positive assessment of the role of the State and the establishment of new forms of action and interaction with the civil society, including indigenous and tribal peoples.

The major challenge is to establish and consolidate a framework and rules of action agreed upon by governments, indigenous peoples and other relevant social actors to ensure a peaceful and constructive co-existence, and sustainable growth. The challenge is to reconcile local aspirations and needs with the welfare of the nation as a whole. This requires:
– a common platform of discussion;
– opportunities, fora and channels for discussion and dialogue; and
– a strong indigenous organisation.

Consensus-building over the costs entailed by the development process and their sharing among different social actors is an essential component of this new strategy.

International standards

The ILO was created in 1919 (at the same time as the League of Nations) and began to work on protection of what it then called "native populations" as early as 1921. It was not until after World War II, however, that the new United Nations system turned to the more experienced ILO to lead a new effort in the international arena.

In 1953 the ILO published its book *Indigenous Peoples*,[4] a pioneering work that still remains a valuable source of reference. This was part of the preparations for the *Andean Indian Programme*, a multidisciplinary effort that has never been equalled by the United Nations system. It was carried out jointly by the United Nations, ILO, FAO, UNESCO, UNICEF and WHO, under the ILO's general coordination.

At the same time, the ILO began to consider the adoption of international legal standards to protect these vulnerable groups. This had been the ILO's principal tool for social protection since its founding, and by the early 1950s, the ILO had already adopted more than 100 international Conventions.

With its growing interest in indigenous and tribal peoples as economically active, but often non-wage earning elements of national populations, came the decision to adapt the ILO's traditional tools to their protection. At the same time, the ILO turned to the other parts of the new international system to widen the scope of its mandate in this vast area. Thus it was that the ILO began work with a view to the adoption in 1957 of what was to become the Indigenous and Tribal Populations Convention, 1957 (No.107) and its accompanying Recommendation No.104, which were to remain the only international legal instruments adopted specifically on these peoples for more than 30 years.[5] Since the 1953 book mentioned above, the ILO decided to add detailed information on "tribal and semi-tribal" groups in addition to the simpler — and narrower — designation of "indigenous populations". Both elements of the definition were later included in Convention No.107.

The discussions led to the adoption in 1957 of Convention No.107. Convention No.107 was eventually ratified by 27 States.[6]

Criticism began to be felt in about 1975 regarding the integrationist approach of Convention No.107, in that it favoured integrating indigenous and tribal parts of a country's population above the preservation of their traditional cultures and traditional ways of life. This, in turn, reflected the fact that the international view of the correct approach had changed.

This was in very large part due to the establishment of indigenous organisations at the international level. They began speaking for themselves at about this time in the United Nations and other international fora. They said repeatedly — and of course they were correct — that Convention No.107 did not respond to their present needs and aspirations, and should be brought up to date.

Urged by indigenous peoples and various bodies in the UN system, the Governing Body of the International Labour Office decided to begin the work that led to the adoption of a revised Convention in 1989. The Indigenous and

Tribal Peoples Convention, 1989 (No.169) has become the primary instrument in international law in this field.

The fundamental difference between Convention No.169 and the earlier instrument is its approach of respect for cultures, ways of life and traditional organisations of indigenous and tribal peoples. Convention No.169 is based on the premise that these peoples will survive whereas Convention No.107 assumed that they would eventually be integrated.

In this same context, Convention No.169 refers to indigenous and tribal "peoples" and not "populations". It also includes the fundamental concept that indigenous and tribal peoples shall be closely involved in the planning and implementation of development projects that affect them. This takes account of the fact that most of the "development" projects that had affected them in the past were decided upon without consultation of indigenous people. The Convention stops short of assigning "a right of veto" over development projects to indigenous people, which probably would have reduced the chances of ratification, but insisted on the provision of consultations thus offering a real chance for these peoples to be heard and to have an effect on decisions.

The Convention also includes numerous mentions of the traditional organisations of these peoples as the instrument of choice for consulting them. This is intended to reinforce their own ways of taking decisions, and to prevent unscrupulous "consultations" with non-representative groups, a favoured tactic for obtaining consent where the people concerned have never actually been consulted. Customary law and the methods traditionally used for decision-making are both recognised in the Convention.

Land rights is of course the most important factor in the continued survival of these peoples. The Convention provides for the recognition of the rights of ownership and possession by these peoples of the lands they have traditionally occupied and for the effective protection of these rights to be guaranteed (Article 14). In Article 15, the rights of these peoples to the natural resources pertaining to their lands is guaranteed, as well as their participation in the benefits of exploration and exploitation of these resources. Article 16 states that they shall not be removed from their lands; but that if such removal is necessary as an exceptional measure it shall take place only with their free and informed consent or after appropriate procedures. It also guarantees their right to return once the emergency has past. Other provisions deal with protection from unauthorised intrusions, transfer of rights in these lands and provision for future growth.

The Convention deals also with labour, vocational training, social security, health and education. There are important provisions for these peoples to be granted control over their own health and education programmes, when they are able to assume this responsibility. Finally, it requires ratifying States to encourage contacts and cooperation between indigenous and tribal peoples across national borders.[7]

The ILO has a well-developed supervisory mechanism to ensure that ratified Conventions are implemented by the States bound by them. Once a Convention has been ratified, the government is required to submit an annual report on its implementation in law and in practice. The initial examination of the implementation of ratified Conventions is carried out by the *Committee of*

Experts on the Application of Conventions and Recommendations, a body of independent experts in law and social sciences. If the Committee finds it necessary, it may make comments or ask for further information from governments. Its annual report[8] contains information on the situation in several countries each year.

The International Labour Conference may then invite certain governments to appear before it to discuss the situation. Such discussions have taken place on a number of occasions in recent years as concerns the application of Convention No.107 — for instance, by Bangladesh, Bolivia, Brazil, India, etc. The Conference Committee's report includes a detailed description of each discussion, and any remaining questions are followed-up by the Committee of Experts.

The comments made by the supervisory bodies usually have the effect of obliging the government to re-examine its own situation in the light of these comments. They are also often followed up by offers of technical assistance by the ILO, which can lead to an improvement in the situation. If satisfactory action is not taken, then the ILO continues the examination until the situation is resolved.

Technical cooperation and standards: a dialectic relationship

The principles and provisions of Convention No.169 guide ILO's activities in the field of technical cooperation and standards. These are the principal tools of the ILO to eliminate discrimination and differential treatment against indigenous and tribal peoples in terms of access to production supplies, to technological assets and skills; of wage differentials and levels of income; of occupational segregation; and of degree and levels of participation in political life.

Through the promotion of the Convention, the ILO seeks to:
- provide opportunities for different levels of government and other parties to develop a shared understanding of the major problems and aspirations of indigenous and tribal peoples and collaborate on diagnosis, prescriptions and implementation;
- establish the basic grounds for discussion between governments and indigenous peoples;
- encourage the gradual harmonisation of approaches and policy guidelines concerning indigenous and tribal peoples within the UN system; and
- help develop a common language among states with regard to the treatment of indigenous and tribal peoples.

To combat the legal dimension of disadvantage and discrimination against indigenous and tribal peoples, the ILO strategy relies on a set of measures focusing on (i) changing discriminatory policies; (ii) improving the enforcement of national and international law; and (iii) education and awareness raising among indigenous and tribal peoples.

For legal reform to be effective, it has to be accompanied, supported and monitored by the people concerned. For the people to back this process of transformation, it is necessary that they understand the constraints and possibilities of the law and the relationship between law and socio-economic development. Another crucial factor is to change the perception that the dominant society has of indigenous peoples and vice-versa, and often to change the perception that indigenous and tribal peoples have of themselves.

The ILO has always taken the position that a purely legal response is not sufficient. For people who suffer from precarious living and working conditions, law may appear meaningless and its application insensitive.

To change discriminatory attitudes against indigenous and tribal peoples, the economic and social environment surrounding them has to change as well. To persuade the dominant society that it is worthwhile "investing" in these peoples, not only for humanitarian reasons but also for social and economic gains, and political stability, their actual and potential contributions to national development and welfare need to be made visible. The material conditions of their existence have to improve. Indigenous and tribal peoples have to re-gain self-esteem and self-confidence.

To ensure that these peoples have access to the national political and economic system on an equal footing, they must be able to (a) articulate their grievances, by building up persuasive and functional arguments, (b) exert influence, by lobbying and establishing alliances, and (c) become self-sufficient and capable of sound economic management.

This explains the high importance attached by the ILO to initiatives geared towards the improvement of their living and working conditions, by promoting a more equitable asset ownership structure, building on organisational capacities, developing constituencies for change, and generating employment and income opportunities.

Land rights: strategies to increase indigenous and tribal peoples' access to land

The critical importance of land for the livelihood and survival of indigenous and tribal peoples as distinct societies is very well documented. It is widely recognised that land tenure security is instrumental to enhanced productivity and sounder environmental management, and that traditional systems and patterns of land use, distribution and transfer have proved more sustainable in fragile and harsh environments than have systems designed for other situations.

However, land and resource rights are very sensitive and complex issues. This explains the variety and diversity of legal and administrative forms by which access of indigenous and tribal peoples to and control over their traditional territories have been regulated worldwide. In Asian countries where there is a long tradition of management and control of forest resources by the State, there is a certain resistance towards the recognition of special rights for indigenous peoples or granting some degree of control over these resources. In Latin America, the normative framework is much more favourable, and provides a significant degree of indigenous self-government over their traditional lands.

In the former case, the entry point might be the provision of technical assistance to strengthen community-based forest management and conservation schemes, allowing for rights over minor forest products. In the latter, the enforcement of existing laws and the strengthening of the organisation and technical skills of indigenous communities, might represent the most effective way of reaching the same objective.

In both cases the recognition and protection of these rights under national law is necessary to accord greater security for indigenous and tribal peoples over their lands. It is not, however, sufficient. Facilities and opportunities have to be provided to indigenous communities to allow them to manage and benefit from these resources on a long-term basis. This requires the establishment of adequate research and investigation systems on traditional knowledge in collaboration with indigenous and tribal peoples, extension services, marketing facilities and access to information. This also requires communities to be organised and capable of defending their territories from encroachment. For example:

In **India**, through the "Wasteland Development through Women's Organisation" project, the ILO has sought to address the dual objective of creating collective access to land for tribal women and improving the environmental conditions in degraded areas of two States, West Bengal and Gujarat. By gaining access to wasteland and proving their organisational and technical capacity to turn barren lands in economic assets, tribal women have been able to (i) meet their basic fuel and food needs; (ii) improve their long-term income and employment opportunities; (iii) increase their consumer and credit credibility; (iv) enhance their self-esteem and self-confidence; and (v) increase their status and participation in local and State-level decision-making bodies.

Working in two separate areas characterised by different political, institutional and economic contexts, and different target groups (in West Bengal the group was more homogeneous culturally and socially, whereas in Gujarat it was much more stratified), the ILO was able to test and refine approaches and methodologies. Special efforts were made to capitalise on and share experience with other development actors working on the same subject. Through dissemination, discussion and exchange of experience, a policy dialogue was stimulated to work out policy recommendations for future wasteland development programmes on ways to facilitate women's access to land.

In **Bolivia**, within the framework of the UNDP-sponsored project "Assistance in the formulation of policies for indigenous peoples of Bolivia's lowlands", proposals were formulated for draft laws on policies targeting indigenous peoples nationwide, and on the reform of the agency responsible for the well-being of indigenous peoples. Diagnostic surveys of the territorial situation and ecological conditions of indigenous territories and their legal situation were conducted. In collaboration with indigenous representatives, field visits were carried out to assess on the spot the quality of the lands, to discuss land demarcation procedures and techniques, and to identify projects allowing the local communities to enhance their livelihood in a sustainable fashion. Experience gained in other countries of the region, including Colombia, was shared with the Bolivian Government, as a means to reinforce local human resources and help develop a sub-regional common policy towards the conservation of the Amazon, reconciling environmental protection with respect for the rights of indigenous peoples. The collaboration and support of other inter-governmental and non-governmental agencies was sought to obtain the necessary financial and technical support, to harmonise guidelines and programmes in this area, and to increase influence on national policies.

A regional development initiative: the Regional Development Fund of Indigenous Peoples in Latin America

The Statute of the Fund explicitly relies on Convention No.169 as the legal and moral framework of reference of the Fund and calls upon the governments of the region to ratify the Convention. Consultations with indigenous organisations were undertaken prior to and during the design of the Fund. They participated and made their voices heard in all inter-agency meetings geared towards the definition of the role and scope of the Fund (see chapter III.2 on the Regional Development Fund of Indigenous Peoples).

Building consensus: Indigenous peoples in the Philippines

In the **Philippines**, it is only very recently that the Government has started to pay attention to the precarious living and working conditions of indigenous peoples, who represent around 17 per cent of the total population. A number of important provisions ranging from political representation to the recognition of indigenous peoples' rights to their ancestral lands and respect for their diversity can be found in the 1987 Constitution. But there is still a long way to go. The major challenge is to ensure that national policies take into consideration the cultural specificities of indigenous peoples, and their needs and aspirations. During the past three decades, tremendous pressure has been exerted on their ancestral lands by economic and political development.

Another big challenge is to reach consensus, or at least more points of convergence, within the Philippines indigenous movement. Divisions exist in terms of objectives, strategies, and alliances. Differences are rooted in the origins and history of indigenous organisations in the Philippines. Indigenous peoples started to organise and mobilise in response to the Marcos regime. With the restoration of democracy and the opening of the political arena, the need has emerged for new tactics and strategies, complementing advocacy and political work with more action and development-oriented activities. Guidance is needed both to articulate suitable models of development for and by indigenous peoples, and to generate the internal consensus required to lobby and push for their implementation.

It was within this framework that a multi-disciplinary fact-finding mission was carried out in early 1993, with the support of UNDP. The findings and recommendations of the mission were shared with indigenous representatives, the NGO community and the Government during a National Workshop and the national Technical Seminar on Convention No.169, organised by the ILO. After these discussions, they were revised.

These events permitted the major indigenous organisations to sit together for the first time and discuss their divergences and measure the implications and costs for the indigenous cause. They were able to present to the Government and other social actors a common position concerning their major problems and possible ways to tackle them. One of the major outcomes of the workshop and seminar was the decision by the indigenous representatives to set up an Indigenous Committee, comprising all participating organisations and open to further affiliation. The principal task of this Committee is to continue the consensus building process.

Conclusions

The ILO is only one of the actors in the unfolding story of international development assistance for indigenous and tribal peoples — but it is a key actor. We believe that these peoples, wherever they may live, have the right to their continued existence in conditions of respect, equality, freedom and dignity. We believe that international assistance, whether through standards or direct help, must respect these characteristics. The ILO is ready to share its experience with others, learn from these peoples themselves how to improve our own work, and work with them to make the contribution we can to their future. We hope that the International Year and Decade will help establish the grounds for a concerted and long-term effort engaging as equal partners the indigenous and tribal peoples and the governments and international community.
May, 1993.

LEE SWEPSTON, Chief of the Equality of Rights Branch, International Labour Standards Department
Tel: 41.22.7997151.
MANUELA TOMEI, Focal point for technical cooperation for indigenous and tribal peoples (E/DEV), Employment and Development Department
Tel: 41.22.7996931.

International Labour Office,
1211 Geneva 22, PO Box 500, Switzerland
Fax: 41.22.7988685.

B. Convention 169 Concerning Indigenous and Tribal Peoples in Independent Countries

The General Conference of the International Labour Organisation,
   Having been convened at Geneva by the Governing Body of the ILO,
   Having met in its 76th Session on 7 June 1989, and
   Noting the international standards contained in the Indigenous and Tribal Populations Convention and Recommendation, 1957, and
   Recalling the terms of the Universal Declaration of Human Rights, the International Covenant on Economic, Social and Cultural Rights, the International Covenant on Civil and Political Rights. and the many international instruments on the prevention of discrimination, and
   Considering that the developments which have taken place in international law since 1957, as well as developments in the situation of indigenous and tribal peoples in all regions of the world, have made it appropriate to adopt new international standards on the subject with a view to removing the assimilationist orientation of the earlier standards, and
   Recognising the aspirations of these peoples to exercise control over their own institutions, ways of life and economic development and to maintain and develop their identities, languages and religions, within the framework of the States in which they live, and

Noting that in many parts of the world these peoples are unable to enjoy their fundamental human rights to the same degree as the rest of the population of the States within which they live, and that their laws, values, customs and perspectives have often been eroded, and

Calling attention to the distinctive contributions of indigenous and tribal peoples to the cultural diversity and social and ecological harmony of humankind and to international co-operation and understanding, and

Noting that the following provisions have been framed with the co-operation of the United Nations, the FAO, UNESCO, WHO as well as the Inter American Indian Institute, at appropriate levels and in their respective fields, and that it is proposed to continue this co-operation in promoting and securing the application of these provisions. and

Having decided upon the adoption of certain proposals with regard to the partial revision of the Indigenous and Tribal Populations Convention, 1957 (No.107), which is the fourth item on the agenda of the session, and

Having determined that these proposals shall take the form of an international Convention revising the Indigenous and Tribal Populations Convention. 1957; adopts this twenty-seventh day of June of the year one thousand nine hundred and eighty-nine the following Convention, which may be cited as the Indigenous and Tribal Peoples Convention, 1989:

PART I. GENERAL POLICY

Article I

1. This Convention applies to:

(a) tribal peoples in independent countries whose social, cultural and economic conditions distinguish them from other sections of the national community and whose status is regulated wholly or partially by their own customs or traditions or by special laws or regulations;

(b) peoples in independent countries who are regarded as indigenous on account of their descent from the populations which inhabited the country, or a geographical region to which the country belongs, at the time of conquest or colonisation or the establishment of present state boundaries and who, irrespective of their legal status, retain some or all of their own social, economic, cultural and political institutions.

2. Self-identification as indigenous or tribal shall be regarded as a fundamental criterion for determining the groups to which the provisions of this Convention apply.

3. The use of the term "peoples" in this Convention shall not be construed as having any implications as regards the rights which may attach to the term under international law.

Article 2

1. Governments shall have the responsibility for developing, with the participation of the peoples concerned, co-ordinated and systematic action to protect the rights of these peoples and to guarantee respect for their integrity.

2. Such action shall include measures for:

(a) ensuring that members of these peoples benefit on an equal footing from the rights and opportunities which national laws and regulations grant to other members of the population;

(b) promoting the full realisation of the social, economic and cultural rights of these peoples with respect for their social and cultural identity, their customs and traditions and their institutions;

(c) assisting the members of the peoples concerned to eliminate socio-economic gaps that may exist between indigenous and other members of the natio-nal community, in a manner compatible with their aspirations and ways of life.

Article 3

1. Indigenous and tribal peoples shall enjoy the full measure of human right and fundamental freedoms without hindrance or discrimination. The provisions of the Convention shall be applied without discrimination to male and female members of these peoples.

2. No form of force or coercion shall be used in violation of the human rights and fundamental freedoms of the peoples concerned, including the rights contained in this Convention.

Article 4

1. Special measures shall be adopted as appropriate for safeguarding the persons, institutions, property, labour, cultures and environment of the peoples concerned.

2. Such special measures shall not be contrary to the freely-expressed wishes of the peoples concerned.

3. Enjoyment of the general rights of citizenship, without discrimination. shall not be prejudiced in any way by such special measures.

Article 5

In applying the provisions of this Convention:

(a) the social, cultural, religious and spiritual values and practices of these peoples shall be recognised and protected, and due account shall be taken of the nature of the problems which face them both as groups and as individuals;

(b) the integrity of the values, practices and institutions of these peoples shall be respected;

(c) policies aimed at mitigating the difficulties experienced by these peoples in facing new conditions of life and work shall be adopted, with the participation and co-operation of the peoples affected.

Article 6

1. In applying the provisions of this Convention, governments shall:

(a) consult the peoples concerned, through appropriate procedures and in particular through their representative institutions, whenever consideration is being given to legislative or administrative measures which may affect them directly;

(b) establish means by which these peoples can freely participate, to at least the same extent as other sectors of the population, at all levels of decision-making in elective institutions and administrative and other bodies responsible for policies and programmes which concern them;

(c) establish means for the full development of these peoples' own institutions and initiatives, and in appropriate cases provide the resources necessary for this purpose.

2. The consultations carried out in application of this Convention shall be undertaken, in good faith and in a form appropriate to the circumstances, with the objective of achieving agreement or consent to the proposed measures.

Article 7

1. The peoples concerned shall have the right to decide their own priorities for the process of development as it affects their lives, beliefs, institutions and spiritual well-being and the lands they occupy or otherwise use, and to exercise control. to the extent possible, over their own economic, social and cultural development. In addition, they shall participate in the formulation, implementation and evaluation of plans and programmes for national and regional development which may affect them directly.

2. The improvement of the conditions of life and work and levels of health and education of the peoples concerned, with their participation and co-operation, shall be a matter of priority in plans for the overall economic development of areas they inhabit. Special projects for development of the areas in question shall also be so designed as to promote such improvement.

3. Governments shall ensure that, whenever appropriate, studies are carried out, in co-operation with the peoples concerned, to assess the social, spiritual, cultural and environmental impact on them of planned development activities. The results of these studies shall be considered as fundamental criteria for the implementation of these activities.

4. Governments shall take measures, in co-operation with the people concerned, to protect and preserve the environment of the territories they inhabit.

Article 8

1. In applying national laws and regulations to the peoples concerned, due regard shall be had to their customs or customary laws.

2. These peoples shall have the right to retain their own customs and institutions, where these are not incompatible with fundamental rights defined by the national legal system and with internationally recognised human rights. Procedures shall be established, whenever necessary, to resolve conflicts which may arise in the application of this principle.

3. The application of paragraphs 1 and 2 of this Article shall not prevent members of these peoples from exercising the rights granted to all citizens and from assuming the corresponding duties.

Article 9

1. To the extent compatible with the national legal system and internationally recognised human

rights, the methods customarily practised by the peoples concerned for dealing with offences committed by their members shall be respected.

2. The customs of these peoples in regard to penal matters shall be taken into consideration by the authorities and courts dealing with such cases.

Article 10

1. In imposing penalties laid down by general law on members of these peoples account shall be taken of their economic, social and cultural characteristics.

2. Preference shall be given to methods of punishment other than confinement in prison.

Article 11

The exaction from members of the peoples concerned of compulsory personal services in any form, whether paid or unpaid, shall be prohibited and punishable by law, except in cases prescribed by law for all citizens.

Article 12

The peoples concerned shall be safeguarded against the abuse of their right and shall be able to take legal proceedings, either individually or through their representative bodies, for the effective protection of these rights. Measures shall be taken to ensure that members of these peoples can understand and be understood in legal proceedings, where necessary through the provision of interpretation or by other effective means.

PART II. LAND

Article 13

1. In applying the provisions of this Part of the Convention governments shall respect the special importance for the cultures and spiritual values of the peoples concerned of their relationship with the lands or territories, or both as applicable, which they occupy or otherwise use, and in particular the collective aspects of this relationship.

2. The use of the term "lands" in Articles 15 and 16 shall include the concept of territories, which covers the total environment of the areas which the peoples concerned occupy or otherwise use.

Article 14

1. The rights of ownership and possession of the peoples concerned over the lands which they traditionally occupy shall be recognised. In addition, measures shall be taken in appropriate cases to safeguard the right of the peoples concerned to use lands not exclusively occupied by them, but to which they have traditionally had access for their subsistence and traditional activities. Particular attention shall be paid to the situation of nomadic peoples and shifting cultivators in this respect.

2. Governments shall take steps as necessary to identify the lands which the peoples concerned traditionally occupy, and to guarantee effective protection of their rights of ownership and possession.

3. Adequate procedures shall be established within the national legal system to resolve land claims by the peoples concerned.

Article 15

1. The rights of the peoples concerned to the natural resources pertaining to their lands shall be specially safeguarded. These rights include the right of these peoples to participate in the use, management and conservation of these resources.

2. In cases in which the State retains the ownership of mineral or sub-surface resources or rights to other resources pertaining to lands, governments shall establish or maintain procedures through which they shall consult these peoples, with a view to ascertaining whether and to what degree their interests would be prejudiced, before undertaking or permitting any programmes for the exploration or exploitation of such resources pertaining to their lands. The peoples concerned shall wherever possible participate in the benefits of such activities. and shall receive fair compensation for any damages which they may sustain as a result of such activities.

Article 16

1. Subject to the following paragraphs of this Article, the peoples concerned shall not be removed from the lands which they occupy.

2. Where the relocation of these peoples is considered necessary as an exceptional measure, such relocation shall take place only with their free and informed consent. Where their consent cannot be obtained, such relocation shall take place only following appropriate procedures established by

national laws and regulations, including public inquiries where appropriate, which provide the opportunity for effective representation of the peoples concerned.

3. Whenever possible, these peoples shall have the right to return to their traditional lands, as soon as the grounds for relocation cease to exist.

4. When such return is not possible, as determined by agreement or, in the absence of such agreement, through appropriate procedures, these peoples shall be provided in all possible cases with lands of quality and legal status at least equal to that of the lands previously occupied by them, suitable to provide for their present needs and future development. Where the peoples concerned express a preference for compensation in money or in kind, they shall be so compensated under appropriate guarantees.

5. Persons thus relocated shall be fully compensated for any resulting loss or injury.

Article 17

1. Procedures established by the peoples concerned for the transmission of land rights among members of these peoples shall be respected.

2. The peoples concerned shall be consulted whenever consideration is being given to their capacity to alienate their lands or otherwise transmit their rights outside their own community.

3. Persons not belonging to these peoples shall be prevented from taking advantage of their customs or of lack of understanding of the laws on the part of their members to secure the ownership, possession or use of land belonging to them.

Article 18

Adequate penalties shall be established by law for unauthorised intrusion upon. or use of, the lands of the peoples concerned, and governments shall take measures to prevent such offences.

Article 19

National agrarian programmes shall secure to the peoples concerned treatment equivalent to that accorded to other sectors of the population with regard to:

(a) the provision of more land for these peoples when they have not the area necessary for providing the essentials of a normal existence, or for any possible increase in their numbers;

(b) the provision of the means required to promote the development of the lands which these peoples already possess.

PART III. RECRUITMENT AND CONDITIONS OF EMPLOYMENT

Article 20

1. Governments shall, within the framework of national laws and regulations and in co-operation with the peoples concerned, adopt special measures to ensure the effective protection with regard to recruitment and conditions of employment of workers belonging to these peoples, to the extent that they are not effectively protected by laws applicable to workers in general.

2. Governments shall do everything possible to prevent any discrimination between workers belonging to the peoples concerned and other workers, in particular as regards:

(a) admission to employment. including skilled employment, as well as measures for promotion and advancement;

(b) equal remuneration for work of equal value;

(c) medical and social assistance. occupational safety and health, all social security benefits and any other occupationally related benefits. and housing:

(d) the right of association and freedom for all lawful trade union activities, and the right to conclude collective agreements with employers or employers' organisations.

3. The measures taken shall include measures to ensure:

(a) that workers belonging to the peoples concerned, including seasonal, casual and migrant workers in agricultural and other employment. as well as those employed by labour contractors, enjoy the protection afforded by national law and practice to other such workers in the same sectors, and that they are fully informed of their rights under labour legislation and of the means of redress available to them;

(b) that workers belonging to these peoples are not subjected to working conditions hazardous to their health, in particular through exposure to pesticides or other toxic substances;

(c) that workers belonging to these peoples are not subjected to coercive recruitment systems, including bonded labour and other forms of debt servitude;

(d) that workers belonging to these peoples enjoy equal opportunities and equal treatment in employment for men and women, and protection from sexual harassment.

4. Particular attention shall be paid to the establishment of adequate labour inspection services in areas where workers belonging to the peoples concerned undertake wage employment, in order to ensure compliance with the provisions of this Part of this Convention.

PART IV. VOCATIONAL TRAINING, HANDICRAFTS AND RURAL INDUSTRIES

Article 21

Members of the peoples concerned shall enjoy opportunities at least equal to those of other citizens in respect of vocational training measures.

Article 22

1. Measures shall be taken to promote the voluntary participation of members of the peoples concerned in vocational training programmes of general application.

2. Whenever existing programmes of vocational training of general application do not meet the special needs of the peoples concerned, governments shall, with the participation of these peoples, ensure the provision of special training programmes and facilities.

3. Any special training programmes shall be based on the economic environment, social and cultural conditions and practical needs of the peoples concerned. Any studies made in this connection shall be carried out in co-operation with these peoples, who shall be consulted on the organisation and operation of such programmes. Where feasible, these peoples shall progressively assume responsibility for the organisation and operation of such special training programmes, if they so decide.

Article 23

1. Handicrafts, rural and community-based industries. and subsistence economy and traditional activities of the peoples concerned. such as hunting, fishing, trapping and gathering, shall be recognised as important factors in the maintenance of their cultures and in their economic self-reliance and development. Governments shall, with the participation of these people and whenever appropriate, ensure that these activities are strengthened and promoted.

2. Upon the request of the peoples concerned, appropriate technical and financial assistance shall be provided wherever possible, taking into account the traditional technologies and cultural characteristics of these peoples, as well as the importance of sustainable and equitable development.

PART V. SOCIAL SECURITY AND HEALTH

Article 24

Social security schemes shall be extended progressively to cover the peoples concerned, and applied without discrimination against them.

Article 25

1. Governments shall ensure that adequate health services are made available to the peoples concerned, or shall provide them with resources to allow them to design and deliver such services under their own responsibility and control, so that they may enjoy the highest attainable standard of physical and mental health.

2. Health services shall, to the extent possible, be community-based. These services shall be planned and administered in co-operation with the peoples concerned and take into account their economic, geographic, social and cultural conditions as well as their traditional preventive care, healing practices and medicines.

3. The health care system shall give preference to the training and employment of local community health workers, and focus on primary health care while maintaining strong links with other levels of health care services.

4. The provision of such health services shall be co-ordinated with other social, economic and cultural measures in the country.

PART VI. EDUCATION AND MEANS OF COMMUNICATION

Article 26

Measures shall be taken to ensure that members of the peoples concerned have the opportunity to acquire education at all levels on at least an equal footing with the rest of the national community.

Article 27
1. Education programmes and services for the peoples concerned shall be developed and implemented in co-operation with them to address their special needs, and shall incorporate their histories, their knowledge and technologies, their value systems and their further social, economic and cultural aspirations.
 2. The competent authority shall ensure the training of members of these peoples and their involvement in the formulation and implementation of education programmes, with a view to the progressive transfer of responsibility for the conduct of these programmes to these peoples as appropriate.
 3. In addition, governments shall recognise the right of these peoples to establish their own educational institutions and facilities, provided that such institutions meet minimum standards established by the competent authority in consultation with these peoples. Appropriate resources shall be provided for this purpose.

Article 28
1. Children belonging to the peoples concerned shall, wherever practicable, be taught to read and write in their own indigenous language or in the language most commonly used by the group to which they belong. When this is not practicable, the competent authorities shall undertake consultations with these peoples with a view to the adoption of measures to achieve this objective.
 2. Adequate measures shall be taken to ensure that these peoples have the opportunity to attain fluency in the national language or in one of the official languages of the country.
 3. Measures shall be taken to preserve and promote the development and practice of the indigenous languages of the peoples concerned.

Article 29
The imparting of general knowledge and skills that will help children belonging to the peoples concerned to participate fully and on an equal footing in their own community and in the national community shall be an aim of education for these peoples.

Article 30
1. Governments shall adopt measures appropriate to the traditions and cultures of the peoples concerned, to make known to them their rights and duties, especially in regard to labour, economic opportunities, education and health matters, social welfare and their rights deriving from this Convention.
 2. If necessary, this shall be done by means of written translations and through the use of mass communications in the languages of these peoples.

Article 31
Educational measures shall be taken among all sections of the national community, and particularly among those that are in most direct contact with the peoples concerned, with the object of eliminating prejudices that they may harbour in respect of these peoples. To this end, efforts shall be made to ensure that history textbooks and other educational materials provide a fair. accurate and informative portrayal of the societies and cultures of these peoples.

PART VII. CONTACTS AND CO-OPERATION ACROSS BORDERS

Article 32
Governments shall take appropriate measures, including by means of international agreements, to facilitate contacts and co-operation between indigenous and tribal peoples across borders, including activities in the economic, social, spiritual and environmental fields.

PART VIII. ADMINISTRATION

Article 33
1. The governmental authority responsible for the matters covered in this Convention shall ensure that agencies or other appropriate mechanisms exist to administer the programmes affecting the peoples concerned, and shall ensure that they have the means necessary for the proper fulfilment of the functions assigned to them.
 2. These programmes shall include:
  (a) the planning, co-ordination, execution and evaluation, in co-operation with the peoples concerned, of the measures provided for in this Convention;

(b) the proposing of legislative and other measures to the competent authorities and supervision of the application of the measures taken, in co-operation with the peoples concerned.

PART IX. GENERAL PROVISIONS

Article 34
The nature and scope of the measures to be taken to give effect to this Convention shall be determined in a flexible manner. having regard to the conditions characteristic of each country.

Article 35
The application of the provisions of this Convention shall not adversely affect rights and benefits of the peoples concerned pursuant to other Conventions and Recommendations, international instruments, treaties, or national laws, awards, custom or agreements.

PART X. FINAL PROVISIONS

Article 36
This Convention revises the Indigenous and Tribal Populations Convention, 1957.

Article 37
The formal ratifications of this Convention shall be communicated to the Director-General of the International Labour Office for registration.

Article 38
1. This Convention shall be binding only upon those Members of the International Labour Organisation whose ratifications have been registered with the Director-General.
    2. It shall come into force twelve months after the date on which the ratifications of two Members have been registered with the Director-General.
    3. Thereafter, this Convention shall come into force for any Member twelve months after the date on which its ratification has been registered.

Article 39
1. A Member which has ratified this Convention may denounce it after the expiration of ten years from the date on which the Convention first comes into force, by an act communicated to the Director-General of the International Labour Office for registration. Such denunciation shall not take effect until one year after the date on which it is registered.
    2. Each Member which has ratified this Convention and which does not, within the year following the expiration of the period of ten years mentioned in the preceding paragraph, exercise the right of denunciation provided for in this Article, will be bound for another period of ten years and, thereafter, may denounce this Convention at the expiration of each period of ten years under the terms provided for in this Article.

Article 40
1. The Director-General of the International Labour Office shall notify all Members of the International Labour Organisation of the registration of all ratifications and denunciations communicated to him by the Members of the Organisation.
    2. When notifying the Members of the Organisation of the registration of the second ratification communicated to him, the Director-General shall draw the attention of the Members of the Organisation to the date upon which the Convention will come into force.

Article 41
The Director-General of the International Labour Office shall communicate to the Secretary-General of the United Nations for registration in accordance with Article 102 of the Charter of the United Nations full particulars of all ratifications and acts of denunciation registered by him in accordance with the provisions of the preceding Articles.

Article 42
At such times as it may consider necessary the Governing Body of the International Labour Office shall present to the General Conference a report on the working of this Convention and shall examine the desirability of placing on the agenda of the Conference the question of its revision in whole or in part.

Article 43
1. Should the Conference adopt a new Convention revising this Convention in whole or in part. then, unless the new Convention otherwise provides-

   (a) the ratification by a Member of the new revising Convention shall *ipso jure* involve the immediate denunciation of this Convention, notwithstanding the provisions of Article 39 above, if and when the new revising Convention shall have come into force:

   (b) as from the date when the new revising Convention comes into force this Convention shall cease to be open to ratification by the Members.

2. This Convention shall in any case remain in force in its actual form and content for those Members which have ratified it but have not ratified the revising Convention.

Article 44
The English and French versions of the text of this Convention are equally authoritative.

UPDATE ON THE PROCESS OF RATIFICATION OF CONVENTION 169 AND RELATED MATTERS

1. Ratifications

Mexico: September, 1990.
An amendment to Article 4 of the Constitution proposed to the National Legislature by the President of Mexico was approved in 1991. The amendment recognises the pluri-ethnic composition of Mexican society.

In April, 1991, the Codigo de Procedimientos Penales was revised by the National Legislature, which incorporates provisions regarding customary law and practices of indigenous communities, in application of parts of Articles 8-12 of Convention 169.

Colombia, March 1991. Became National Law 21/91.
July 6, 1991, the new Constitution of Colombia adopted in full by the Constituent Assembly. Incorporates some far-reaching provisions on the rights of indigenous peoples.

Bolivia, July, 1991. Signed into National Law by the President of Bolivia on July ll, after ratification by the National Legislature (June 13, 1991).

August 6, 1991, the President introduced a National Law on Indigenous Rights, recognising further provisions relating to the specific rights of the tropical lowland indigenous peoples.

Argentina, April, 1992. Not yet registered with the Director General (ILO).

Norway, June 1990, *Costa Rica,* April 1993, *Paraguay,* August 1993, *Peru,* February 1994.

2. Submitted to the Legislature for ratification:

Brazil (July, 1991)

Chile (December, 1990)
Also, a National Law on Indigenous Peoples' rights and a constitutional amendment, introduced to the National Legislature (October 1991).

Ecuador (May, 1991)
The National Legislature accepted to consider ratification of Convention 169 and a proposal for amending the Constitution, submitted by the Confederaci6n de

Nacionalidades del Ecuador (CONAIE) in May, 1991. The National Legislature also is discussing a National Indigenous Law.

Guatemala, Venezuela, Denmark, Finland, Philippines, Fiji, Austria and Argentina decided to ratify Convention 169.

3. Consultations toward ratification:

Venezuela

The Ministry of Labour sponsored an initial consultation seminar on Convention 169 in September, 1991. The Ministry of Education, the Dirección Nacional de Asuntos Indigenas, the Consejo Nacional de Indigenas de Venezuela and the Confederacion de Trabajadores de Venezuela (CTV), have submitted to the President of Venezuela and the Ministry of Labour their respective recommendations that Convention 169 should be ratified.

The President established in March 1991, a special Office for Indigenous Peoples within the Fiscalia General de la Nacion, to monitor human rights of indigenous peoples.

Guatemala

The President of Cuatemala, on November 29, 1991, at a National Forum on Convention No.169, which culminated a five-month process of consultations with the organisations of indigenous peoples, ngo's, government agencies, worker and employer organisations, announced his Government's intention to submit the convention to the National Congress for ratification in early 1992. In his speech at the UN General Assembly (September 1991), he also made a similar reference.

Convention 169 is being considered as part of the framework for discussions on the rights of indigenous peoples in the peace negotiations with the armed opposition.

Honduras

The Ministry of Labour and the President are completing consultations to submit Convention 169 for ratification in the National Legislature.

The National Legislature is discussing a National Law for Indigenous Peoples.
The National Legislature is discussing the draft of a National Indian Law.

El Salvador

The Ministry of Labour has scheduled a consultation workshop on Convention 169 in September, 1991, jointly with the two national indigenous organisations and the World Council of Indigenous Peoples.

Panama

The Ministry of Labour held a consultation seminar in January, 1991 jointly with the General Congress of the Guaymi. The Ceneral Congresses of the Embera and Kuna peoples have submitted requests to the Covernment for ratification of Convention 169.

Fiji. The Government of Fiji has decided to ratify the Convention but has not yet proceeded to deposit the relevant instrument of ratification.

Shri Lanka. The Government of Shri Lanka has set up a National Committee for the World's Indigenous People under the Ministry of Environment and Parliamentary Affairs. The Chairman of this Committee, Mr. Devanesan Nesiah has requested the ILO for an in-depth briefing on Convention No.169 as the Committee intends to propose this Convention to the Cabinet for ratification.

References
1. P. Sheeten: *Global Governance for Human Development* Occasional paper for Human Development, UNDP 1992. While not accurate as a fact, it is as a trend.
2. M. Haq: *Human Development in a Changing World*, Occasional Paper on Human Development, UNDP.
3. Manifesto de Tiahuanacu in *Oppressed but not defeated*, UNRISD Participation Programme, Geneva, 1987.
4. ILO: *Indigenous Peoples: Living and Working Conditions of Aboriginal Populations in Independent Countries* (Geneva, 1953).
5. The only exception is the 1940 international agreement creating the Inter-American Indian Institute (Patzcuaro, Mexico). This Convention is, however, of regional character and is principally devoted to creating indigenous institutes in ratifying countries.
6. It should be noted that Convention No.107 has been closed to new ratifications since the revising Convention No.169 came into force on 5 September 1991. However, ratifications of Convention No.107 will remain in force unless the countries concerned ratify Convention No.169 — a kind of replacement ratification.
7. Copies of the Convention are available from the International Labour Office, 1211 Geneva, Switzerland, or from ILO offices around the world.
8. Report III (4A) to each session of the International Labour Conference.

2. The World Bank and Operational Directive 4.20

A. The World Bank and Indigenous Peoples[1]
by Shelton H. Davis

Introduction

In 1982, the World Bank issued a brief operational policy statement which outlined procedures for protecting the rights of so-called "tribal people" in Bank-financed development projects. "Experience has shown," the World Bank directive stated, "that, unless special measures are adopted, **tribal people are more likely to be harmed than helped by development projects that are intended for beneficiaries other than themselves**. Therefore, whenever tribal peoples may be affected, the design of projects should include measures or components necessary to safeguard their interests, and, whenever feasible, to enhance their well being."[2] The directive further stated that, "As a general policy, the Bank will not assist development projects that knowingly involve encroachment on traditional territories being used or occupied by tribal people, unless adequate safeguards are provided. In those cases where environmental and/or social changes promoted through development projects may create undesired effects for tribal people, the project should be designed so as to prevent or mitigate such effects."[3]

While the World Bank has been criticised by non-governmental organisations for the adverse impacts upon indigenous or tribal populations of some of the projects that it finances, there is little doubt, as one source put it, that the World Bank "has become the first international development agency to recognise that economic development places in jeopardy the survival of tribal people".[4]

Over the past decade, the World Bank has financed numerous projects which contain special programmes or components for the protection of the lands and other resources of these peoples. As a result of this experience, the World Bank has revised its original policy toward indigenous peoples, bringing it more in line with current thinking on the role of these peoples as active participants in and beneficiaries of development projects.

The following article describes the policies and experience of the World Bank in relationship to indigenous peoples. The article opens with a discussion of the Bank's 1982 policy statement. It then describes the findings of a five-year implementation review of Bank-financed projects with tribal programmes. Lastly, it discusses the Bank's new policy towards indigenous peoples, and places this policy within the larger framework of the Bank's increasing concern for social and economic rights.[5]

A major theme of the article is that **there has been a fundamental change in the World Bank's thinking about indigenous peoples** from an early concern with protecting small, isolated tribal societies (many of them forest-dwelling tribes in the lowlands of South America) from the negative impacts of development to the promotion of conditions among its Borrowers for the active participation of indigenous peoples in the development process itself. This new approach is reflected in the Bank's current policy directive, as well as several recent projects being prepared and financed by the Bank. It is also reflected in the Bank's growing emphasis upon participatory forms of development and the increasing incorporation of social and cultural analysis into its investment program and other development work.

Tribal people in Bank-financed projects

The first policy directive of the World Bank concerning indigenous peoples (Operational Manual Statement, OMS 2.34) was issued in February 1982 under the title "Tribal People in Bank financed Projects." Actually, even previous to the release of this directive, the Bank's Office of Environmental and Scientific Affairs, which was then responsible for the Bank's environmental assessment work, had initiated a study of the effects of economic development on the lands and cultures of tribal peoples. A major emphasis of this study was that there was an historical continuum or range of types of tribal societies from those which are geographically and culturally isolated from national societies (so-called "uncontacted" tribes of which there are relatively few remaining in the world) to those which have been fully integrated into the wider political economies and rural societies of the country's which they form part (the so-called "indigenous peasant populations"). In between, the study noted, there is a continuum of societies from "semi-isolated tribal groups" to those in "permanent contact" but still not "fully integrated" with their respective national societies.[6]

This notion of a "continuum of acculturation" or integration of tribal societies came from two sources. One, the experience of the Bank in financing frontier development and colonisation programmes in lowland tropical forest areas of Brazil and other countries of South America where, at the time, there were still a number of uncontacted or only recently contacted, forest-dwelling tribal groups. And, two, the notion then prevalent among some government indigenist agencies in Latin America that it was inevitable that these relatively remote tribal societies would, if adequately protected during a transition period, forsake their traditional cultures and tribal identities and eventually integrate into the wider society. Much of this viewpoint was based upon the "integrationist" assumptions and "protectionist" provisions of International Labour Organisation Convention No. 107 which was drafted in the 1950s and ratified by several Latin American countries in the 1960s and early 1970s.[7]

If one analyses the 1982 directive, it is clear that some of the protectionist and integrationist premises of the early ILO Convention found their way into the Bank's policy statement. Although more limited in scope than the ILO definition, the term "tribal" peoples in the Bank's policy directive referred to those ethnic groups that have "stable, low-energy, sustained-yield economic systems," and exhibit in varying degrees the following characteristics:

(a) geographically isolated or semi-isolated;

(b) unacculturated or only partially acculturated into the societal norms of the dominant society;
(c) nonmonetised, or only partially monetised; production largely for subsistence, and independent of the national economic system;
(d) ethnically distinct from the national society;
(e) nonliterate and without a written language;
(f) linguistically distinct from the wider society;
(g) identifying closely with one particular territory;
(h) having an economic lifestyle largely dependent on the specific natural environment;
(i) possessing indigenous leadership, but little or no national representation, and few, if any, political rights as individuals or collectively, partly because they do not participate in the political process; and,
(j) having loose tenure over their traditional lands, which for the most part is not accepted by the dominant society nor accommodated by its courts; and, having weak enforcement capabilities against encroachers, even when tribal areas have been delineated.[8]

The directive also contained an important footnote indicating that the Bank's policy was "not concerned with projects designed specifically for tribal people as the direct beneficiaries, but rather with other types of projects that *impact on* (emphasis mine) tribal people".[9] While the Bank policy recognised that it was the responsibility of governments to implement measures that will "effectively safeguard the integrity and well-being of the tribal people," it also stated that it would not support policies at either extreme: "either those that perpetuate isolation from the national society and needed social services; or, those promoting forced, accelerated acculturation unsuited to the future well being of the affected tribal people."[10]

The guiding principle behind the Bank's policy was that development projects that affect tribal people should provide "adequate time and conditions for acculturation".[11] To be successful, the operational directive stated, such acculturation needed to be "slow and gradual".[12] Furthermore, projects should contain special tribal components or parallel programmes which would mitigate the adverse effects of the wider development project and provide tribal peoples with adequate conditions and time to adapt to the national society at their own pace. The design of tribal components or parallel programmes, which formed the essence of the Bank's operational response to the adverse effects of development projects on tribal peoples, should be "**based upon detailed, contemporary knowledge of the peoples to be affected**",[13] and contain four elements:

(a) the recognition, demarcation and protection of tribal areas containing those resources required to sustain the tribal people's traditional means of livelihood;
(b) appropriate social services that are consonant with the tribe's acculturation status, including, especially, protection against diseases and the maintaining of health;
(c) the maintenance, to the extent desired by the tribe, of its cultural integrity and embodiments thereof; [and,]
(d) a forum for the participation of the tribal people in decisions affecting them,

and providing for adjudication and redress of grievances.[14]

The remainder of the policy directive indicated ways in which Bank project officers and Borrowers could incorporate tribal components and parallel programmes into the Bank's project cycle. During project identification, for example, the directive stated, the "approximate numbers, location, and degree of acculturation of tribal people in the general region of the project should be ascertained".[15] At this stage, assessments should be made of relevant government agencies and their policies, the status of indigenous lands, and the enforcement capabilities of the government. The actual tribal component or parallel programme was to be designed before or during project preparation, the second stage of the Bank's project cycle. This should include the incorporation of information provided by pre-feasibility anthropological studies and site visits, ways of institutionally strengthening government agencies responsible for indigenous affairs, and the design of special programmes for the demarcation of tribal lands and protection of the health of tribal populations.[16]

At project appraisal, the third stage in the project cycle, project officers were responsible for assessing the "adequacy and appropriateness of the tribal component, the need for legislation concerning the relevant government agency and other aspects, and the capability of the designated agency to implement the component".[17]

Finally, during project implementation and the Bank supervision stage, specialist input (mainly by anthropologists and "indigenists") would again need to be called upon to evaluate the performance of the tribal component.[18] In general, OMS 2.34 provided a set of guidelines for assuring that tribal people's needs were met in Bank-financed projects. Without such guidelines, past experience had demonstrated that development projects would have negative, and sometimes permanently damaging, effects on the lands, subsistence resources, health and cultures of tribal populations.

The Five-Year Implementation Review

In 1986, the Office of Environmental and Scientific Affairs conducted a desk review of the Bank's experience in implementing the policy directives contained in OMS 2.34. The implementation review found that the issuing of OMS 2.34 had significantly increased the identification by Bank staff of tribal or indigenous peoples affected by Bank-financed projects. Until the late 1970s, it was standard Bank practice to assume that all rural populations in developing countries were essentially alike (i.e., economically underdeveloped and poor) and that there was no need to make special provisions in project design for ethnically or culturally distinct populations. The effects of OMS 2.34 in changing this practice were reflected in the increasing number of Bank-financed projects that were indicated as having consequences for the general health, cultural integrity and economic well-being of tribal or indigenous groups. In 1983, for example, only 15 Bank-financed projects were identified as having tribal peoples in their areas of influence and hence coming under the purview of the new Bank guidellnes. This number increased to 36 projects in 1984, and to 53 projects by 1986. The number of projects with special tribal components or parallel programmes also increased from 8 projects in 1983 to 15 projects in 1986. The majority of these projects, as already noted, were in the lowland tropical forest areas of South America where the Bank was increasingly financing road construction and land settlement programmes.[19]

The implementation review also indicated that Bank staff generally assumed (justifiably given the definition contained in the original operational statement) that the Bank's policy mainly applied to relatively small, isolated and unacculturated tribal societies (what were euphemistically termed "vulnerable ethnic minorities"), such as the rainforest Indians of South America or the pygmies or bushmen of Central and South Africa; and, not to larger and more heterogeneous tribal populations, such as the nomadic pastoral societies of the Sahel region or of Eastern and Western Africa or the "tribal" peoples of India and Southeast Asia. This staff perception of the limited applicability of OMS 2.34 was noted in earlier implementation reviews as well as the 1987 review. A 1983 review, for example, stated that "the idea that certain tribal peoples (e.g., in Asia and Africa) are outside the scope of OMS 2.34 because they are 'acculturated' appears in several documents. In some of these cases, such judgments are not supported by data or analysis." Similarly, a 1984 review, noted that "principles contained in OMS 2.34 can be applied to projects where the tribal populations are dominant and heterogeneous, rather than vulnerable ethnic minorities targeted by the OMS."[20]

The implementation review also indicated that while the Bank had some success in convincing its Borrowers to include special tribal components or parallel programmes in its projects, many of these components were being designed on an *ad hoc* basis and not with the rigor assumed in the policy directive. For example, of the 15 projects containing tribal components analysed in the review, only two contained all of the four protective measures (land demarcation and protection, adequate health and social services, measures for protecting tribal cultural integrity, and tribal participation and adjudication mechanisms) outlined in OMS 2.34. Furthermore, land demarcation and protection, which are so vital to the integrity and survival of tribal or indigenous populations, only occurred in six of the 15 projects and, even in these cases, they were severely delayed or out of pace with the progress of the overall project.[21]

The Bank was successful in convincing Borrowers to provide social, health and other services to tribal populations (programmes of this nature existed in 13 of the 15 Bank-financed projects). However, even in these cases, the social services and health programmes were not designed in terms of the cultural needs and preferences of the tribal population, nor did these peoples participate in their preparation or implementation. In fact, participation by the tribal peoples only occurred in three of the 15 projects, and this resulted from the presence of strong regional or tribal federations which pressured their governments and the Bank to take into account their needs and wishes. Lastly, the implementation review found that many of the government agencies responsible for designing and implementing tribal components were institutionally weak, under-funded and lacked adequate anthropological personnel. While NGOs, such as missionary groups and grassroots development organisations, were providing needed social services and legal support to some tribal and indigenous groups, government agencies often saw themselves in conflict with these organisations and seldom invited them to participate in the planning process.

The revised Police Directive

Based upon the findings of the Five-Year Implementation Review and several more years of experience with projects containing special tribal components or programmes, in 1991, the Bank issued a revised Operational Directive (OD 4.20) on "Indigenous Peoples." The new directive (see attached) is much more detailed than the first and more in keeping with current international thinking on indigenous peoples rights. Several changes and shifts in emphasis in the revised Bank policy are important to note.

First, the definitional criteria used to identify indigenous peoples in the revised directive are much broader than those in OMS 2.34. The revised directive notes that for purposes of Bank work, the term "indigenous peoples" (or other equivalent terms such as "indigenous ethnic minorities" "tribal groups," and "scheduled tribes") refers to "social groups with a social and cultural identity distinct from the dominant society that makes them vulnerable to being disadvantaged in the development process."[22] It also notes that there are varying national legal contexts and socio-cultural criteria for identifying "indigenous peoples", and that "no single definition can capture their diversity." Some people are truly isolated from mainstream culture and society, while others are integrated into the wage labour force and national markets. In particular geographical areas, indigenous peoples can be identified by some characteristics, such as:

(a) a close attachment to ancestral territories and to the natural resources in these areas;
(b) self-identification and identification by others as members of distinct cultural groups;
(c) an indigenous language, often different from the national language;
(d) presence of customary social and political institutions;
(e) primarily subsistence-oriented production.[23]

Second, the revised Bank policy recognises the need to both protect indigenous peoples against the potential harm or damage caused by development projects, as well as to provide them (if they so wish) with new opportunities to participate in the benefits of the development process. The revised policy states:

> The Bank's broad objective towards indigenous peoples, as for all the people in its member countries, is to ensure that the development process fosters full respect for their dignity, human rights, and cultural uniqueness. More specifically, the objective at the canter of this directive is to ensure that indigenous peoples do not suffer adverse effects during the development process, particularly from Bank-financed projects, and that they receive culturally compatible social and economic benefits.[24]

The directive notes that there is great controversy about how to approach indigenous peoples within the development process, with some advocating their total insulation from the forces of modernisation and others promoting their rapid acculturation into the dominant society's values and economic activities. Rather than taking a position on this issue, which in many cases is only of theoretical or historical interest, **the Bank's policy calls for the informed participation and recognition of the preferences of indigenous peoples**.

> The Bank's policy is that the strategy for addressing the issues pertaining to indigenous peoples must be based on the *informed participation* (emphasis in original) of the indigenous peoples themselves. Thus, identifying local preferences through direct consultation, incorporation of indigenous knowledge into project approaches, and appropriate use of experienced specialists are core activities for any project that affects indigenous peoples and their rights to natural and economic resources.[25]

A third innovation of the Bank's revised policy is the incorporation of indigenous people's concerns into several other aspects of Bank work besides that of investment projects. For example, the revised directive notes that issues concerning indigenous peoples, including threats to their environments and natural resources, should be identified through environmental assessments, which since 1989 have been mandated for all Bank projects which have a significant impact on the environment.[26] Bank Country Departments are also mandated, under the new directive, to "maintain information on trends in government policies and institutions that deal with indigenous peoples," and to address issues relating to indigenous peoples in country economic and sector work and in the Bank's country dialogue with its Borrowers.[27]

Another area where the revised directive breaks new ground is in indicating the willingness of the Bank to provide funds for technical assistance to improve Borrower abilities to respond to the needs of indigenous peoples. "Technical assistance," the revised directive states, "is normally given within the context of project preparation, but technical assistance may also be needed to strengthen the relevant government institutions or to support development initiatives taken by indigenous peoples themselves".[28]

Finally, the revised directive devotes its major attention to ways of incorporating indigenous people's concerns into Bank financed investment projects. The main innovation here is the requirement that special Indigenous Peoples Development Plans (IPDPs) be prepared, consistent with Bank policies, for all Bank funded projects which affect the lands, resources and cultures of indigenous peoples. These IPDP's can either form the basis of special components or provisions within broader Bank-funded development projects, or in certain cases be the entire project, when the main beneficiaries are indigenous peoples. Numerous paragraphs in the new directive outline the prerequisites, contents and technical, institutional and financial arrangements for designing these IPDPs.[29]

Since the issuing of OD 4.20, the Bank has prepared and appraised several projects which contain IPDPs and are based on the active participation of the affected tribal or indigenous populations. These include, among others, a special plan for the incorporation of tribal peoples (many of them tribal women) in a rubber cultivation project in India, an agricultural and rangelands management project with Bedouin tribes in the western desert of Egypt, and a natural resource management and forestry project with indigenous and Afro-American communities in the Choco region of Colombia. The Bank is also involved in a number of sector studies relating to indigenous peoples, including a statistical survey of poverty and indigenous peoples in Latin America, a study of tribal health and nutrition pro grams in India, and several country-level forestry sector reviews which discuss indigenous peoples land rights.[30] The findings and recommendations of these studies promise to increase the Bank and Borrower Country knowledge of indigenous peoples issues and eventually to be incorporated into investment projects that the Bank finances.

Conclusion

In conclusion, *there has been a fundamental shift in the way in which the Bank is conceptualising and approaching the concerns of indigenous peoples in its policy and project work*. Rather than focusing solely on attempting to mitigate the adverse impacts of its projects on relatively small and isolated tribal groups, it has broadened the definition of the subject population to include a much more diverse assemblage of peoples and to seek ways in which these peoples might both participate in and benefit from the development process itself. This policy is more in keeping with current international thinking on the rights of indigenous peoples, as well as with the general trend to recognising the social and economic rights of poor and marginalised peoples throughout the world.

The past decade has witnessed a growing interest on the part of the Bank, as well as other multilateral agencies, in increasing the amount and quality of local participation in development projects, not only of indigenous peoples but also of other social groups, such as the poor, women, and NGOs. One of the reasons for this focus on local participation is because of the failure of traditional top down or statist approaches to economic development and poverty alleviation. Much of the Bank's current work with indigenous peoples must be seen within this broader framework of the search for alternative strategies or models of development in which the rights and aspirations of local populations are taken into account.[31]

The past decade has also witnessed a growing awareness on the part of the Bank and other development agencies that environmentally sustainable development will not come about unless indigenous and other traditional peoples are brought into the effort to solve the world's urgent environmental problems. Numerous international reports and conferences, including the report of the World Commission on Environment and Development, the World Conservation Strategy, and the Agenda 21 document of the United Nations Conference on Environment and Development, have highlighted the important role that indigenous peoples and their traditional environmental knowledge can play in the conservation of biodiversity and fragile ecosystems. The Bank is in a pivotal position to promote the participation of indigenous peoples in the implementation of the recommendations of these reports and conferences, because of its central role in such institutions as the Global Environmental Facility (GET) and its more than a decade of experience attempting to promote among its Borrowers the rights of tribal and indigenous peoples.

Recently, the Bank has established a new Vice-Presidency for Environmentally Sustainable Development the purpose of which is to increase the Bank's institutional capacity to deal with issues in this area. As part of this effort, a new division on Social Policy and Resettlement has been established in the Bank's central Environment Department. This division will be working closely with the Bank's regional and country operational departments to increase the social soundness and performance of the Bank's investment projects. It will also be developing new guidelines for social assessment and for increasing local peoples participation in natural resource management and biodiversity conservation. A focus on indigenous peoples will be a major thrust of these new initiatives, both because of the large number of indigenous peoples who live in the Bank's member countries and their potentially significant cultural contribution to the search for a more socially and environmentally sustainable development path.

SHELTON DAVIS,
Senior Sociologist of the Environment Department, ENVSP S-5109,
Tel: 1.202.4733413

The World Bank
Headquaters:
Washington, D.C.
20433 U.S.A.
Tel: 1.202.4771234 and Fax: 1.202.4776391

B. Operational Directive 4.20: Indigenous Peoples

September 17, 1991[32]
The directive emphasises the need for:
 a) adopting broader definitional criteria than the existing OMS to reflect the diversity of definitions and sensitivities found in member countries;
 b) ensuring that Indigenous People are not adversely affected by Bank projects and that the social and economic benefits they receive are in harmony with their cultural preferences;
 c) addressing issues concerning Indigenous Peoples in economic and sector work;
 d) including project components on Indigenous Peoples in Bank-financed projects
 d) ensuring the "informed participation" of Indigenous People in the preparation of development plans and in the design and implementation of projects.
 Questions on this directive should be referred to the Senior Adviser, Social Policy and Sociology, Environment Department.

Introduction
1. This directive describes Bank policies and processing procedures for projects that affect Indigenous Peoples. It sets out basic definitions, policy objectives, guidelines for the design and implementation of project provisions or components for Indigenous Peoples, and processing and documentation requirements. (**'Bank' includes IDA, and 'loans' include credits**).
 2. The directive provides policy guidance to (a) ensure that indigenous people benefit from development projects, and (b) avoid or mitigate potentially adverse effects on Indigenous People caused by Bank-assisted activities. Special action is required where Bank investments affect Indigenous Peoples, tribes, ethnic minorities, or other groups whose social and economic status restricts their capacity to assert their interests and rights in land and other productive resources.

Definitions
3. The terms "Indigenous Peoples", "Indigenous ethnic minorities", "tribal groups," and "scheduled

tribes", describe social groups with a social and cultural identity distinct from the dominant society that makes them vulnerable to being disadvantaged in the development process. For the purposes of this directive, *"Indigenous Peoples" is the term* that will be used to refer to these groups.

4. Within their national constitutions, statutes, and relevant legislation, many of the Bank's borrower countries include specific definitional clauses and legal frameworks that provide a preliminary basis for identifying Indigenous Peoples.

5. Because of the varied and changing contexts in which Indigenous Peoples are found, *no single definition can capture their diversity*. Indigenous People are commonly among the poorest segments of a population. They engage in economic activities that range from shifting agriculture in or near forests to wage labour or even small-scale market-oriented activities. Indigenous Peoples can be identified in particular geographical areas by the presence in varying degrees of the following *characteristics*:
(a) a close attachment to ancestral territories and to the natural resources in these areas;
(b) self-identification and identification by others as members of a distinct cultural group;
(c) an indigenous language, often different from the national language;
(d) presence of customary social and political institutions; and
(e) primarily subsistence-oriented production.

Task managers (TMs) must exercise judgment in determining the populations to which this directive applies and should make use of specialized anthropological and sociological experts throughout the project cycle.

Objective and policy

6. The Bank's broad objective towards Indigenous People, as for all the people in its member countries, is to ensure that the development process fosters full respect for their dignity, human rights, and cultural uniqueness. More specifically, the objective at the center of this **directive is to ensure that indigenous peoples do not suffer adverse effects during the development** process, particularly from Bank-financed projects, and that they receive culturally compatible social and economic benefits.

7. How to approach indigenous peoples affected by development projects is a controversial issue. Debate is often phrased as a choice between two opposed positions. One pole is to insulate indigenous populations whose cultural and economic practices make it difficult for them to deal with powerful outside groups. The advantages of this approach are the special protections that are provided and the preservation of cultural distinctiveness; the costs are the benefits foregone from development programmes. The other pole argues that indigenous people must be acculturated to dominant society values and economic activities so that they can participate in national development. Here the benefits can include improved social and economic opportunities, but the cost is often the gradual loss of cultural differences.

8. The Bank's policy is that the strategy for addressing the issues pertaining to Indigenous Peoples must be based on the *informed participation* of the indigenous people themselves. Thus, identifying local preferences through direct consultation, incorporation of indigenous knowledge into project approaches, and appropriate early use of experienced specialists are core activities for any project that affects Indigenous Peoples and their rights to natural and economic resources.

9. Cases will occur, especially when dealing with the most isolated groups, where adverse impacts are unavoidable and adequate mitigation plans have not been developed. In such situations, the Bank will not appraise projects until suitable plans are developed by the borrower and reviewed by the Bank. In other cases, Indigenous People may wish to be and can be incorporated into the development process. In sum, a full range of positive actions by the borrower must ensure that Indigenous People benefit from development investments.

Bank role

10. The Bank addresses issues on Indigenous Peoples through;
   a) country economic and sector work,
   b) technical assistance, and,
   c) investment project components or provisions.

Issues concerning indigenous peoples can arise in a variety of sectors that concern the Bank; those involving, for example, agriculture, road construction, forestry, hydropower, mining, tourism, education, and the environment should be carefully screened (displacement of Indigenous Peoples can be particularly damaging, and special efforts should be made to avoid it. See Operational Directive 4.30 Involuntary Resettlement, for additional policy guidance on resettlement issues involving Indigenous People) Issues related to Indigenous Peoples are commonly identified through the environmental assessment or social impact assessment processes, and appropriate measures should be taken under environmental mitigation actions (see Operational Directive 4.01, *Environmental Assessment*).

11. *Country Economic and Sector Work.* Country departments should maintain information on trends in government policies and institutions that deal with Indigenous Peoples: Issues concerning Indigenous Peoples should be addressed explicitly in sector and subsector work and brought into the Bank-country dialogue. National development policy frameworks and institutions for Indigenous Peoples often need to be strengthened in order to create a stronger basis for designing and processing projects with components dealing with Indigenous Peoples.

12. *Technical Assistance.* Technical assistance to develop the borrower's abilities to address issues on Indigenous Peoples can be provided by the Bank. Technical assistance is normally given within the context of project preparation, but technical assistance may also be needed to strengthen the relevant government institutions or to support development initiatives taken by indigenous people themselves.

13. *Investment Projects.* For an investment project that affects indigenous peoples, the borrower should prepare an indigenous peoples development plan that is consistent with the Bank's policy. Any project that affects Indigenous Peoples is expected to include components or provisions that incorporate such a plan. When the bulk of the direct project beneficiaries are Indigenous People, the Bank's concerns would be addressed by the project itself and the provisions of this Operational Directive would thus apply to the project in its entirety.

Indigenous Peoples development plan

Prerequisites

14. Prerequisites of a successful development plan for Indigenous Peoples are as follows:
(a) The key step in project design is the preparation of a culturally appropriate development plan based on full consideration of the options preferred by the indigenous people affected by the project.
(b) Studies should make all efforts to *anticipate adverse trends* likely to be induced by the project and develop the means to avoid or mitigate harm (for guidance on Indigenous Peoples and environmental assessment procedures, see Operational Directive 4.01 Environmental Assessment, and Chapter 7 of the World Bank Environmental Assessment Sourcebook, Technical Paper No.139, Washington, D.C., 1991)
(c) The institutions responsible for government interaction with Indigenous Peoples should possess the social, technical, and legal skills needed for carrying out the proposed development activities. Implementation arrangements should be kept simple. They should normally involve appropriate existing institutions, local organizations, and non governmental organisations (NGOs) with expertise in matters relating to indigenous peoples.
(d) Local patterns of social organization, religious beliefs, and resource use should be taken into account in the plan's design.
(e) Development activities should support production systems that are well adapted to the needs and environment of Indigenous Peoples, and should help production systems under stress to attain sustainable levels.
(f) The plan should avoid creating or aggravating the dependency of indigenous people on project entities. Planning should encourage early handover of project management to local people. As needed, the plan should include general education and training in management skills for indigenous people from the onset of the project.
(g) Successful planning for Indigenous Peoples frequently requires long lead times, as well as arrangements for extended follow-up. Remote or neglected areas where little previous experience is available, often require additional research and pilot programs to fine-tune development proposals.
(h) Where effective programmes are already functioning, Bank support can take the form of incremental funding to strengthen them rather than the development of entirely new programmes.

(Regionally Specific technical guidelines for preparing Indigenous Peoples components, and case studies of best practices, are available from the Regional environment divisions (REDs).

Contents

15. The development plan should be prepared in tandem with the preparation of the main investment. In many cases, proper protection of the rights of indigenous people will require the implementation of special project components that may **lie outside the prirnary project's objectives**. These components can include activities related to health and nutrition, productive infrastructure, linguistic and cultural preservation, entitlement to natural resources, and education. The project component for Indigenous Peoples development should include the following elements, as needed:

(a) Legal Framework

The plan should contain an assessment of

  (i) the legal status of the groups covered by this Operational Directive, as reflected in the country's constitution, legislation, and subsidiary legislation (regulations, administrative orders, etc.); and

  (ii) the ability of such groups to obtain access to and effectively use the legal system to defend their rights. Particular attention should be given to the rights of Indigenous Peoples to use and develop the lands that they occupy, to be protected against illegal intruders, and to have access to natural resources (such as forests, wildlife, and water) vital to their subsistence and reproduction.

(b) Baseline Data

Baseline data should include;

  (i) accurate, up-to-date maps and aerial photographs of the area of project influence and the areas inhabited by indigenous peoples;

  (ii) analysis of the social structure and income sources of the population;

  (iii) inventories of the resources that Indigenous People use and technical data on their production systems; and

  (iv) the relationship of indigenous peoples to other local and national groups. It is particularly important that baseline studies capture the full range of production and marketing activities in which indigenous people are engaged. Site visits by qualified social and technical experts should verify and update secondary sources.

(c) Land Tenure

When local legislation needs strengthening, the Bank should offer to advise and assist the borrower in establishing legal recognition of the customary or traditional land tenure systems of indigenous peoples. Where the traditional lands of Indigenous Peoples have been brought by law into the domain of the state and where it is inappropriate to convert traditional rights into those of legal ownership, alternative arrangements should be implemented to grant long-term, renewable rights of custodianship and use to indigenous peoples. These steps should be taken before the initiation of other planning steps that may be contingent on recognized land titles.

(d) Strategy for Local Participation

Mechanisms should be devised and maintained for participation by Indigenous People in decision making throughout project planning, implementation, and evaluation. Many of the larger groups of indigenous people have their own representative organisations that provide effective channels for communicating local preferences. Traditional leaders occupy pivotal positions for mobilising people and should be brought into the planning process, with due concern for ensuring genuine representation of the indigenous population. (See also Community Involvement and the Role of NGOs in Environmental Assessment in *World Bank, Environmental Sourcebook*, Technical Paper No.139, Washington, D.C., 1991). No foolproof methods exist, however, to guarantee full local-level participation. Sociological and technical advice provided through the Regional environment divisions (REDs) is often needed to develop mechanisms appropriate for the project area.

(e) Technical Identification of Development or Mitigation Activities

Technical proposals should proceed from on-site research by qualified professionals acceptable to the Bank. Detailed descriptions should be prepared and appraised for such proposed services as education, training, health, credit, and legal assistance. Technical descriptions should be included for the planned investments inproductive infrastructure. Plans that draw upon Indigenous knowledge are often more successful than those introducing entirely new principles and institutions. For example, the potential contribution of traditional health providers should be considered in planning delivery systems for health care.

(f) Institutional Capacity

The government institutions assigned responsibility for indigenous peoples are often weak. Assessing the track record, capabilities, and needs of those institutions is a fundamental requirement. Organisational issues that need to be addressed through Bank assistance are the;

(i) availability of funds for investments and field operations;
(ii) adequacy of experienced professional staff;
(iii) ability of Indigenous Peoples' own organisations, local administration authorities, and local NGOs to interact with specialised government institutions;
(iv) ability of the executing agency to mobilize other agencies involved in the plan's implementation; and
(v) adequacy of field presence.

(g) Implementation Schedule

Components should include an implementation schedule with benchmarks by which progress can be measured at appropriate intervals. Pilot programs are often needed to provide planning information for phasing the project component for indigenous peoples with the main investment. The plan should pursue the long-term sustainability of project activities subsequent to completion of disbursement.

(h) Monitoring and Evaluation (see Operational Directive 10.70, Project Monitoring and Evaluation)

Independent monitoring capacities are usually needed when the institutions responsible for indigenous populations have weak management histories. Monitoring by representatives of Indigenous Peoples' own organizations can be an efficient way for the project management to absorb the perspectives of indigenous beneficiaries and is encouraged by the Bank. Monitoring units should be staffed by experienced social science professionals, and reporting formats and schedules appropriate to tbe project's needs should be established. Monitoring and evaluation reports should be reviewed jointly by the senior management of the implementing agency and by the Bank. The evaluation reports should be made available to the public.

(i) Cost Estimates and Financing Plan

The plan should include detailed cost estimates for planned activities and investments. The estimates should be broken down into unit costs by project year and linked to a financing plan. Such programs as revolving credit funds that provide indigenous people with investment pools should indicate their accounting procedures and mechanisms for financial transfer and replenishment. It is usually helpful to have as high a share as possible of direct financial participation by the Bank in project components dealing with Indigenous Peoples.

Project processing and documentation

Identification

16. During project identification, the borrower should be **informed of the Bank's policy for** Indigenous Peoples. The approximate number of potentially afffected people and their location should be determined and shown on maps of the project area. The legal status of any affected groups should also be discussed. TMs should ascertain the relevant government agencies, and their policies, procedures, programmes, and plans for Indigenous Peoples affected by the proposed project (see paras. 11 and 15(a)). TMs should also initiate anthropological studies necessary to identify local needs

and preferences (see para. 15(b)). TMs, in consultation with the REDs, should signal Indigenous Peoples issues and the overall project strategy in the Initial Executive Project Summary (IEPS).

Preparation

17. If it is agreed in the IEPS meeting that special action is needed, the indigenous peoples development plan or project component should be developed during project preparation. As necessary, the Bank should assist the borrower in preparing terms of reference and should provide specialised technical assistance (see para. 12). Early involvement of anthropologists and local NGOs vith expertise in matters related to Indigenous Peoples is a useful way to identify mechanisms for effective participation and local development opportunities. In a project that involves the land rights of Indigenous Peoples, the Bank should work with the borrower to clarify the steps needed for putting land tenure on a regular footing as early as possible, since land disputes frequently lead to delays in executing measures that are contingent on proper land titles (see para. 15(c)).

Appraisal

18. The plan for the development **component for** indigenous peoples should be submitted to the Bank along **with the project's overall feasibility** report, prior to project appraisal. Appraisal should assess the adequacy of the plan, the suitability of policies and legal frameworks, the capabilities of the agencies charged with implementing the plan, and the adequacy of the allocated technical, financial, and social resources. Appraisal teams should be satisfied that indigenous people have participated meaningfully in the development of the plan as described in par. 14(a) (also see par. 15(d)). It is particularly important to appraise proposals for regularising land access and use.

Implementation and Supervision

19. Supervision planning should make provisions for including the appropriate anthropological, legal, and technical skills in Bank supervision missions during project implementation (see paa. 15(g) and (h), and OD 13.05, *Project Supervision*). Site visits by TMs and specialists are essential. Midterm and final evaluations should assess progress and recommend corrective actions when necessary.

Documentation

20. The borrower's commitments for implementing the Indigenous Peoples development plan should be reflected in the loan documents; legal provisions should provide Bank staff with clear benchmarks that can be monitored during supervision. The Staff Appraisal Report and the Memorandum and Recommendation of the President should summarise the plan or project provisions.

References
1. An extended version of this paper was prepared for a panel discussion on Indigenous Peoples and Ethnic Minorities at the Denver Initiative Conference on Human Rights, University of Denver Law School, Denver Colorado, April 16-17, 1993, and has been submitted for publication in the *Denver Journal of International Law and Policy*. The interpretations contained in the paper are solely those of the author and should not be attributed to the World Bank, its Executive Directors or its Member Countries.
2. "Tribal Peoples in Bank-Financed Projects," Operational Manual Statement 2.34, February 1982, para. 4.
3. OMS 2.34, para. 5.
4. *Guardian*, London, 12 August 1981.
5. For a broader discussion of the limits and challenges which the World Bank faces in dealing with human rights issues, see: Ibrahim F.I. Shihata, "The World Bank and Human Rights: An Analysis of the Legal Issues and the Record of Achievements," *Denver Journal of International Law and Policy*, Vol.17, No.1, 1988, pp.39-66. Reproduced in Ibrahim F.I. Shihata, *The World Bank in a Changing World*, Dordrecht, Martinus Nijhoff Publishers, 1991, Chapter 3, pp.97-134.
6. See, Robert Goodland, Tribal Peoples and Economic Development: *Human Ecologic Considerations*, Washington, World Bank, 1982.
7. For background on the role of ILO Convention No.107 in Latin American indigenist policies, see: Lee Swepston, "Latin American Approaches to the 'Indian Problem'," *International Labour*

Review, Vol.117, No.2, March-April 1978, pp.179-196.
8. OMS 2.34, para. 2.
9. OMS 2.34, footnote 2.
10. OMS 2.34, para. 5.
11. OMS 2.34, para. 6.
12. OMS 2.34, para. 7.
13. OMS 2.34, para. 8.
14. OMS 2.34, para. 7.
15. OMS 2.34, para. 10.
16. OMS 2.34, para. 11.
17. OMS 2.34, para. 12.
18. OMS 2.34, para. 13.
19. Office of Environmental and Scientific Affairs, *A Five-Year Implementation Review of OMS 2.34 (1982-1986)*, World Bank, Projects Policy Department, June 1987.
20. Cited in Office of Environmental and Scientific Affairs, *Five Year Implementation Review*, pp.15 and 16.
21. For a detailed analysis of Bank-financed indigenous land regularisation programmes introduced under OMS 2.34, see, Alaka Wali and Shelton Davis, Protecting Amerindian Lands: *A Review of World Bank Experience with Indigenous Land Regularisation programmes* in Lowland South America, Latin America and Caribbean Region, Technical Department, Regional Studies Programme Series, Report 19 (Washington, World Bank, 1992).
22. "Indigenous Peoples," Operational Directive 4.20, September 1991, para. 3.
23. OD 4.20, para. 5.
24. OD 4.20, para. 6.
25. OD 4.20, para. 8.
26. Operational Directive 4.01 ("Environmental Assessment", 1991; originally issued as Operational Directive 4.00, Annex A, 1989) makes specific reference to the need to consult local populations, including indigenous peoples, when environmental assessments are being conducted for projects on or in the areas of influence of their communities and lands.
27. OD 4.20, para. 10.
28. OD 4.20, para. 12.
29. OD 4.20, paras. 14 and 15. Footnote 3 of the OD notes that "regionally specific technical guidelines for preparing indigenous peoples components, and case studies of best practice, are available from the Regional environment divisions." The Africa region has initiated a process of drafting such technical guidelines, the purpose of which is to adapt the OD to the specific political and cultural conditions of the African continent.
30. In March 1993, the Bank issued a new Forestry Policy which makes specific reference to the need to incorporate local people (including "forest dwellers") in environmentally sound forestry conservation and development plans. See, Operational Policy 4.36, para. l(d)(ii).
31. For a discussion of these issues, especially as they relate to the participation of NGOs in Bank-financed projects, see, Ibrahim F.I. Shatterer, "The World Bank and Non-Governmental Organisations," *Cornell International Law Journal*, Vol.25, No.3, Spring 1992, pp.623-641.
32. This directive was prepared for the guidance of staff of the World Bank and is not necessarily a complete treatment of the subjects covered. This new directive 4.20 replaced the OMS on Tribal People in Bank-Financed Projects.

3. United Nations Working Group on Indigenous Populations

A. The United Nations and Indigenous Peoples

by Julian Burger

"Until this moment, we have had our place in world civilisation determined by the so-called 'modern' industrial nations and ranked according to their values — values which have placed indigenous people at the very bottom of the human family. Today, the United Nations begins the process of knowing us, not through the distorted history of the colonisers, but by hearing our own voices, looking into our own hearts, and coming to understand our humanity. Today, you begin learning the important past and potential contributions of indigenous people to the world. Today, you begin the process of seeing indigenous peoples of the world not as primitive and backward, but rather as human beings with our own dreams and aspirations, our own value systems, our own yearning for international recognition of our human rights, including the right of self-determination."

Russell Means, International Indian Treaty Council, addressing the General Assembly, 12 December 1992.

For two weeks in July, the United Nations Office at Geneva becomes the setting of a unique exercise in international affairs: the annual meeting of the Working Group on Indigenous Populations. Hundreds of indigenous people leave their communities, make sometimes arduous journeys to an international airport, and settle down for 12 hour flights or more. The costs are plenty. Geneva is one of the most expensive cities in the world, and the rituals of the meeting are both perplexing and frustrating. For many participants it may seem like an awfully big effort for not very much. But there are rewards and that is why, with every year that passes, more and more indigenous people make the pilgrimage to the United Nations to push open the door of the international arena a little bit more.

The Working Group on Indigenous Populations was established in 1982 to review developments affecting indigenous people and elaborate standards for the protection of their rights. Both parts of the mandate are important. The review of developments provides an opportunity to hear first-hand about the specific problems faced by indigenous people and occasionally about their solutions. The work on standard-setting, which has accelerated considerably in the past three years, has focused on the drafting of a declaration on the rights of indigenous peoples.

The United Nations has been formally involved with the question of indigenous peoples and their rights since 1972 when the Economic and Social Council authorized a special study on discrimination against indigenous populations.[1] The report covered a range of issues, including health, culture, religion, employment, land and political rights. It concluded that existing international instruments were not adequate to protect the rights of indigenous people.[2] The five-member Working Group on Indigenous Populations composed of independent experts of the Sub-Commission on Prevention of Discrimination and Protection of Minorities — was one of the results of the study.

The creation of the Working Group coincided with a growing internationalisation of activities by indigenous peoples. Two nongovernmental conferences bringing together indigenous peoples from the Western Hemisphere took place in 1977 and 1981. In 1977, the International Indian Treaty Council requested and gained consultative status with the Economic and Social Council thereby making it the first indigenous organization to have rights of participation in United Nations meetings. Several other indigenous peoples' organizations also received similar credentials. Pressure was, thus, present from indigenous peoples themselves for action by the United Nations system.

The past decade has seen a major change in the international situation of indigenous people. Once neglected and totally excluded from the international scene, indigenous people now have a number of possibilities for political action. Their public criticism of the only existing international instrument protecting the rights of indigenous people — the International Labour Organisation's Convention No.107 — as assimilationist and paternalist contributed to its review by the organization and its subsequent revision. Since 1989 a new ILO Convention on indigenous and tribal peoples (No.169) has been adopted which recognises the distinct cultures and right to self-development of indigenous peoples. Pressures by indigenous peoples and lobby groups active in human rights and environmental protection have led to changes in policy by the World Bank.[3] Most recently several hundred indigenous people from the Americas, Asia, Africa, Australia, Europe and the Pacific were active at the United Nations Conference on Environment and Development (UNCED) ensuring that the Final Declaration and Agenda 21, the action plan to implement the recommendations of the Conference, reflected at least some of their concerns.[4]

The Working Group on Indigenous Populations has played an important role, albeit unintentionally, in this global movement. As the only United Nations meeting formally addressing indigenous peoples' concerns, it has attracted worldwide participation. Its first session in 1982 was attended by some 30 people; at its last session in 1992 attendance had risen to over 600. The opportunity for indigenous people to meet, exchange ideas and plan future cooperation is unprecedented. But the formal deliberations of the Group are also vital. At its last session, 120 separate oral presentations were made on different country situations, making the Working Group a potential source of first-hand testimony on the state of the 300 million indigenous people of the world unparalleled. The Working Group has generated critical studies, expert meetings, and various kinds of practical action. These include the study on treaties, agreements and other constructive arrangements by the Special Rapporteur, Miguel Alfonso Martinez[5] and the study on the cultural and intellectual property of indigenous peoples by the Special Rapporteur, Erica-Irene Daes.[6] Three United Nations expert seminars have given rise to a range of comprehensive recommendations on racism, self-government and environment.[7] The proposal to proclaim an International Year of the World's Indigenous People also began its course in the Working Group. The Working Group is a forum where indigenous people have relatively free access and are able to launch a number of ideas and calls for action. Indeed it is the only place in the United Nations where they have an established right to speak as indigenous peoples, nations and organisations.

No one has any doubts, however, that despite the successes of the last years, indigenous peoples still find themselves treated as second-class citizens in the international arena. The Working Group, open as it is, is not a policy-making body of the United Nations. It reports to a Sub-Commission of independent experts which in turn reports to the Commission on Human Rights. Every recommendation emanating from the Working Group must make its way through its parent bodies until authority is given by the Economic and Social Council or the General Assembly itself. And this process will be critical for the future of the draft declaration on the rights of indigenous peoples.

A first reading of the draft declaration on the rights of indigenous peoples began at the Working Group session in 1991. In the 1992 session the first reading was completed and a second reading was initiated. In view of the proclamation by the United Nations of the International Year of the World's Indigenous People in 1993, the Chairperson/Rapporteur of the Working Group, EricaIrene Daes, has pledged to make every effort to complete the draft at second reading during the eleventh session in July 1993. This course of action has brought into focus a number of questions about the future place of indigenous peoples in the United Nations system. How will the Governments react to the draft declaration when it leaves the Working Group to make its way to the General Assembly? Will indigenous people have the same rights of participation as they do in the Working Group in any new body which might be set up by the Commission on Human Rights? What will be the fate of the Working Group itself if it is relieved of responsibility for one of its two principal mandates? These questions and others will not be resolved during 1993 but they will be hotly debated.

But what does the draft declaration say and why is it so important to indigenous peoples? The first thing to note is that the way in which the declaration is being drafted is unique in United Nations history. There has never been an international instrument discussed so intensely by the very people it is meant to benefit. The recently adopted Declaration on Minority Rights was drafted with virtually no participation by representatives minorities themselves.[8] The Working Group on Indigenous Populations has, on the contrary, benefited from the participation of indigenous leaders as well as of representatives of communities. Since 1986 the Voluntary Fund for Indigenous Populations has provided funds for travel and subsistence of indigenous people precisely so that they can share their experiences and viewpoints with the members of the Working Group. This active participation in the drafting of the declaration represents a new departure for the United Nations.

The draft declaration as it stands at the time of writing contains 17 preambular and 39 operational paragraphs.[9] No doubt when it is restructured and revised at second reading the number will be marginally larger. As declarations go, the draft declaration on the rights of indigenous peoples is long, longer than any existing comparable instrument. The operational paragraphs may be grouped perhaps under eight major themes and, although any detailed discussion would require almost book-length commentary, some of the main features of the draft declaration can be identified. First, in the area of general policy, indigenous peoples have insisted on recognition of their right of self-determination. A formulation was agreed upon by members of the Working Group in 1992 as follows:

"Indigenous peoples have the right of self-determination, in accordance with international law, by virtue of which they may freely determine their political status and institutions and freely pursue their economic, social and cultural development. An integral part of this is the right to autonomy and self-government." (Paragraph 1)

The question of the self-determination of peoples has generated a gargantuan literature and increasingly scholars and jurists are considering the right as it appertains to indigenous peoples. At the heart of the debate is a political question rather than a juridical one. States, almost without a dissenting voice, consider that recognition of the right to self-determination opens up possibilities of secession.[10] Indigenous peoples without exception consider the right fundamental to the achievement of every other right. As the representative of the Nordic Saami Council stated at the Working Group on Indigenous Populations in 1988: "Our rights to self-determination must be expressly acknowledged. In addition, self-determination should be the primary theme of the Declaration . . ." Similar affirmations have been made by indigenous people at every meeting of the Working Group. The formulation of paragraph 1 as it stands at present is derived from the recommendations of the United Nations expert meeting on self-government of indigenous peoples which took place in Nuuk, Greenland, in September 1991.

By way of balancing this paragraph on self-determination, reference is made in a later paragraph to the Declaration on Principles of International Law concerning Friendly Relations and Cooperation among States in accordance with the Charter of the United Nations which stresses the preeminence of the principle of territorial integrity of States.

A critical distinction claimed by indigenous peoples is that they have a right to maintain their differences and to determine their future development collectively. Such a right should not deny them full participation in the political, economic, social and cultural life of the State and nor should it, of course, deny them their full enjoyment of the rights established by international human rights law.

The second group of rights elaborated by the draft declaration concern *the rights to life and physical integrity of indigenous peoples.* It is well understood that indigenous peoples in some countries face violations of their right to life. Abuses against indigenous people include extrajudicial executions, "disappearances" and torture and other forms of ill-treatment. The rights to life and physical integrity are guaranteed by the International Bill of Human Rights and other international instruments such as the Convention against Torture. However, indigenous peoples as a group are sometimes the victims of State-orchestrated campaigns of violence, including of genocide. Furthermore, indigenous peoples consider that any form of forced assimilation or the deprivation of their distinct cultural characteristics constitutes cultural genocide.

The right to protection against cultural genocide is specifically recognized in the draft declaration.[11]

The third group of rights in the draft declaration concern *the rights to cultural, religious and linguistic identity*. The rights include protection of sacred sites and the restitution of cultural property as well as the repatriation of human remains. The revitalization and transmission to future generations of indigenous languages and oral traditions are vital aspects of these rights. The process of colonization has resulted in the loss and debilitation of countless local languages. For a long period national policies were aimed at the assimilation of indigenous people into mainstream society and education programmes tried to eliminate indigenous languages and customs. States now recognize these distinct indigenous cultures but the damage caused by these policies is extensive. Thus, indigenous peoples consider the reestablishment of their own languages and cultural traditions as a priority.

A fourth group of rights promote *education and public information*. In most countries, indigenous people have less opportunities to education than other groups. The draft declaration, therefore, recognises "the right to all levels and forms of education, including access to education in their own languages, and the right to establish and control their educational systems and institutions".

The principles of *greater access by indigenous people to services* as well as their right to control where appropriate policies and institutions affecting them are also reflected in the fifth group of rights dealing with economic and social matters. It is generally recognised that indigenous people face discrimination and disadvantage in all countries and in all areas. According to every socio-economic indicator, whether dealing with health, housing, education, employment, life expectancy or social welfare, indigenous people fare far worse than any other group in society. Broadly speaking there are two causes: a lack of access to services, often as a result of discriminatory practices, and the delivery of services which are inappropriate, alien and sometimes culturally unacceptable. The draft declaration gives voice to what is becoming in some countries national policy, namely a system of services which is planned and implemented by indigenous people themselves.[12] Finally, the right to engage in traditional economic activities, including hunting, fishing, herding, gathering, forestry and cultivation is recognised.

Land for indigenous peoples means the total environment of the lands, air, water, sea, sea-ice, flora and fauna and other resources they have used. The sixth group of rights addresses this most important question. Recognition is given to the distinctive and profound relationship which indigenous people have to their lands. There is also recognition of indigenous peoples right to own, control and use their lands and territories as well as recognition of their land-tenure systems and institutions for the management of resources. The right of recognition of the intellectual property of indigenous peoples is promoted. This right is of particular concern to indigenous peoples who live in what are sometimes called "wilderness regions" where their technologies and knowledge of the properties of flora and fauna are subject to exploitation for profit by outsiders.

The draft declaration also reflects the concern many indigenous people have about development projects on their lands. Many indigenous peoples have lost parts of their territories, seen their forests or mountains turned into barren wastelands, or been forced to move altogether when mining, hydro-electric, logging, ranching or some other scheme take place. The destructive impact of much large-scale development on indigenous people is well documented.[13] States are, thus, required by the draft declaration to obtain the free and informed consent of indigenous peoples before any project commences.

The seventh group of rights addresses the *question of self-government of indigenous peoples*. The draft declaration states: "Indigenous peoples have the right to autonomy and self-government in matters relating to their internal and local affairs . . ." Emphasis is laid on the right of indigenous people to determine their membership, establish their own institutions according to their own practices and retain and develop their own customs, laws and legal systems. The right to maintain and develop contacts with other indigenous peoples across borders is also recognised by the draft declaration. This right is especially important for peoples, such as the Inuit or Saami, who have been divided by international frontiers. Reference is also made to the treaties concluded between States and indigenous peoples and the right to their observance is recognised.

An eighth group of rights, at present less developed, looks at *ways in which the draft declaration could be monitored and implemented*. The declaration sets out the minimum basic human rights of indigenous peoples and will not be binding on States. However, ten years have gone into the making of the draft declaration so far and some time may pass before it is finally adopted by the General Assembly. Indigenous peoples are, therefore, demanding that the draft declaration require States and the United Nations to take effective measures to give effect to the rights contained in the draft declaration.

The adoption of the draft declaration would be an extremely important first step for the world's indigenous peoples. Although not binding on States, it would serve as a reference point for Governments and indigenous peoples and help guide national legislation. The declaration once adopted may also have an impact on the programmes and policies of intergovernmental organizations and multilateral financial institutions.

But what is the timetable for the draft declaration? How long will indigenous people have to wait before they enjoy protection of their rights in international law? No one can predict the answer with accuracy. The United Nations Working Group on Indigenous Populations plans to complete the second reading of the draft declaration in July 1993 and it is hoped that its parent body — the Sub-Commission on Prevention of Discrimination and Protection of Minorities which meets in August of the same year — will recommend the draft to the Commission on Human Rights. If all goes as planned, the Commission will examine the draft declaration at its session in February 1994. The Commission may then set up its own working group to review the draft declaration or else recommend it to the Economic and Social Council, and the General Assembly at its session in December 1994.

Whatever happens to the draft declaration, whether it lingers in the Commission or moves quickly to the General Assembly, indigenous peoples have now put their cause onto the agenda of the United Nations. A symbolic if not substantive recognition of this fact is signalled by the proclamation by the

General Assembly of 1993 as the International Year of the World's Indigenous People. Much more will be expected of the United Nations than can ever be delivered but that is ever the case with international years. Twelve months is not enough time to put right centuries of neglect and oppression. Funds contributed by Governments to assist indigenous people are still extremely modest when compared to those contributed for other vulnerable groups such as children or refugees. But it is important to see beyond 1993. The Working Group on Indigenous Populations, the draft declaration and the International Year are the first building blocks of an international programme. It is only a little over a decade since the United Nations began its first formal contacts with indigenous people. A great deal has happened since then. The next ten years promise to be just as remarkable.

JULIAN BURGER is the Secretary of the Working Group on Indigenous Populations and the focal point at the United Nations Centre for Human Rights on indigenous peoples. He is the author of several books on indigenous peoples including "Report from the frontier: the state of the world's indigenous peoples", Zed Press, 1987 and "First peoples: a future for the indigenous world", Doubleday, 1990. The views expressed in this article are those of the author and do not necessarily reflect those of the United Nations.
April 1993

The Working Group on Indigenous Populations completed its work on the Draft Declaration on Rights of Indigenous Peoples at its eleventh session. The Chairwoman/rapporteur of the Working Group, Mrs. Daes submitted a final text of the draft Declaration to the Subcommission on Prevention of Discrimination and Protection of Minorities in August. The Subcommission, however, decided not to discuss the Declaration, but to transfer it to its next meeting in 1994. The text of the Declaration is final and can no longer be amended. The Working Group recommended that the future role of the Working Group should be considered at its twelfth session.

B. Draft Declaration on the Rights of Indigenous Peoples

As agreed upon by the Members of the Working Group of Indigenous Populations at its eleventh session. E/CN.4/Sub.2/1993/29

Affirming that indigenous peoples are equal in dignity and rights to all other peoples, while recognising the right of all peoples to be different, to consider themselves different, and to be respected as such,

Affirming also that all peoples contribute to the diversity and richness of civilisations and cultures, which constitute the common heritage of humankind,

Affirming further that all doctrines, policies and practices based on or advocating superiority of peoples or individuals on the basis of national origin, racial, religious, ethnic or cultural differences are racist, scientifically false, legally invalid, morally condemnable and socially unjust,

Reaffirming also that indigenous peoples, in the exercise of their rights, should be free from discrimination of any kind,

Concerned that many indigenous peoples have often been deprived of their human rights and fundamental freedoms, resulting, *inter alia*, in their colonisation and dispossession of their lands, territories and resources, thus preventing them from exercising, in particular, their right to development in accordance with their own needs and interests,

Recognising the urgent need to respect and promote the inherent rights and characteristics of indigenous peoples, especially their rights to their lands, territories and resources, which derive from their political, economic and social structures and from their cultures, spiritual traditions, histories and philosophies,

Welcoming the fact that indigenous peoples are organising themselves for political, economic, social and cultural enhancement and in order to bring an end to all forms of discrimination and oppression wherever they occur,

Convinced that control by indigenous peoples over developments affecting them and their lands, territories and resources will enable them to maintain and strengthen their institutions, cultures and traditions, and to promote their development in accordance with their aspirations and needs,

Recognising also that respect for indigenous knowledge, cultures and traditional practices contributes to sustainable and equitable development and proper management of the environment,

Emphasizing the need for demilitarisation of the lands and territories of indigenous peoples, which will contribute to peace, economic and social progress and development, understanding and friendly relations among nations and peoples of the world,

Recognising in particular the right of indigenous families and communities to retain shared responsibility for the upbringing, training, education and well-being of their children,

Recognising also that indigenous peoples have the right freely to determine their relationships with States in a spirit of coexistence, mutual benefit and full respect,

Acknowledging that the Charter of the United Nations, the International Covenant on Economic, Social and Cultural Rights and the International Covenant on Civil and Political Rights affirm the fundamental importance of the right of self-determination of all peoples, by virtue of which they freely determine their political status and freely pursue their economic, social and cultural development,

Bearing in mind that nothing in this Declaration may be used to deny any peoples their right of self-determination,

Encouraging States to comply with and effectively implement all international instruments, in particular those related to human rights, as they apply to indigenous peoples, in consultation and cooperation with the peoples concerned,

Emphasizing that the United Nations has an important and continuing role to play in promoting and protecting the rights of indigenous peoples,

Believing that this Declaration is a further important step forward for the recognition, promotion and protection of the rights and freedom of indigenous peoples and in the development of relevant activities of the United Nations system in this field,

Solemnly proclaims the following United Nations Declaration on the Rights of Indigenous Peoples:

PART I

Article 1
Indigenous peoples have the right to the full and effective enjoyment of all of the human rights and fundamental freedoms recognised in the Charter of the United Nations, the Universal Declaration of Human Rights and in international human rights law.

Article 3
Indigenous peoples have the right of self-determination. By virtue of that right they freely determine their political status and freely pursue their economic, social and cultural development.

Article 4
Indigenous peoples have the right to maintain and strengthen their distinct political, economic, social and cultural characteristics, as well as their legal systems, while retaining their rights to participate fully, if they so choose, in the political, economic, social and cultural life of the State.

Article 5
Every indigenous individual has the right to a nationality.

PART II

Article 6
Indigenous peoples have the collective right to live in freedom, peace and security as distinct peoples and to full guarantees against genocide or any other act of violence, including the removal of indigenous children from their families and communities under any pretext.

In addition, they have the individual rights to life, physical and mental integrity, liberty and security of person.

Article 7
Indigenous peoples have the collective and individual right not to be subjected to ethnocide and cultural genocide, including prevention of and redress for:
 (a) Any act which has the aim or effect of depriving them of their integrity as distinct peoples, or of their cultural values or ethnic identities;
 (b) Any action which has the aim or effect of dispossessing them of their lands, territories or resources;
 (c) Any form of population transfer which has the aim or effect of violating or undermining any of their rights;
 (d) Any form of assimilation or integration by other cultures or ways of life imposed on them by legislative, administrative or other measures;
 (e) Any form of propaganda directed against them;

Article 8
Indigenous peoples have the collective and individual right to maintain and develop their distinct identities and characteristics, including the right to identify themselves as indigenous and to be recognised as such.

Article 9
Indigenous peoples and individuals have the right to belong to an indigenous community or nation, in accordance with the traditions and customs of the community or nation concerned. No disadvantage of any kind may arise from the exercise of such a right.

Article 10
Indigenous peoples shall not be forcibly removed from their lands or territories. No relocation shall take place without the free and informed consent of the indigenous peoples concerned and after agreement on just and fair compensation and, where possible, with the option of return.

Article 11
Indigenous peoples have the right to special protection and security in periods of armed conflict. States shall observe international standards, in particular the Fourth Geneva Convention of 1949, for the protection of civilian populations in circumstances of emergency and armed conflict, and shall not:
 (a) recruit indigenous individuals against their will into the armed forces and, in particular, for use against other indigenous peoples;
 (b) Recruit indigenous children into the armed forces under any circumstances;
 (c) Force indigenous individuals to abandon their lands, territories or means of subsistence, or relocate them in special centres for military purposes;
 (d) Force indigenous individuals to work for military purposes under any discriminatory conditions.

PART III

Article 12
Indigenous peoples have the right to practice and revitalise their cultural traditions and customs. This includes the right to maintain, protect and develop the past, present and future manifestations of their cultures, such as archaeological and historical sites, artifacts, designs, ceremonies, technologies and visual and performing arts and literature, as well as the right to the restitution of cultural, intellectual, religious and spiritual property taken without their free and informed consent or in violation of their elaws, traditions and customs.

Article 13
Indigenous peoples have the right to manifest, practise, develop and teach their spiritual and religious traditions, customs and ceremonies; the right to maintain, protect and have access in privacy to their

religious and cultural sites; the right to the use and control of ceremonial objects; and the right to the repatriation of human remains.

States shall take effective measure, in conjunction with the indigenous peoples concerned, to ensure that indigenous sacred places, including burial sites, be preserved, respected and protected.

Article 14

Indigenous peoples have the right to revitalise, use, develop and transmit to future generations their histories, languages, oral traditions, philosophies, writing systems and literatures, and to designate and retain their own names for communities, places and persons.

States shall take effective measures, whenever any right of indigenous peoples may be threatened, to ensure this right is protected and also to ensure that they can understand and be understood in political, legal and administrative proceedings, where necessary through the provision of interpretation or by other appropriate means.

PART IV

Article 15

Indigenous children have the right to all levels and forms of education of the State. All indigenous peoples also have this right and the right to establish and control their educational systems and institutions providing education in their own languages, in a manner appropriate to their cultural methods of teaching and learning.

Indigenous children living outside their communities have the right to be provided access to education in their own culture and language.

States shall take effective measures to provide appropriate resources for these purposes.

Article 16

Indigenous peoples have the right to have the dignity and diversity of their cultures, traditions, histories and aspirations appropriately reflected in all forms of education and public information.

States shall take effective measures, in consultation with the indigenous peoples concerned, to eliminate prejudice and discrimination and to promote tolerance, understanding and good relations among indigenous peoples and all segments of society.

Article 17

Indigenous peoples have the right to establish their own media in their own languages. They also have the right to equal access to all forms of non-indigenous media.

States shall take effective measures to ensure that State-owned media duly reflect indigenous cultural diversity.

Article 18

Indigenous peoples have the right to enjoy fully all rights established under international labour law and national labour legislation.

Indigenous individuals have the right not to be subjected to any discriminatory conditions of labour, employment or salary.

PART V

Article 19

Indigenous peoples have the right to participate fully, if they so choose, at all levels of decision-making in matters which may affect their rights, lives and destinies through representatives chosen by themselves in accordance with their own procedures, as well as to maintain and develop their own indigenous decision-making institutions.

Article 20

Indigenous peoples have the right to participate fully, if they so choose, through procedures determined by them, in devising legislative or administrative measures that may affect them.

States shall obtain the free and informed consent of the peoples concerned before adopting and implementing such measures.

Article 21

Indigenous peoples have the right to maintain and develop their political, economic and social systems, to be secure in the enjoyment of their own means of subsistence and development, and to engage freely in all their traditional and other economic activities. Indigenous peoples who have been deprived of their means of subsistence and development are entitled to just and fair compensation.

Article 22
Indigenous peoples have the right to special measures for the immediate effective and continuing improvement of their economic and social conditions, including in the areas of employment, vocational training and retraining, housing, sanitation, health and social security.

Particular attention shall be paid to the rights and special needs of indigenous elders, women, youth, children and disabled persons.

Article 23
Indigenous peoples have the right to determine and develop priorities and strategies for exercising their right to development. In particular, indigenous peoples have the right to determine and develop all health, housing and other economic and social programmes affecting them and, as far as possible, to administer such programmes through their own institutions.

Article 24
Indigenous peoples have the right to their traditional medicines and health practices, including the right to the protection of vital medicinal plants, animals and minerals.

They also have the right to access, without any discrimination, to all medical institutions, health services and medical care.

PART VI

Article 25
Indigenous peoples have the right to maintain and strengthen their distinctive spiritual and material relationship with the lands, territories, waters and coastal seas and other resources which they have traditionally owned and otherwise occupied or used, and to uphold their responsibilities to future generations in this regard.

Article 26
Indigenous peoples have the right to own, develop, control and use the lands and territories, including the total environment of the lands, air, waters, coastal seas, sea-ice, flora and fauna and other resources which they have traditionally owned or otherwise occupied or used. This includes the right to the full recognition of their laws and customs, land-tenure systems and institutions for the development and management of resources, and the right to effective measures by States to prevent any interference with alienation or encroachment upon these rights.

Article 27
Indigenous peoples have the right to the restitution of the lands, territories and resources which they have traditionally owned or otherwise occupied or used, and which have been confiscated, occupied, used or damaged without their free and informed consent. Where this is not possible, they have the right to just and fair compensation. Unless otherwise freely agreed upon by the peoples concerned, compensation shall take the form of lands, territories and resources equal in quality, size and legal status.

Article 28
Indigenous peoples have the right to conservation, restoration and protection of the total environment and the productive capacity of their lands, territories and resources, as well as to assistance for this purpose from States and through international cooperation. Military activities shall not take place in the lands and territories of indigenous peoples, unless otherwise freely agreed upon by the peoples concerned.

States shall take effective measures to ensure that no storage or disposal of hazardous materials shall take place in the lands and territories of indigenous peoples.

States shall also take effective measures to ensure, as needed, that programmes for monitoring, maintaining and restoring the health of indigenous peoples, as developed and implemented by the peoples affected by such materials, are duly implemented.

Article 29
Indigenous peoples are entitled to the recognition of the full ownership, control and protection of their cultural and intellectual property.

They have the right to special measures to control, develop and protect their sciences, technologies and cultural manifestations, including human and other genetic resources, seeds, medicines, knowledge of the properties of fauna and flora, oral traditions, literatures, designs and visual and performing arts.

Article 30
Indigenous peoples have the right to determine and develop priorities and strategies for the development or use of their lands, territories and other resources, including the right to require that States obtain their free and informed consent prior to the approval of any project affecting their lands, territories and other resources, particularly in connection with the development, utilisation or exploitation of mineral, water or other resources, compensation shall be provided for any such activities and measures taken to mitigate adverse environmental, economic, social, cultural or spiritual impact.

PART VII

Article 31
Indigenous peoples, as a specific form of exercising their right to self-determination, have the right to autonomy or self-government in matters relating to their international and local affairs, including culture, religion, education, information, media, health, housing, employment, social welfare, economic activities, land and resources management, environment and entry by non-members, as well as ways and means for financing these autonomous functions.

Article 32
Indigenous peoples have the collective right to determine their own citizenship in accordance with their customs and traditions. Indigenous citizenship does not impair the right of indigenous individuals to obtain citizenship of the States in which they live.

Indigenous peoples have the right to determine the structures and to select the membership of their institutions in accordance with their own procedures.

Article 33
Indigenous peoples have the right to promote, develop and maintain their institutional structures and their distinctive juridical customs, traditions, procedures and practices, in accordance with internationally recognised human rights standards.

Article 34
Indigenous peoples have the collective right to determine the responsibilities of individuals to their communities.

Article 35
Indigenous peoples, particular those divided by international borders, have the right to maintain and develop contacts, relations and cooperation, including activities for spiritual, cultural, political, economic and social purposes with other peoples across borders.

States shall take effective measures to ensure the exercise and implementation of this right.

Article 36
Indigenous peoples have the right to the recognition, observance and enforcement of treaties, agreements and other constructive arrangements concluded with States or their successors, according to their original spirit and intent, and to have States honour and respect such treaties, agreements and other constructive arrangements. Conflicts and disputes which cannot otherwise be settled should be submitted to competent international bodies agreed to by all parties concerned.

Article 37
States shall take effective and appropriate measures, in consultation with the indigenous peoples concerned, to give full effect to the provisions of this Declaration. The rights recognised herein shall be adopted and included in national legislation in such a manner that indigenous peoples can avail themselves of such rights in practice.

Article 38
Indigenous peoples have the right to have access to adequate financial and technical assistance, from States and through international cooperation, to pursue freely their political, economic, social, cultural and spiritual development and for the enjoyment of the rights and freedoms recognised in this Declaration.

Article 39
Indigenous peoples have the right to have access to and prompt decision through mutually acceptable

and fair procedures for the resolution of conflicts and disputes with States, as well as to effective remedies for all infringements of their individual and collective rights. Such a decision shall take into consideration the customs, traditions, rules and legal systems of the indigenous peoples concerned.

Article 40
The organs and specialised agencies of the United Nations system and other intergovernmental organisations shall contribute to the full realisation of the provisions of this Declaration through the mobilisation, *inter alia*, of financial cooperation and technical assistance. Ways and means of ensuring participation of indigenous peoples on issues affecting them shall be established.

Article 41
The United Nations shall take the necessary steps to ensure the implementation of this Declaration including the creation of a body at the highest level with special competence in this field and with the direct participation of indigenous peoples. All United Nations bodies shall promote respect for and full application of the provisions of this Declaration.

PART IX

Article 42
The rights recognised herein constitute the minimum standards for the survival, dignity and well-being of the indigenous peoples of the world.

Article 43
All the rights and freedoms recognised herein are equally guaranteed to male and female indigenous individuals

Article 44
Nothing in this Declaration may be construed as diminishing or extinguishing existing or future rights in indigenous peoples may have or acquire.

Article 45
Nothing in this Declaration may be interpreted as implying for any State, group or person any right to engage in any activity or to perform any act contrary to the Charter of the United Nations.

References
1. United Nations, "Study on the problem of discrimination against indigenous populations" (José R. Martinez Cobo, Special Rapporteur of the Sub-Commission on Prevention of Discrimination and Protection of Minorities) E/CN.4/Sub.2/1986/7 and Add.1-4, Geneva: UNO, 1972-83.
2. *Ibid*, E/CN.4/Sub.2/1986/7/Add.4, para 633.
3. Cf. The World Bank, *Tribal peoples and economic development: human ecological considerations*, Washington, May 1982, and Operations Manual, February 1982. In 1991, the World Bank issued Operational Directive 4.20. It can also be credited, after considerable local and international criticism, with the decision to order an independent review of the Narmada Dam project in India. Cf.Bradford Morse & Thomas Berger, *Sardar Sarovar: Report of the Independent Review*, Resources Future, Ottawa, 1992. The Report was highly critical of the project and the World Bank has since withdrawn.
4. See the text of the Kari-Oca Declaration and Earth Charter, adopted at the World Conference of Indigenous Peoples on Territory, Environment and Development 25-30 May 1992.
5. First progress report submitted by Mr Miguel Alfonso Martinez, Special Rapporteur, United Nations document E/CN.4/Sub.2/1992/32.
6. The study was preceded by a working paper on the question of the ownership and control of the cultural property of indigenous peoples prepared by Ms Erica-Irene Daes, United Nations document E/CN.4/Sub.2/1991/34.
7. The United Nations seminar on the effects of racism and racial discrimination on the social and economic relations between indigenous peoples and States was held in Geneva, in January 1989; the United Nations Meeting of Experts to review the experiences of countries in the operation of schemes of internal self-government for indigenous peoples was held in Nuuk, Greenland, in September 1991 (cf E/CN.4/1992/42); the United Nations Technical Conference on practical experience in the realization of sustainable and environmentally sound self-development of indigenous peoples was held in Santiago, Chile, in May 1992, (cf. E/CN.4/Sub.21992/31).

8. The Declaration on the Rights of Minorities was adopted by the General Assembly in December 1992.
9. See the text of the 1992 draft declaration on Indigenous Peoples in this chapter.
10. The representative of the Government of Canada, for example, stated at the 1992 Working Group session that "Canada does not recognise this rights of self-determination . . . as that term is understood in international law."* The representatives of Australia and the Nordic countries were more conciliatory suggesting that the term might be acceptable if carefully elaborated. Indigenous peoples have not presented their claims to self-determination in terms of secession from the State. See for example *Fourth World Bulletin*, Vol.2, No.2, February 1993, p.3: "Although few indigenous nations actually aspire to become independent states, many would not regard their aspirations for self-determination as secessionist in any case, since they never gave their informed consent to integration into the State and so should not be understood to be seceding if they ever should want to separate and become states in their own right."
11. The right reflects the conclusions of the UNESCO Meeting of Experts on Ethno-development and Ethnocide in Latin America, San José, Costa Rica, December 1981, where ethnocide was defined as the condition under which an ethnic group is denied the right to enjoy, develop and transmit its own culture and its own language.
12. For example, the Aboriginal and Torres Strait Islander Commission in Australia, established in 1991, is run by an elected body of indigenous commissioners who are responsible for the delivery of approximately A$1000 million of health, housing, vocational and other services.
13. Cf. the extensive bibliography in Julian Burger, *Report from the frontier: the state of the world's indigenous peoples*, Zed Press, 1987.

4. United Nations Development Programme (UNDP)

A. United Nations Development Programme and Indigenous Peoples

by Marcel Viergever

Introduction

Only a few decades ago, indigenous people were largely considered a 'hindrance' to development. They were seen as part of a backward, pre-industrial, traditional sector whose interests, especially in the case of land rights, were in conflict with the interests of the modern, industrial sector of society. A number of developments, such as general acceptance of the concept of sustainability and renewed emphasis on basic needs and participatory approaches, are changing that view.

The concept of sustainable development (i.e. development that seeks to meet present needs without compromising the capacity to meet the needs of future generations), brought development and environment into one logical framework and built an "ideological bridge" between the 'traditional' and the 'modern' sector by recognising the significance of indigenous people's holistic traditional knowledge of the environment and management of natural resources.

A sharp deterioration in living conditions, especially in Africa and Latin America, the failure of traditional development strategies and the mushrooming and growing influence of non governmental and community based organisations, jointly caused a reorientation of some bilateral and multilateral donor organisations in their policies and strategies towards greater involvement of the 'beneficiaries' in the design and implementation of programmes.

Within UNDP this resulted in the emergence of the concept of *sustainable human development*. This is an approach to overall development that regards people simultaneously as both means and ends of social and economic policy; that sees development as a *process* that should aim at enlarging peoples' capabilities, promoting their *empowerment* and allowing them to *participate* in local and national decision-making processes to determine priorities, needs and aspirations and in the implementation of strategies and programmes to achieve those aspirations; finally, it is *inclusive* and, necessarily, *multi-sectoral*.

Both developments were further reinforced by the adoption, at the United Nations Conference on Environment and Development, of Agenda 21, an action plan for the 1990s and into the 21st century. In chapter 26, "Recognising and strengthening the role of Indigenous People and their communities", Agenda 21 calls for *". . . recognition of their [indigenous people] values, traditional knowledge and resource management practices with a view to promoting environmentally sound and sustainable development"* and for *"establishment, [. . .], of arrangements to strengthen the active participation of indigenous people and their communities in the national formulation of policies, laws and programmes relating to resource management and other development processes that may affect them, and their initiation of proposals for such policies and programmes"*.[1]

In 1992, UNDP's Administrator presented a paper to the Governing Council on the International Year for the World's Indigenous People. On the basis of a process of consultations with a range of indigenous people's organisations and experts, the report suggested that UNDP support should be guided by the overall framework of human development and be made part of two of UNDP's most relevant major areas of focus for 1992-1996, i.e. poverty eradication and grass-roots participation, and Environmental and natural resources management. The following types of activities were identified:[2]

a) *Cultural revitalisation*, through, for example, (i) the recovery, strengthening and dissemination of indigenous traditions and languages; (ii) acquisition of skills in handling official languages; and (iii) networking and replication of successful approaches and projects.

b) *Improvement of living standards*, through: (i) nutrition, including, the recovery of knowledge of nutrition and related changes in dietary habits; (ii) health, in particular health education for healers, midwives and other indigenous health specialists, immunisation and primary health care, and infrastructural support for health projects, combining small-scale modern technology and traditional experience; and (iii) social security, the introduction of community-based health-care systems articulated with services available form the State, local governments and the private sector;

c) *Preservation of natural resources and environmental conservation* through (i) recovery, consolidation and dissemination of traditional knowledge and skills in the use and maintenance of natural habitats and resources; (ii) participation of indigenous communities in resource management and conservation strategies and practices; and (iii) preservation of indigenous people's territories from environmentally unsound or socially and culturally inappropriate activities;

d) *Economic and technological development* through, for example, (i) the removal of obstacles to creativity, the promotion of entrepreneurial capacity and the articulation of indigenous people's economic processes with existing structures and markets; (ii) greater participation in decision-making on, and management of, territories and resources; articulation of traditional and modern know-how in order to raise incomes through small capital investments and better use of labour and natural resources; and (iv) dissemination and replication of successful approaches and projects and exchanges of skills and experience.

UNDP projects and programmes for and with Indigenous Peoples

UNDP is the world's largest channel for multilateral development co-operation. It is active in more than 150 developing countries and territories and it operates in virtually every economic and social sector. UNDP assistance, like that of the other UN system agencies, is made available at the request of Governments and in response to their needs as identified in five-year country and intercountry programmes. This means that in countries where governments overlook the needs of indigenous people, indigenous communities' access to UNDP funding will be limited. But, even in those countries, the UN Resident Coordinator may be in a position to support and promote a dialogue between indigenous peoples and governments and raise government officials' and institutions' awareness about the needs of indigenous communities.

Also, governments that are reluctant to allocate UNDP's regular country programme resources to projects supporting Indigenous Peoples, may be more amenable to accept support for indigenous peoples funded from Special Programme Resources or special funds, e.g. Capacity 21, the Global Environment Facility, and several small-grants programmes.

Capacity 21 is a facility to assist capacity-building programmes in support of Agenda 21. It aims to assist developing countries in the task of integrating environment and development and in the transition to more sustainable development paths. It may also be able to consider funding for grassroots initiatives within a national policy framework. It is for example, considering a proposal for support to Indigenous Peoples in the most ecologically fragile forest areas of Honduras, to (i) develop a legal framework for indigenous settlements located within ecologically fragile forests, to create buffer zones to contain deforestation by cattle ranchers and migrant farmers; (ii) strengthen traditional community administration systems practised by native tribes through training in community development, natural resource management, etc.; (iii) develop a package of "demonstration" micro-projects at the village level, encompassing sustainable resource management, agro-forestry, food security, primary health care, bicultural education, revitalization of traditional crafts, etc.

Another programme that may be of relevance to Indigenous People is the **Global Environment Facility (GEF).** This is a three-year experiment to help developing countries protect the global environment by addressing four main global environment problems: 1) Global warming, particularly the effects on the worlds's climate of greenhouse gas emissions resulting from the use of fossil fuels and the destruction of carbon-absorbing forests; 2) Destruction of biological diversity through the degradation of natural habitats and depletion of natural resources; 3) Pollution of international waters, including oceans and international river systems; and 4) Depletion of the stratospheric ozone layer from emissions of chloro-fluorocarbons (CFCs), halons and other gases. The GEF is implemented by three agencies: UNDP, UNEP and the World Bank. UNDP is responsible for technical assistance and for the GEF small-grants programme (see below). In 1992, GEF approved a project, 'Regional Strategies for the Conservation and Management of Natural Resources in the Amazon', which contains a component of support for indigenous grassroots communities management of their natural resources. It is also examining the feasibility of funding another project that would identify and support ongoing initiatives being undertaken by indigenous people that benefit their community while at the same time benefitting the environment in which they live.

Small-grants programmes are intended mainly to support grassroots and community-based groups and NGOs. These programmes are offered in a limited number of countries, and individual grants do not exceed US$50,000. UNDP small-grants programmes that may be relevant to indigenous people' organisations include:

Africa 2000 Network. This programme helps mobilise and support community groups, NGOs and technical institutions through direct project assistance, training and communication exchange, in a regional effort to protect Africa's environment and promote ecologically sustainable development at the grassroots level.

Partners in Development Programme. This programme is offered in 1992-93 in 73 developing countries. Its main objectives are to (a) support community-based self-help initiatives; (b) strengthen the institutional capacity of local NGOs and community groups to respond effectively to critical development needs; and (c) promote networking with a view to strengthening dialogue among NGOs, Governments and UNDP.

Global Environment Facility (GEF) Small-Grants Programme. This programme, which is in its pilot phase, provides support to small-scale activities, undertaken by NGOs and networks, people's associations and community groups, that address the same global environmental problems as the GEF itself (see above).

Education for All — PULSE Small-Grant Facility. The general purpose of this new facility is to encourage innovation in meeting basic learning needs through cooperation between developing countries and among governments and non-governmental organisations. Activities eligible for funding include: alternative systems to primary schooling; non-formal learning; operational linkages of the formal education system with other sector activities; introduction of new and useful content into the curriculum.

Through a process of consultations with the UN Centre for Human Rights in Geneva and the Working Group on Indigenous Populations, UN agencies, NGOs and indigenous peoples' organisations, it has been suggested that an important approach to improving the living standards of indigenous peoples would be through better **recognition of indigenous knowledge** and contributions to science and technology. Supporting special measures for the protection of their traditional medicine and knowledge of useful properties of the fauna and flora would also be a way to preserve this knowledge for future generations and possible medical applications.

UNDP already has experience in the related fields of inter alia biodiversity, ethnobotany, e.g.: the Ethno-botanical Exchange between Asia and the Amazon, a meeting with the objective, among others, to establish more rigorous criteria for the collection of ethno-botanical information; support to the seminar and publication on Indigenous Territorial Rights and Ecology in the Tropical Forests of America; support to the Amazon Commission on Development and Environment. Recently, the first steps for the preparation of a new programme have been taken to identify and implement concrete measures to protect indigenous intellectual property and or ensure that indigenous communities benefit from the commercialisation and application of their knowledge.

How to apply for UNDP support

UNDP has country offices in some 120 developing countries. To apply for UNDP support through regular country programmes or Special Programme Resources, or small-grants programmes, Indigenous People should contact either the governmental organisation responsible for coordination of multilateral co-operation or UNDP's Country Office. Addresses of the UNDP Country Office and/or information about UNDP programmes supporting Indigenous Peoples may be obtained from the Government or from the focal point at UNDP Headquarters at the following address:

MARCEL VIERGEVER
Focal Point for Indigenous People
United Nations Development Programme
Programme Development and Support Division (PDSD)
One UN Plaza New York, N.Y. 10017. US
Tel: (212) 906 5347, Fax: (212) 906 5313
April 1993

B. International Year for the World's Indigenous People Report of the Administrator[3]

1. Introduction

2. There are clear indications of the growing commitment on the part of the international community to address the problems faced by indigenous communities. Actions are being encouraged which: (a) protect and promote the rights of indigenous people; (b) recognise and make use of their skills and knowledge in critically important areas; and (c) enable them to participate in all areas of development.

II. Experience with indigenous communities

3. In association with developing country governments and UN specialised agencies, UNDP has long been concerned with the concerns and issues of indigenous people. Examples of recent and current activities include;

(a) *The funding*, in association with the ILO and the World Bank. of a workshop convened by the Government of Colombia in March 1991 on land-tenure issues and the management of natural resources by indigenous communities. The workshop was attended by indigenous representatives and experts from eight countries of Latin America;

(b) *The participation of Indigenous people in the brainstorming session organised in 1991* on governance, the State and civil society in Latin America and the Caribbean, with a view to broadening the participation of indigenous communities in project formulation and programme revision and to securing such participation in the technical group and Commission on environment and development in the Amazon region;

(c) *Two preparatory assistance projects in the Latin America and Caribbean region* on (a) the management of natural resources by indigenous communities and the promotion of alternatives for the management of timber and non-timber resources by indigenous tribes living in forests and (b) technical assistance to the Government of Bolivia, acting on behalf of other governments in the region, for the establishment of a fund for the development of indigenous peoples in Latin America and the Caribbean;

(d) *The funding*, in 1990, of a *seminar on Pygmy life* in the Central African Republic, which was attended by government officials and NGOs to explore ways in which the health and education needs of the Pygmies in the Central African Republic could be met without disrupting their culture and relationship to the environment;

(e) *The funding*, in *Southern Laos*, of a rural development project that seeks to improve the living conditions of isolated hill tribes and to integrate them more fully in the mainstream of Lao life, in particular through better access to health and educational services and the development of the forest and water resources of the region;

(f) *The UNDP contribution* to the preparatory process of the United Nations Conference on Environment and Development (UNCED), consisting in (i) the organisation, in March 1991, of an international NGO consultation on poverty, environment and development, with participation from indigenous people's organisations and (ii) support to Brazilian indigenous people's organisations for activities related to UNCED.

III. Proposed Directions for Future Activities

4. Indigenous communities around the world vary greatly from demographic, economic and other points of view. However, they share several common characteristics which, taken together, define indigenous people as vulnerable groups often living in extreme poverty. These characteristics are: subordinate position within national societies; marginal and inhospitable territories; subsistence economies; languages which are, for the most part, unwritten; cultural marginalisation; maladjustments due to migration from rural to urban areas; and threatened ancestral habitats particularly rain forests.

5. As regards emphases and activities, UNDP will be guided by its previous experience and by Governing Council decision 90/34, in which the Council mandated the Programme to establish human development as the framework for all its activities and identifies the six major areas of focus for the fifth cycle. On this basis, the two areas which are most relevant to the needs of indigenous people are (i) poverty eradication and grass-roots participation in development and (ii) environmental problems and natural resource management. Following a process of consultations which have taken place since 1991 with a range of indigenous people's organisations and experts, it is suggested that UNDP could support the following types of activities;

(a) *Improvement of living standards*, through (i) nutrition including in particular the recovery of knowledge of nutrition and related changes in dietary habits; (ii) health, in particular health education for healers, midwives and other indigenous health specialists, immunisation and primary health care, and infrastructural support for health projects, combining small-scale modern technology and traditional experience; and (ii) social security, the introduction of community-based health-care systems articulated with services available from the State, local governments and the private sector;

(b) *Economic and technological development* through (i) the removal of obstacles to creativity, the promotion of entrepreneurial capacity and the articulation of indigenous people's economic processes with existing structures and markets; (ii) greater participation in decision-making on, and management of, territories and resources; (ii) articulation of traditional and modern know-how in order to raise incomes through small capital investments and better use of labour and natural resources; and (iv) dissemination and replication of successful approaches and projects and exchanges of skills and experience;

(c) *Preservation of natural resources and environmental conservation* through (i) recovery, consolidation and dissemination of traditional knowledge and skills in the use and maintenance of natural habitats and resources; (ii) participation of indigenous communities in resource management and conservation strategies and practices; (iii) preservation of indigenous people's territories from environmentally unsound or socially and culturally inappropriate activities;

(d) *Cultural revitalisation* through (i) recovery, strengthening and dissemination of indigenous traditions and languages; (ii) acquisition of skills in handling official languages; and (iii) networking and replication of successful approaches and projects.

6. Like other activities undertaken by UNDP to promote human development, those concerned with improving the condition of indigenous people should be participatory in their design, implementation and evaluation. They should also be based on the concept of reciprocity, which will make it possible to utilise the knowledge and skills of indigenous communities, in particular in natural resource management, environmental conservation and health (e.g., medicinal plants), on a broader societal base. Where appropriate, collaboration with NGOs working with indigenous people will be encouraged.

References
1. Agenda 21, chapter 26, pp.3.
2. Report of the Administrator (1992). Programme-Level Activities, International Year for the World's Indigenous People. UNDP Governing Council document DP/1992/61, 15 April 1992.
3. The present report on the International Year for the World's Indigenous People has been prepared in response to Governing Council decision 01/12 of 25 June 1991. Report of the Administrator (1992). Programme-Level Activities, International Year for the World's Indigenous People. UNDP Governing Council document DP/1992/61, 15 April 1992.

5. United Nations Educational, Scientific and Cultural Organisation (UNESCO)

by Barbara Ischinger

UNESCO has recently reinforced its activities in the area of indigenous peoples in conformity with the proclamation by the United Nations of 1993 as International Year of the World's Indigenous People. The profound changes which have modified international relations and transformed social interaction within nations, underline the importance of cultural identities in multi-cultural societies. The present situation reveals that recognition of the equal dignity of peoples and cultures is essential to a world of peace.

UNESCO's objectives in the period leading up to and during this United Nations year are to stimulate the debate and contribute to the establishment of greater inter-cultural dialogue.

The following activities were organised:

Amerindia '92 Meeting (Paris, 13-17 March 1989)
A meeting of experts in indigenous affairs from different countries of America and Europe analyzed indigenous matters and suggested that themes directly related to the various cultural identities should be developed.

"Amerindia towards the IIIrd Millennium" (San Cristobal de las Casas, State of Chiapas, Mexico, 14-16 June 1991)
This meeting, brought together about 60 participants, indigenous leaders and intellectuals from 22 countries, to examine the relationship between Indigenous Peoples and the Nation States of Latin America.

Strengthening the Spirit — beyond Five Hundred Years (Ottawa, Canada, 10-14 November 1991)
The Conference brought together 400 participants, delegates and observers from the various countries of the American continent. Representatives of Indigenous Peoples of Australia, South Africa, the Philippines, Scandinavia and Russia also took part in this conference. Topics including the process of acculturation, bilingual inter-cultural education and the role of the family were discussed.

In March 1993, UNESCO co-organised in Chichicastenango, Guatemala, an International Seminar-Workshop on plans and perspectives for sustainable development in the Maya World regions. The Seminar also brought to light the extreme environmental, cultural, social, economic and political complexity of the Maya region. The cultural dimension revealed not only diversity (22 linguistic ethnic groups) but also the need to integrate peacefully the Mayan Peoples and other groups such as inter-ethnic groups who also claim their place in the development efforts. The cultural identity of these populations could thus provide an opening to dialogue and collaboration with other cultures, provided that these are focused on the mutual respect of all actors involved.

Education, Work and Cultural Pluralism (Oaxaca, Mexico, 1923 May 1993)
A seminar took place in the framework of the World Day for Cultural Development with the participation of indigenous leaders and experts on indigenous matters. The themes of cultural pluralism and inter-cultural dialogue were stressed in the final Declaration of this meeting.

World Summit of Indigenous Peoples (Chimaltenango, Guatemala, 24-28 May 1993)[1]
This meeting was organised by the Nobel Laureate Rigoberta Menchú with the support of UNESCO.

Human Rights of indigenous peoples in the context of the New Partnership (Campeche, Mexico, 3-6 June 1993)
Indigenous participants from North, Central and South America participated in this Seminar of which the final Declaration, "Open letter of Ah-Kim-Pech (Campeche)" was submitted to the World Conference on Human Rights in Vienna.

Since 1991, UNESCO has also been collaborating in the creation of the Fund for Development of Indigenous Peoples of Latin America and the Caribbean.[2] The Organisation advocates that the approach of the Fund should take into account the promotion of human rights, stressing the need for respect of cultural diversity as a fundamental factor in development projects.

In 1993, UNESCO launched a project to celebrate the International Year in the framework of its Associated Schools Project. Teaching materials intended for secondary school teachers on "The importance of teaching about indigenous peoples" are presently being prepared by educators from different continents. These materials are to be translated into several languages and will be distributed to teacher-training institutions belonging to the UNESCO Associated Schools network worldwide.

Although UNESCO has not adopted any standard setting instrument on indigenous peoples, funds have been allocated to many projects concerning the preservation of the culture of indigenous peoples. Through projects which aim at the establishment of new forms of dialogue between people and at the promotion of a culture for peace, UNESCO will continue to support the cause of the world's Indigenous Peoples in their search for cultural development, justice and peace.

BARBARA ISCHINGER, Director of the Division of International Cultural Cooperation, and enrichment of cultural identities. The Division is one of the two Focal Points for the Year of Indigenous People in UNESCO, the other being the Latin-America Caribbean 2000 Unit.

UNESCO 7, Place de Fontenoy
75352 Paris 07 SP France
Tel: 33.1.45681000. Fax: 33.1.45671690

References
1. See Annex IV: B'okob' Declaration of the First World Summit of Indigenous Peoples, Chimaltenango, Guatemala.
2. See Chapter III.2 on the Indigenous Peoples Fund.

6. United Nations High Commission for Refugees (UNHCR)

by Kate Jastram Balian

The Office of the United Nations High Commissioner for Refugees welcomes the opportunity to contribute to the goals and objectives of the International Year for the World's Indigenous People, as set forth in the United Nations General Assembly resolution 47/75.

The mandate of the UNHCR is to provide international protection to refugees and to seek permanent solutions to their problems. In this context, UNHCR planned and carried out a number of activities to raise awareness among its staff on issues relating to indigenous peoples and promoted the participation of indigenous persons in activities of the Office.

A brief review of these activities is set forth below.

Recognising the importance of linking indigenous refugee communities with activities related to the International Year, UNHCR made possible the participation of an indigenous refugee from Guatemala in the opening ceremonies of the International Year which took place in New York in December 1992.

UNHCR has been encouraging indigenous persons to apply to its internship programme, which provides an opportunity for a small number of graduate or post graduate students specialising in international law or international relations with a strong legal background and experience in refugee related issues to work at UNHCR Headquarters in Geneva for a three month period. The Office would welcome such applications; interested persons should address a curriculum vitae and a request for an application form to Mr. Jean-Francois Durieux, Chief, Promotion of Refugee Law Section, Division of International Protection, Case Postale 2500 — CH-1211 Geneva 2. Tel: 41.22.7398339 and Fax: 41.22.7398263.

In preparing for the International Year, the Office engaged a consultant to prepare a report on indigenous peoples for internal use. On the basis of the report, UNHCR is finalising a memorandum concerning assistance and protection issues relating to indigenous peoples for distribution to UNHCR branch and field offices.

Considering that violations of human rights are one of the major factors generating refugee flows, and bearing in mind that refugee protection and the search for durable solutions to the problem of refugees are inextricably linked with the larger system of human rights protection, UNHCR has recognised the increasing importance of promoting awareness of the relationship between situations giving rise to refugee flows and lack of respect for human rights as well as the role of human rights in preventing the need for people to become refugees and in seeking durable solutions to their plight.

Ms KATE JASTRAM BALIAN, Senior Human Rights Liaison Officer, Promotion of Refugee Law Section, Geneva and focal point for all questions related to indigenous peoples.
Tel: 41.22.7398664.
Fax: 41.22.7398263.

7. International Fund for Agriculture and Development (IFAD)

A way of contributing to the sustainable development of Amazonia

by Roberto Haudry de Soucy

The IFAD, the 'International Fund for Agricultural Development', is a United Nations financial institution with its headquarters in Rome. The Fund supports projects to combat rural poverty. As IFAD principally works with rural people, fishermen and landless labourers, it stands to reason therefore that it would also work with indigenous peoples.

Over the past years, IFAD implemented several projects that were aimed at strengthening indigenous organisations and initiatives. Ninety per cent of IFAD operations are loans. For methodological purposes, IFAD distinguishes between indigenous campesinos (farmers) on the one hand, (Mexico, Guatemala, Ecuadorian Andes, Peru and Bolivia) and indigenous peoples in tropical areas on the other (Panama, Peruvian forest, low lands of Bolivia, etc.). Approximately 40% of IFAD rural development projects in Latin America are targeted at indigenous peoples (e.g. in Oaxaca, Mexico rural development project developed jointly with IBRD). The objective of such projects is "ethno-development", that is, to provide an opportunity to ndigenous people to be part of mainstream national economic life without sacrificing their lands and cultures. IFAD is preparing a new project in the *Arca del Beni in Bolivia* and has been developing actions in Panama, Ngobo and Alto Peru, Mayo. The *Regional Programme for Indigenous Peoples of the Amazon*, described below, is basically a pre-investment programme to facilitate the transmission of funds and guarantee the survival and autonomous growth of indigenous peoples. Its purpose is to: (i) strengthen indigenous organisations (ii) help formalise their ideas and projects (iii) support consolidation of their territories.

"Amazonia" in its widest possible sense, can be taken to cover the tropical rainforests of the Amazon and Orinoco basins and parts of the northern Rio de la Plata basin. The area comprises almost half of South America and is effectively being "re-discovered", thus inviting "new conquests". This "new land" is considered as somewhere to be "explored", somewhere to be "exploited" at a time when biodiversity is discovered by the West as a new wealth.

Just as occurred 500 years ago, "wealth" is only being seen in terms of its commercial value. The true wealth of Amazonia, i.e. its inhabitants who for centuries have lived in harmony with nature, is being forgotten. Amazonia is not uninhabited, and its riches cannot be "discovered" because they belong to its inhabitants. It is from these peoples, these cultures, that we have to learn, with humility, the "secrets" of the greatest reserve of the biosphere. Indigenous peoples have shown that they know how to administer and reproduce this wealth and they may be willing to share it, first with the States in the area, and then with the rest of the world.

The exact number and size of the indigenous peoples of the Amazon is unknown: estimates vary from 400-500 peoples, with a total population of about one million. Some 360 peoples have a population of less than 250 persons and are in danger of dying out. If they do, their language and their culture, including "appropriate Amazon" technology, will disappear with them. In Bolivia, for example, the Pacawara have dwindled to about eleven people, and the group will not live to see the 21st century.

For several years, citizens of the Amazon countries and of the rest of the world, including members of public and private institutions and international agencies, have made efforts to learn about indigenous peoples and to support their self-development through various activities, some of which may be described as development projects. Over the years we have received more from indigenous peoples than we have been able to give them. We have learned, for example, that a ten-year-old Aguarunian is able to identify over 300 different plants, explain how they are related and describe some of their properties. We have also learned that the cultivation of Amazon crops is highly profitable for the following reasons:

(i) It is an extraction-replacement operation:

When the production cycle is over nature recovers the area and reproduces its cycle.

(ii) It is an activity that does not generate external costs:

It does not contaminate water, degrade soil, or have other detrimental effects. In other words, a hectare cultivated by an indigenous people costs the rest of society nothing.

(iii) It has maximum profitability:

Since the costs are negligible, the internal rate of return for the products sold is practically unlimited.

(iv) Its overall productivity/cost ratio is higher than that of modern agriculture:

The short-term productivity may be lower (yields are below the national averages), but after all goods are harvested and gathered during the agricultural cycle (which lasts at least ten years) the productivity/cost ratio is higher.

(v) Its technologies are dynamic:

The indigenous peoples are not repeating "age-old technologies", but innovating, making mistakes, and learning. Moreover, in the programmes being implemented by the Inter-Ethnic Association for the Development of the Peruvian Forest (AIDESEP) and the INPA of Manaos, qualified scientists and indigenous experts are sharing and systemising their knowledge.

What can be done?

First and foremost, we should appreciate that indigenous peoples, through their organisations have clearly indicated their needs and objectives. The first of these is land demarcation: a people without territory is not a people; a farmer who has no guarantee that he will not be deprived of the fruits of his labour will not look after his land. In accordance with this, indigenous men, women and their organisations will behave as investors do; i.e. asking for legal protection of their land rights, techniques and products. Once the territorial question is settled, inventories should be compiled of the wild plants and animals, waterways and other resources existing in the territory under the guidance of indigenous organisations.

The next priorities are health and education. Health because indigenous peoples are being killed off by diseases not previously known to them. Education, because it provides a means of consolidating and developing their culture. Most indigenous peoples have drawn up proposals for bilingual education in both indigenous and national languages. It is considered desirable to continue education to the highest possible level. A case in point are the Shuar of Ecuador who regularly send their children to university. Territory, organisation, health and education are the foundations of cultural development and the improvement of production, technology and living conditions. They constitute a necessary condition for long-term thinking.

Parallel to the essential elements described above is another aspect: micro-projects proposed by the indigenous peoples for food processing and conservation, reforestation, resin collection, semi-cultivation of medicinal plants, joint research on forest and biological resources, river transport, and so on. When these micro-projects are formulated, indigenous peoples implement them autonomously. With the support of national governments and local institutions (public or private) they can formulate larger-scale projects that will bring benefits to the national society and economy.

A good example of such a reciprocal approach is to be found in the Regional Programme in Support of Indigenous Peoples in the Amazon Basin, financed by an IFAD technical assistance grant of US$2 million. The programme aims to help the indigenous peoples and governments of four countries (Bolivia, Brazil, Colombia and Venezuela) put their proposals into effect and strengthen their organisations. The Andean Development Corporation (CAF) has contributed an additional US$150,000 and will administer the Programme. The Programme will be managed by the Coordinating Body of the Indigenous Peoples' Organisations of the Amazon Basin (Coordinadora de Organizaciones Indigenas de la Cuenca Amazonica — COICA), the Special Commission for Amazon Indigenous Affairs (Comision Especial de Asuntos Indigenas de la Amazonia — CEAIA) of the Amazon Cooperation Treaty (TCA) and the International Labour Organisation (ILO). The Programme will be open to all institutions that wish to contribute resources and know-how.

The Programme will provide indigenous peoples with resources to enable them to identify, prepare and carry out actions for land demarcation and consolidation, studies and micro-projects in health, education, and areas specifically requested by them. Grass-root organisations will receive the funds and contract out the services and goods that will be needed in the public or private sector. The Programme will not "offer" any type of model or service, or employ experts of its own.

This may not be the best or the only way of learning to work with indigenous peoples. It is, however, a way of not depending on outside institutions and of giving priority to the indigenous peoples we claim to "help".
February 1993

ROBERTO HAUDRY DE SOUCY, IFAD Project Controller
107 Via del Serafico 00142, Rome, Italy.
Tel: 39.6.54591. Fax: 39.6.5043463.

8. 1993, Year of the World's Indigenous People — A New Partnership

The International Year of the World's Indigenous People

by Helen McLaughlin

An historic event took place on 10 December 1992 in New York. Twenty indigenous persons from around the world addressed the General Assembly of the United Nations at the official inauguration of the International Year of the World's Indigenous People. Some may consider it a fitting conclusion to the long hard struggle by indigenous peoples, for recognition by the United Nations. However, to indigenous peoples, this occasion was but a milestone, significant indeed, but nevertheless *a milestone which marks the beginning of a new era in international relationships*, the beginning of a new struggle for 300 million of the world's most disadvantaged peoples.

Indigenous peoples are distinct peoples living in many countries. They are as diverse as the Inuit of the circumpolar regions, the Aboriginal peoples of Australia and the Indian peoples of South America. Indigenous peoples are working together to draw world attention to their situation. Indicative of this accord, a Hopi leader, Thomas Banyacya, a representative of the first peoples of the North American continent at the General Assembly on 10 December 1992 called upon the United Nations to keep its doors open so that the world might hear indigenous spiritual elders from the four corners of the world.

Almost without exception, *the world's indigenous peoples face threats to their ways of life*. Since the commencement of the spread of modern colonialism in 1492 their cultures and their lifestyles have been disrupted and they have been displaced from their lands. This dispossession has been followed by poverty, poor health, exploitation and in some cases, the threat of extinction. But indigenous peoples believe that in the destruction of their societies, lies the seeds of the destruction of the world. Only now, is the world as a whole becoming aware of the repercussions of this unrelenting bid for progress, as the deterioration of the environment becomes a major problem with severe implications for all the world's peoples. Indigenous peoples hope that a new understanding between themselves and non-indigenous peoples will begin to develop. Indigenous peoples have much to teach the world in general, and about environmental management in particular, but these lessons may not be passed on without an atmosphere of mutual respect and understanding, the concept reflected in the theme of the International Year of the World's Indigenous People.

The International Year of the World's Indigenous People was proclaimed by the General Assembly of the United Nations on 18 december 1990 in resolution 45/164. In resolution 46/128 of 17 December 1991, the General Assembly adopted the theme "Indigenous people — a new partnership". *The proclamation of 1993 as the International Year of the World's Indigenous People comes as the result of the efforts of the many indigenous organisations which have fought for years to achieve international recognition.* Thus, in proclaiming the Year the General Assembly has finally recognised the problems faced by these people, and the value and diversity of the cultures that they represent.

In resolution 46/128, the General Assembly also appointed the Under-Secretary-General for Human Rights as Coordinator of the Year and assigned responsibilities for implementing the activities of the Year to the Centre for Human Rights in conjunction with the International Labour Office.

The purposes of the Year are to strengthen international cooperation for the solution of problems faced by indigenous communities in areas such as human rights, the environment, development, education and health and to raise public awareness of indigenous cultures through special international and national activities. These purposes are to be achieved through honouring the objective of enhancing the participation of indigenous people in the planning, implementation and evaluation of projects affecting them.

In accordance with General Assembly resolution 46/128 the Coordinator of the International Year of the World's Indigenous People convened a Technical Meeting of agencies, regional commissions and other relevant organisations of the United Nations system with representatives of States, organisations of indigenous peoples and other non-governmental organisations having a special interest in indigenous matters. The meeting was held in Geneva from 9 to 11 March 1992. The six major categories of activities for the Year which were identified at this Technical Meeting were human rights, development and environment, education and culture, health, self-management and self-government and public events and information. Public awareness campaigns should aim, where ever possible, to increase information to indigenous communities about the United Nations, to raise public awareness about the situation of indigenous people and to promote understanding of the position of indigenous people.

Unfortunately, it was not possible for many representatives of indigenous peoples to attend this meeting, and a second Technical Meeting was held 3-5 August 1992 to further develop the planning for the Year. As this meeting was held immediately after the Working Group on Indigenous Populations, it was possible for a greater number of indigenous peoples to attend it. A third Technical Meeting will be held in July 1993 to consider the progress already made, and to plan strategies for the future beyond 1993.

As is usual practice in International Years, the Secretary General of the United Nations opened a Voluntary Fund for the International Year of the World's Indigenous People and appealed to governments, intergovernmental and non-governmental organisations for contributions. A target of US$500,000 was set, and the funds raised will be distributed to small scale projects of direct benefit to indigenous peoples, located mainly in developing nations. Projects are expected to encourage self-development by ensuring that they are planned, implemented and evaluated by indigenous peoples. Overall, the response to the Fund has been disappointing. Although three governments have generously assisted the United Nations with staff and resources, and several have supported specific projects, these contributions are not associated with the Voluntary Fund.

The majority of governments have been slow to contribute to the Fund itself. Consequently, at the time of writing, less than US$100,000 has been made available for projects, whilst the Fund has attracted over US$6.5 million worth of proposals. It is perplexing to consider that governments have supported the Year through various General Assembly resolutions on the one hand, but on the other, have failed to provide the concrete, practical support that will assist indigenous communities to establish small-scale community projects which will be of positive value at the grass-roots level. The Coordinator, now the Assistant-Under-Secretary-General for Human Rights and the secretariat for the Year, continue to urge governments to contribute the Voluntary Fund.

Because of the poor response to the Voluntary Fund, the secretariat has sought to involve governments, intergovernmental organisations, NGOs and the private sector in other ways. It is preparing a portfolio of projects from those received from indigenous peoples, and this will be available upon request to interested governments to consider whether assistance might be given more directly, through bilateral or other aid programmes. The secretariat is also following up interests in the private sector which may consider adopting projects during 1993. There are many imaginative ways that both governments and the private sector may explore to find new ways to assist, through working directly with the communities involved.

Indigenous people have made the point that the UN system, and all bodies, governmental or others, should ensure that indigenous peoples be treated as equal partners in dignity and mutual respect in all matters concerning them. In particular, it has been stressed that indigenous peoples should participate in the planning, management, execution and evaluation of projects to be carried out in the International Year of the World's Indigenous People. A number of initiatives have been taken to encourage the United Nations agencies to meet with indigenous peoples and develop programmes for their benefit. The Centre for Human Rights has been instrumental in organising various meetings between the agencies and indigenous peoples. These include the two technical meetings on the Year (March and August 1992), an inter-agency meeting (August 1992), and an informal consultation of indigenous peoples and agencies in New York on 11 December 1992. The third technical meeting to be held in July 1993 will continue this process.

Indigenous peoples have requested that the agencies of the United Nations system appoint indigenous people as experts and advisers and as staff members on a permanent basis. Strong representations have been made already, to the World Health Organisation, suggesting that it consult with indigenous experts on health matters affecting indigenous peoples. Furthermore, the Centre for Human Rights which has the responsibility for the administration of the Year, has sought to employ indigenous staff. The governments of Australia, Denmark and Norway have supported the secondment of indigenous staff to the secretariat for the year which is located in Geneva. This small team of indigenous administrators is fully involved in all the projects being developed for the Year by the Centre for Human Rights, and in the general administration of the Year's activities. A practical programme of activities has been developed and the indigenous staff are available to advise all sectors of the United Nations on matters relating to the International Year.[1]

In consultation with the International Labour Office, the Centre for Human Rights has engaged a consultant to research and write a manual on indigenous peoples and self-government. This project is a direct response to the recommendation by indigenous peoples for the publication of such a manual. The recommendation was made at the conference concerning indigenous peoples and self government held in Nuuk, Greenland in September 1991.[2]

The 1992 Nobel Peace Prize winner, Rigoberta Menchu, has agreed to be the Goodwill Ambassador for the Year. In her capacity as Goodwill Ambassador, Ms Menchu will be in a position to draw world attention to the Year and to the situation of indigenous peoples.

Indigenous peoples are anxious to see some positive outcomes from this Year. The theme is "A New Partnership", and indigenous peoples have expressed the hope that the United Nations system should be committed to ensuring that there is a genuine recognition of the concerns of indigenous peoples. It was suggested that a significant outcome for the Year could be a move towards the building of a **new and meaningful relationship between indigenous peoples and the United Nations**. Indigenous leaders have requested that events and projects specifically directed towards the celebration of the Year should be meaningful, and not just window-dressing focusing on indigenous folk-lore. Activities that reinforce the popular "folkloric" images that surround indigenous peoples should be avoided at all costs. There is a strong consensus that the Year should support meaningful priorities identified by indigenous peoples.

Many indigenous representatives have proposed **the establishment of a permanent forum for indigenous peoples**, supported by a permanent functional secretariat and officially recognised within the UN system. Indigenous people could use such a forum to debate concerns freely, and respond to international issues in an atmosphere of equality and mutual respect.

It is essential that activities and projects for the Year should aim to have an impact over many years. There are many issues common to indigenous people such as displacement from their lands, loss of property rights, and lack of respect for their cultures and the contributions that they have made to the world. Governments have been encouraged to support initiatives to ensure a high profile for the International Year of the World's Indigenous People. At the two technical meetings held to discuss activities for the Year, they were urged to keep in mind that the main purposes of the Year are to further international cooperation between States and intergovernmental bodies, to solve problems faced by indigenous peoples, and to increase the participation of indigenous peoples in the development of projects and policies affecting them, and generally, to raise public awareness about indigenous people.

It is pleasing to note that a great deal of interest has been shown in the Year. The secretariat has received many invitations to speak to groups about indigenous affairs and many requests for interviews from the media. The indigenous staff, in particular, are endeavouring to accept as many of these engagements as possible. Ensuring the dissemination of accurate information about indigenous peoples, their circumstances and their causes, is a secretariat priority.

As 1993, the International Year of the World's Indigenous People unfolds, it is important to reflect upon what it really means for indigenous peoples everywhere, and what may realistically be achieved. The Year began with the official inauguration held in the General Assembly on 10 December 1992. This event was significant. For the first time in the history of the United Nations a space was opened for indigenous peoples as twenty representatives from the four directions of our planet, took their places, one by one, at the podium to make statements about the situations of indigenous peoples and their relationship with the world. Thousands of years of distilled wisdom about the care and usage of land, the protection of the environment, human relationships, governance, traditional values and spirituality were encapsulated in the speeches of these twenty people. Yet this was a "special" meeting of the General Assembly. As the rules of the Assembly allow only for governments to speak, the formal meeting was suspended, to enable the indigenous persons to speak. Their words do not form part of the official record. The importance of giving indigenous peoples a formal place within the international framework of the United Nations is indeed highlighted by the underlying circumstances governing this historic occasion.

The International Year of the World's Indigenous People will end on 31 December 1993. A Year is just that: twelve short months, and not a great deal may be achieved in concrete terms. However, it is realistic to expect that the world community will be more aware of the circumstances of indigenous peoples, and will be willing to continue the dialogue that has commenced. The International Year of the World's Indigenous People is the platform from which indigenous peoples will launch the next phase in their long struggle to gain the recognition due to them in the world of today.

HELEN MCLAUGHLIN is an Aboriginal woman from Australia. She is a senior officer with the Aboriginal and Torres Strait Islander Commission of Australia, who has been seconded to the Centre for Human Rights in Geneva for 18 months. Ms McLaughlin holds a Diploma in Social Studies from the University of Queensland, and was one of the first Aboriginal people in Australia to gain University qualifications. Ms McLaughlin practised professionally as a Social Worker, before taking up an appointment in the former Department of Aboriginal Affairs 20 years ago. During the past 20 years, Ms McLaughlin has worked for indigenous people in Australia in traditional and urban locations in Queensland, the Northern Territory and the Australian Capital Territory.

Secretariat International Year of the World's Indigenous People.
April, 1993

The International Year for the World's Indigenous People,
Centre for Human Rights,
United Nations,
1211 Geneva 10,
Switzerland
or:
Department of Public Information,
Room S-1040,
United Nations,
New York, N.Y. 10017, USA.

References

1. In preparing public awareness materials for the Year, the United Nations Department of Public Information worked closely with the Centre for Human Rights and the indigenous staff. A poster, two brochures, and a press kit containing information sheets on indigenous peoples and the issues facing them in the world of today have been produced by the UNDP and are available for world-wide distribution. Since the team of indigenous administrators has been in place, the Centre for Human Rights has been preparing a world calendar of events, a newsletter and an international directory of indigenous organisations. The newsletter will be published in English and Spanish several times during 1993 and will contain information about activities being undertaken by the United Nations, The *directory of indigenous organisations* will contain up-to-date information about indigenous organisations throughout the world and will be an important communications and reference tool not only for indigenous peoples but for governments and all the bodies of the United Nations system.
2. The Centre has also been successful in attracting sponsorship from the private sector for the publication of an educational resource to be used in schools. This resource is in the form of a wall chart with interesting information about indigenous peoples, superimposed upon a map of the world indicating generally where they live. Interested groups or governments may purchase the art work, and adapt the text to regional requirements. Translations into local languages is encouraged.

III. The Inter-American System

1A. Human Rights Protection for the Indigenous Peoples in the Inter-American System

by Felipe Sanchez Rodriguez and
Denise Gilman[1]

The Inter-American System for the protection and promotion of human rights

When national remedies fail, the people of the Americas can resort to additional protection for their basic rights. The indigenous people, individually and as communities can and do use that protection. The Inter-American system for the protection of human rights (or the OAS human rights system) has been working for more than three decades, legally sustained by three international legal instruments: the Charter of the Organisation of American States ("the Charter"), the American Declaration on the Rights and Duties of Man ("the Declaration") and the Inter-American Convention on Human Rights ("the Convention").

These legal instruments cover a broad spectrum of rights which all States have to respect and guarantee. "Respect" is vital as it indicates a commitment by State agents, such as the police, the military, the judiciary and even the legislature and political authorities in complying with these instruments. "Guarantee" is important because it shows that if human rights are not thus respected, then necessary legal measures will be enforced.

The organs of the system

The "Inter-American System" is composed primarily of the Inter-American Commission ("the Commission") and an Inter-American Court ("the Court"). The Inter-American system works by reinforcing and supplementing what the local institutions in each country do, and in that sense it is subsidiary to the domestic remedies for human rights violations. The political organs of the OAS are kept informed of the decisions and reports of the Commission and the Court, and can adopt measures based upon them.

The NGOs, while not formal organs of the system, also play an important role as they are, in most cases, the ones that present petitions to the Commission or bring attention to specific problems and cooperate in its investigations or *in loco* visits by the Commission to the countries (see the example of CEJIL).

The fundamental rights protected

Basically, the Declaration and the Convention recognise and specify a list of rights and freedoms all Member-States must respect and guarantee. The States shall provide guarantees for the free and full exercise of those rights for everyone under its jurisdiction. It is the task of the Commission and the Court, each in its own defined level of action, to promote and enforce the respect and full enjoyment of those rights when and only if the institutions at the national level fail to do so.

The definition of which rights shall be promoted and protected by the system originates basically from the Inter-American Convention of Human Rights and related international legal instruments, which also limit and qualify the scope of those rights. Those rights are, in brief:[2]

- the right to juridical personality (to be recognised as person before the law.
- the right to respect for life.
- the right to have one's physical, mental and moral integrity respected.
- freedom from being subject to slavery or involuntary servitude.
- the right to personal liberty and security.
- the right to a fair trial.
- freedom from *ex-post facto* laws.
- the right to compensation for miscarriage of justice.
- the right to privacy, including respect for and dignity of the person, private life, home and correspondence.
- freedom of conscience and religion, including freedom to maintain or to change one's religion or beliefs, to profess and disseminate them, in public or private.
- freedom of thought and expression, without prior censorship[3]
- the right to reply to offensive statements disseminated by the press.
- the right to peaceful assembly without arms.
- freedom of association for ideological, religious, political, economic, labour, social, cultural, sports or other purposes.
- the rights of the family, considered the natural and fundamental group unit of society[4]
- the right to a name.
- the rights of the child to measures of protection required by his condition as a minor.
- the right of nationality, including the right to the nationality of the state in whose territory one was born if one does not have the right to any other nationality.
- the right to property, its use and enjoyment.
- freedom of Movement and residence, including the right to leave any country freely, including one's own.
- the right to participate in government directly or through freely chosen representatives and to have access to public service positions under conditions of equality with all other citizens.
- the right to equal protection before the law, without discrimination.
- the right to judicial protection through a simple and prompt recourse against acts that violate fundamental rights, even if such violation have been committed by persons acting in the course of their official duties.

The Convention also states that the Members shall adopt measures in order to achieve the realisation of the rights implicit in the economic, social, educational, scientific and cultural standards set forth in the Charter of the OAS.

While the Convention recognises that in time of war, public danger or any other emergency, states may have their obligations temporarily lifted under the Convention, there are restrictions. These include derogations which are not inconsistent with other obligations under international law, suspensions which involve discrimination, and several rights and freedoms.[5]

The Convention also recognises that there is a relationship between duties and rights, and that the rights of each person are limited by the rights of others, by the security of all, and by the just demands of the general welfare in a democratic society.

By June 1993, 26 of the 35 OAS member-countries had ratified the Convention and 15 had accepted the jurisdiction of the Court.[6] All OAS member-countries are bound however by the American Declaration and the Charter.

The workings of the Commission and the Court

The Commission is the nerve-centre of the Inter-American System. It initiates the different processes of the Inter-American Convention on Human Rights, either in response to an individual petition, or by its own decision. These processes relate either to individual cases of violations, to human rights threats, or to general situations. The individual cases are generally initiated in response to petitions made to the Commission by individuals or NGOs. General cases are undertaken directly by the Commission when it deems necessary.

Under the Convention, the Commission has three major tasks: (i) to attend to individual complaints; (ii) to monitor and report upon the human rights situations in individual countries and (iii) to develop human rights, international agreements or other legal instruments. The Commission receives and investigates complaints of human rights abuses that may have been committed by Government authorities or officers. Where the Commission finds that human rights abuses have occurred, it makes recommendations to the government responsible to ensure that the occurrences are investigated, the victims are compensated, and that measures are taken to prevent the recurrence of the violation.

The Commission's strength lies in its powers of persuasion and its freedom to publicise human rights abuses, since it can not take any course of action for member states. It can, however, initiate action on behalf of the victim against the States that have accepted the jurisdiction of the Inter-American Court of Human Rights in San José, Costa Rica. The decisions of the Court are mandatory for those States.

The Court has two main functions, one as the authoritative organ to interpret the treaties comprised by the Inter-American System, and the other, to adjudicate cases submitted to it by the Commission or the Members to the Convention.

The rights of indigenous peoples and their communities in the Inter-American System[7]

The Inter-American system has considered issues related to indigenous peoples since 1993.[8] The Commission created in 1959, and strengthened in 1967 by the Convention, issued in 1971 a formal proclamation on human rights violations against indigenous populations, and called upon the member States "to implement the recommendations of Art. 39 of the Inter-American Charter of Social Guarantees". A similar but stronger resolution was passed in 1971 maintaining that "special protection for indigenous populations constitutes a sacred commitment of the States" and encouraging the States officials "to act with the greatest zeal in defence of the human rights of indigenous persons, who should not be the object of discriminations of any kind."

Among the duties of the Commission is to monitor the situation of human rights in individual countries and to report on them. In many of these reports, the situation of the indigenous peoples' rights has been highlighted: report on the situation in Paraguay (1978; 1987); in Nicaragua (1978; 1981), Colombia (1981), Guatemala (1981; 1983; 1985; and 1993); Bolivia (1981); in Suriname (1983; 1985). A special report on the Miskito people in Nicaragua was published in 1983.

The *Report on the Situation in Guatemala* (1991-March 1993) is a good example of the way in which indigenous peoples are treated in their own country. It analyses the situation of the Guatemalan Maya-Quiche people and reviews their demographic and socio-economic conditions as well as the guarantees enshrined in the Guatemalan Political Constitution since 1986. The Commission indicates that, despite the constitutional guarantees "many actions of the Guatemalan State reflect a cultural stereotype that is discriminatory. One of these is the educational system where the history, geographic place names, language of instruction, and even the ethical values disdain or ignore those used by the majority of the population, thereby undermining their cultural integrity and their right to dignity".[9]

The report also points out that the Maya-Quiche are the major segment of the Guatemalan population and that they are discriminated against both by the state and by private institutions. The militarisation of rural areas, the imposed participation in the supposedly "voluntary patrols" controlled by the army, the irregular forced recruitment of indigenous young adults for military service and the disregard for the land and property rights of the Maya-quiche population are analyzed.

Many of the cases dealt with by the Commission are a result of individual complaints for alleged violations of the Convention, the victims often being indigenous persons. This has been especially so in areas where indigenous peoples live and there have been clashes between the Security forces and irregular armed groups. In these cases, the Commission will focus on the possible violations such as the right to life, liberty, personal integrity or judicial guarantees for the alleged victims, regardless of their status as members of an indigenous community or not. Surinamese Indians, members of the traditional Maroon society, for example, were the victims in several cases of killings and disappearances during military rule. The Commission took three such cases to the Inter-American Court in San José, where the new civilian government of Suriname accepted the responsibility of the State in two of them. A third case, regarding Saramacan people, is presently under scrutiny. The particularities of their communities are relevant, such as when a decision has to be made as to which members of their polygamic families are next-of-kin and with rights to receive compensation, or if there is to be a collective compensation to the extended family tribe, the Saramaca. Local authority had been recognised by treaty by the Dutch government during colonial times, the obligations were transferred to the new Surinam state after independence.

In other cases their indigenous heritage is of paramount importance because it relates directly to the understanding of the human rights at issue and the motives for the violation. This is especially so in problems related to land rights. *The three most important cases of this kind involve the Guahibo Indians of Colombia, the Aché and Toba-Maskoy of Paraguay and the Yanomami of Brazil.*

The case of the Guahibo Indians of the las Planas region of Eastern Colombia refers to an armed conflict in 1970 that "had broken out between Indians and settlers" along a frontier area. Davis[10] affirms that the State viewed it as an Indian rebellion organised by a government extension agent, and responded to the conflict by sending the army to the area where, allegedly, the military acted in ways that violated the rights of the Guahibos. The Commission intervened with the Government over these situations and, after several exchanges of information, "satisfied that the Colombian government and judiciary system had adequately investigated the Planas incident, the Commission decided to file the materials...without making any judgment on the facts..."[11]

The case of the Aché Guayaki Indians of Eastern Paraguay concerns allegations of systematic violations of the rights to life and culture during the year 1974. A rapporteur was assigned to the case and during the next three years the Government of Paraguay took action to redress the issue. There was, however, no evidence that the violations were corrected and in May 1977 the Commission recommended that the Paraguayan government adopt "vigorous measures to provide effective protection for the rights of the Aché" and "punish, in accordance with Paraguayan law, those responsible for the events denounced".[12] Since then, the government has taken several measures to provide and guarantee territorial rights for most of the Achés.

The well known plight of the *Yanomami people* was brought to the attention of the Commission in 1980 in a communication backed by several major anthropological and legal institutions[13] sustaining that "the Government had not only failed to protect the Yanomami from the deleterious effects of highway construction, mineral prospecting and other forms of territorial invasion, but had also been an accomplice in serious human rights violations. Despite several measures taken since 1982 by the Brazilian government in defence of the Yanomami, including the demarcation of their land achieved in 1992, pressure from private interests has continuously been exerted upon the tribe and the Commission continues to communicate with the Government about their human rights situation.

Procedures following each petition[14]

Any individual or group of individuals can bring to the attention of the Commission a situation that involves a violation of human rights in a simple communication which is immediately considered by its Secretariat. These communications have to be sent to the Commission headquarters at the OAS

General Secretariat in Washington D.C., USA, either personally, by mail or fax or through the OAS offices in the capital of each member-country.[15]

The Commission receives a petition, examines the complaint and, where appropriate, begins its enquiries.[16] First of all it contacts the government concerned, informs it that a claim has been received against it and invites it to reply to the accusations. The Commission can take various steps to investigate what has happened and discover the truth. It can conduct hearings and on-site investigations.

What is the ultimate goal of processing a complaint or petition? The Commission will recommend that the government redress the injury, investigate what has happened, compensate the victims, and, in general, refrain from further violations of fundamental rights. The Commission cannot force this outcome, but it will try to achieve it in various ways.

Above all, the Commission will, at some point, try to convince the parties (the petitioner and the government) to come to an "amicable understanding". If that fails, it will issue its conclusions on the case and forward them to the government, along with recommendations on how to redress the damage. If the Government concerned does not comply, the Commission may publish its conclusions in its annual report to the General Assembly of the OAS, and in any other form. The threat of publication and public censure can exert considerable political pressure on governments to correct the situation. The Commission also has the option of referring the case — as seen above — to the Inter-American Court in Costa Rica if the State in question has accepted its jurisdiction.

The claimant participates at various stages by providing additional information about what has happened, names of witnesses, etc. The petitioner also has the chance to refute the reply received from the government and take part in any negotiated settlement. If need be, the claimant will be able to appear and speak before the Inter-American Court.

The preparation of a future legal instrument on indigenous rights

Following a recommendation by the OAS General Assembly, the Commission has begun the preparation of a new legal instrument on indigenous rights. In 1992, the Commission sent a questionnaire to governments of all member states as well as to a large number of indigenous and intergovernmental institutions asking their opinion on the issues and approaches that the future instrument should include. Eleven States and twenty indigenous organisations responded to this questionnaire. A fifty-page summary can be consulted in the Commission's 1992-93 Annual Report.[17] The Commission is at present preparing a first draft of the instrument to be the subject of a new round of consultations by States and organisations in 1994.
July 1993

FELIPE SANCHEZ RODRIGUEZ is a Mexican lawyer graduated from the Instituto Tecnológico y de Estudios Superiores de Monterrey.
DENISE GILMAN is a Jurisprudence Doctor candidate at Columbia University.

Organisation of American States,
General Secretariat,
Washington, D.C.
20006-4499.
IACHR — OAS,
Executive Secretariat,
1889 F Street,
N.W. Washington, D.C.
20016, USA
Tel: 1 (202) 458-6002
Fax: 1 (202) 458-3992

B. Presenting cases before the Inter-American System: The example of CEJIL
by Jose Miguel Vivanco

Introduction

An urgent need exists for legal counsel, supervision and representation in cases before the Inter-American system. The Centre for Justice and International Law (CEJIL) established in 1991 as a consortium of nine human rights organisations from North, Central and South America and the Caribbean, tries to respond to this need. *It offers an integrated programme of full-time litigation, free legal advisory service and monitoring of the work of the Inter-American system.* In coordination with local human rights organisations, it presents and litigates cases before the Inter-American Commission and Inter-American Court of Human Rights of the OAS. CEJIL handles urgent actions and precautionary measures before the Commission and the Court and coordinates the participation of NGOs as amicus curiae in adversarial cases as well as in advisory opinions presented to the Court.

The Court and the Commission provide an important forum for debate on fundamental human rights issues. Favourable decisions by those bodies carry great weight with governments. Many petitions and cases are currently before the Commission, some having the possibility of reaching the Court. Their litigation potential, however, often solely depends on long-distance inquiries made to the Commission by the plaintiffs or on the occasional appearance of interested parties before the Commission. CEJIL's consortium members have prepared several important cases for submission to the Commission and have obtained the transfer of some of these cases to the Court. The office assumes the representation of the plaintiff organisations and victims in contentious cases before the Court. Of the five cases currently before the Court, four are part of the CEJIL docket.[18]

Prosecution of a complaint before any international human rights institution needs close and direct monitoring. The filing of individual complaints and the follow-up process established by the Convention is a complicated procedure and requires constant supervision, input of information and creative initiative on the part of the petitioner. Effective prosecution of individual complaints demands permanent contact with the Commission's lawyers charged with reviewing cases. The norms which regulate the process before the Commission and the Court are sufficiently flexible to permit experienced practitioners to take full advantage of the system's potential to protect human rights.

CEJIL's objectives

The primary objective of organisations such as CEJIL whose aim is to seek justice and represent those whose rights have been violated, is to ensure the full implementation of international human rights norms at the domestic level. Through its support of human rights victims and local NGOs, CEJIL seeks to make governments accountable for violations of their international obligations. In view of the fact that the agenda for human rights and litigation is set at the domestic level by NGOs and victims' groups, CEJIL acts as the 'international' counterpart to these organisations, including indigenous peoples. CEJIL sets its priorities in accordance with local needs and realities as each country is victimised by different kinds of human rights abuses.

To accomplish its objectives, CEJIL's work is divided into three programme areas:

Legal Defence: With the presentation of individual complaints before the Commission and their litigation before the Court, CEJIL aims to reverse gross and massive[19] or endemic patterns of human rights violations. Examples of endemic patterns include cases of racial, political, economic and sexual discrimination against minorities. Specifically, CEJIL looks for cases that represent the interests of indigenous people, women, children and the mentally ill.

Legal Advice: CEJIL's legal advisory programme provides counsel to NGOs on substantive and procedural matters in international human rights systems, including the inter-American and United Nation systems. The advisory service is an integral part of CEJIL's objective since it *builds and strengths the capacity of local grassroot organisations to litigate cases of human rights violations at the domestic and international level.*

Publications: CEJIL's publications monitor the work of inter-governmental human rights organisations, particularly within the Inter-American system, as well as actions taken by the political organs of the OAS and UN in relation to their respective inter-governmental human rights organisations.

CEJIL's role within the Inter-American system

While gross and massive violations of human rights have declined in some countries as a result of transitions to democracy[20] more insidious and endemic abuses have come to the forefront.[21] In its legal defence work before the Commission and the Court, CEJIL aims to defeat these patterns of human rights violations. In addition to these continuing violations, the predominance of amnesty laws in the region pose a major obstacle to the full enjoyment of human rights. The tendency to believe that democracies do not commit human rights violations is increasingly and dangerously common. States have replaced many "active" human rights violations with "passive" violations, or acts of omission. When a state fails to prevent, investigate and punish violations, which often happens in cases involving indigenous peoples, it is a direct violation of the American Convention. It is for this reason that CEJIL must play the role of human rights advocate before the Commission. It represents victims of both "active" and "passive" human rights violations.

In the Inter-American system, the Court is the final arbiter. Recently, the Court issued its first two judgments against Honduras for engaging in an official policy to make 150 persons "disappear",[22] including Mr Manfredo Velasquez Rodriguez and Mr Saul Godinez Cruz.[23] The lawyers for the plaintiffs proved that a pattern of disappearances took place in Honduras between 1981-84 with the involvement of state agents. The Court's rulings reaffirmed the work of human rights organisations, which for many years have denounced the systematic policy of forced disappearance in Latin America. The Court's decisions were also the result of a close and successful collaboration between local and international NGOs, the families of the victims, and human rights lawyers.

The Velasquez judgement is especially relevant to the protection of indigenous rights. Although the state involved may have laws to protect indigenous peoples, it often fails to investigate, and punish violations of their rights. Many times, the actual conduct that violates indigenous rights is committed at the hands of private individuals. Under Velasquez, the failure of the state to adequately respond to these actions is in direct violation of the American Convention. The Velasquez decision establishes that states must prevent, investigate, prosecute and punish rights violations, and that the failure to do so contravenes the American Convention. *The Court makes clear that states can be held internationally responsible when they fail to respond to actions taken by private individuals that violate human rights.*[24]

CEJIL's docket

CEJIL seeks full compliance of domestic practices with international standards of human rights protection. In accordance with this, governments have to account for their practices at home in view of what has been agreed on internationally. Guidelines are applied in developing a caseload by looking primarily for cases which are illustrative of a particular phenomenon or pattern of human rights abuses. Factors considered when taking up a case will include:

a) Merits and evidence: cases which represent the most pressing current human rights issues and cases with strong, accessible and available evidence.

b) Ripeness: cases which offer a timely opportunity to expand domestic and international human rights law in substantive and procedural matters;[25]

c) Potential for the development of international human rights jurisprudence: cases which involve new legal challenges for domestic and international human rights law;[26]

d) Domestic significance: cases which will define a country's domestic policies regarding international human rights norms; cases that are politically significant in the country; and cases which allow for follow-up in cooperation with local human rights organisations;

e) Needs of the victims and their relatives: cases which provide a vehicle for fair monetary and ethical compensation[27] to individuals and, if applicable, the restoration of the victim's rights.

In line with the task of seeking international compliance and acting as an impartial monitor, CEJIL also works to encourage governments to respect and expand the rights of their citizens. By monitoring human rights, prosecuting abuses and encouraging the humane treatment of individuals and groups, it aims to contribute to positive social change. The office is currently litigating 65 cases before the Commission, four of which have been referred to the Court.

Recently, CEJIL has been concentrating its efforts on developing creative approaches to utilizing the Court's jurisdiction by making use of the Court's injunctive power to protect Mutual Support Group (GAM) and Consejo de Comunidades Etnicas "Runujel Junam" (CERJ) human rights groups in Chunima, El Quiché, Guatemala. *The **Chunima** case involved the murder of four indigenous human rights activists and the wounding of a fifth.* The principal suspects of the crimes are now convicted and in detention.[28] It was not until the Court issued an injunction to protect human rights monitors that the arrest warrant was carried out. Not only was it the first time that Guatemala had been before the Court, it was also the first time that the Court had issued an injunction to protect human rights monitors. The Court's ruling is a positive step towards making the government of Guatemala accountable for its human rights violations, particularly with regard to the rights of indigenous peoples that constitute the majority of the population and are often victim to the most flagrant atrocities.

JOSE MIGUEL VIVANCO is the executive director of CEJIL, a non-profit corporation composed of some of the leading non-governmental human rights groups in Latin America and the Caribbean: Mariclaire Acosta, Comision Mexicana de Defensa y Promocion de los Derechos Humanos, México; Ligia Bolivar (Secretary) Programa Venezolano de Educacion-Accion en Derechos Humanos (PROVEA), Venezuela; Benjamin Cuellar, Instituto de Derechos Humanos de la Universidad Centro-Americana "José Simeon Canas" (IDHUCA) El Salvador; Gustavo Gallon (Chair), Comision Andina de Juristas-Seccional Colombiana, Colombia; Diego Garcia-Sayan, Comision Andina de Juristas, Peru; Michael McCormack, Guyana Human Rights Association, Guyana; Juan E. Méndez (Vice-Chair) Americas Watch, United States of America; Emilio Mignone, Centro de Estudios Legales y Sociales (CELS), Argentina; Paulo Sérgio Pinheiro, Nucleo de Estudos da Violencia, Universidade de Sao Paulo, Brazil.

CEJIL
1522 K Street, NW
Suite 800, Washington, D.C. 20005-1202
Tel: 1.202.371.6592
Fax: 1.202.371.8032

References
1. The authors want to acknowledge the ideas and information provided by Dr. Osvaldo Kreimer, staff lawyer at the IACHR.
2. The Convention goes into detail about what is or is not covered by each right. We strongly recommend that the reader consults the text of the Convention.
3. Censorship can be applied for the moral protection of childhood and adolescence. Any propaganda for war and any advocacy of national, racial or religious hatred that constitute incitements to lawless violence shall be considered as offenses punishable by law.
4. The Convention does not define the concept of family, and includes both the nuclear and the enlarged family, recognising equal rights both for children born out of wedlock and those born in wedlock.
5. The articles that are not authorized to be suspended are those related to: Right to juridical personality; Right to Life; Right to Humane treatment; Freedom from Slavery; Freedom from *ex post facto* laws; Freedom from Conscience and Religion; Rights of the Family; Right to a Name; Rights of the Child; Right to Nationality; Right to Participate in Government; and the judicial guarantees essential for the protection of such rights.
6. Countries that have ratified the Convention: *Argentina, Barbados, Bolivia, Brazil, *Chile, *Colombia, *Costa Rica, Commonthwelth of Dominica, Dominican Republic, *Ecuador, El Salvador, Grenada, *Guatemala, Haití, *Honduras, Jamaica, México, *Nicaragua, *Panamá, Paraguay, *Perú, *Suriname, *Trinidad and Tobago, United States, *Uruguay, *Venezuela. Those with asterisk have accepted the jurisdiction of the Court.
7. Shelton H. Davis in his book "Land Rights and Indigenous Peoples", published in 1988 (Cultural Survival, Cambridge Mass. 02138) reviews in depth this part of the work of the IACHR. We have used it as a main reference for this article.
8. In 1933, the VIIth. International American Conference called for organising an hemispheric congress to study the problems of indigenous populations. As a result of the first of these Congresses, the Inter-American Indian Institute was created in 1942. The indigenous problems were also adressed in 1936 in the Inter-American Charter of Social Guarantees (Art.39). See Davis S. op.cit.
9. In June 1993, the new Constitutional President Lic. Ramiro de Leon Carpío has appointed a renowned Guatemalan-Maya educator as Minister for Public Education.
10. *Op.cit.* p.10.
11. Davis S., *op.cit.* p1.
12. IACHR Annual Report. 1977. p.36-37.
13. The submission was presented by the American Anthropological Association, the Anthropology Resource Center, the Indian Law Resource Center and Survival International, on behalf of the Yanomami community.
14. Inter-American Commission on Human Rights *How to present a petititon in the Inter-American System* IACHR/IIDH/LCHR; Washington D.C. 1993. This publication in English or Spanish, can be requested free of charge from the Commission at the address given.
15. The petitions addressed to the Commission shall include:
    a. The name, nationality, occupation, postal address or domicile and signature of those making the complaint;
    b. an account of the act or situation that is denounced, specifying the place and date of the alleged violations and, if possible the names of the victims of such violations as well as that of any official that might have been appraised of the act or situation denounced; and the name of the State which the petitioner considers responsible;
    c. information on whether the remedies under domestic law have been exhausted or whether it has been impossible to do so.
16. In case of imminent danger to a person's life or integrity, the Commission has the power to immediately request precautionary measures from the Government. The Commission does not reveal the identity of the person making the petition, unless he or she requests so in writing.
17. Special and Annual Reports shall be requested, and petitions shall be addressed to the IACHR, OAS, Executive Secretariat.
18. CEJIL is the petitioner for the victim in the following cases in current Court docket: *Velasquez* and *Godinez* cases against Honduras (still pending); *Bustios*, precautionary measures against

Peru; *El Fronton* case against Peru; *Cayara* case against Peru; *Isidro Caballero* case against Colombia; *Chunima*, precautionary measures against Guatemala.

19. For instance, arbitrary executions are a serious problem today in Colombia, Guatemala and Peru. In some states, arbitrary executions are in fact more common than disappearances. Usually, both crimes are part of the same policy to the extent that the decrease in disappearances is offset by an increase in executions (as in the Peru today) or vice versa.

20. As in Argentina, Chile and Uruguay, where patterns of disappearances, arbitrary and summary executions and torture for political reasons were widespread and notorious official policies.

21. Police brutality, inhuman prison conditions and constraints on civil liberties are usually considered to be endemic or structural human rights violations. These violations are not the result of the policies of a particular regime but are those actions and attitudes which result from the abusive exercise of power by state authorities.

22. The brutal practice of disappearances is still common in many countries in Latin America. Several states implement this practice as an official method of repression or counter-insurgency. The concept and practice of disappearances started in the 1960s in Guatemala. The policy of disappearances which was common in the infamous Chilean and Argentine dictatorships in the 1970s is still a state practice in Peru, Colombia and Guatemala. The problem is so serious that *the Court asserted that the forced disappearance of persons is one of the gravest violations of human rights that a State Party to the Convention can commit.* The crime of disappearance begins with the abduction of the victim by state agents who normally operate in broad daylight. The victim is transported to a clandestine place or hidden detention centre. These agents systematically deny, to the relatives and to the authorities charged with investigating the disappearance, the detention, the actual condition and the ultimate fate of the victim. The lack of formal recognition of the illegal detention permits the state agents to operate with total impunity, beyond the reach of the law, torturing and eventually executing the victim in most cases. Domestic remedies are ineffective.

23. *Velasquez* Judgment, Inter-Am. Ct.H.R. (ser.C) No.4 (1988); *Godinez* Judgment, Inter-Am. Ct.H.R. (ser.C) No.5 (1989). In December 1990, the Honduran government partially complied with the judgement of the Court by paying the original settlement, not indexed for devaluation and interest. The result was that the plaintiffs received and estimated one-third of the amount due to them in accordance with the judgement. CEJIL is exploring legal options to resolve this issue.

24. "An illegal act which violates human rights and which is initially not directly imputable to a State (for example, because it is the act of a private person or because the person responsible has not been identified) can lead to international responsibility of the State, not because of the act itself, but because of the lack of due diligence to prevent the violation or to respond to it as required by the Convention". Velasquez Judgement, at para.172.

25. For instance, some domestic courts define torture as the use of force to extract information while in detention. In fact, any excessively forceful, degrading, cruel and inhuman physical and/or psychological treatment of persons could constitute torture. Through the litigation of relevant and illustrative cases, CEJIL can help to educate and change public opinion about the incidence of torture, especially when it is committed against non-political prisoners. By bringing particular cases of torture before the Commission and the Court, CEJIL will help set precedents to develop an expansive and progressive concept of human rights that strengthens the broad principles of the Convention.

26. CEJIL will use general principles, such as international human law, in conjunction with human rights treaties to hold state agents and irregular armed forces accountable. This progressive approach includes the protection of such non-derogable rights as a fair trial.

27. Victims of human rights violations deserve to be fairly compensated for their suffering. The victims or their relatives should receive monetary compensation (in an amount equivalent to the material and psychological damage or loss), ethical compensation such as a public apology (to re-establish the dignity and honour of the victim), and punitive damages.

28. The first arrest warrant was issued by Judge Roberto Lemus Garza, but was not executed. The execution of a second arrest warrant was ordered by President Serrano, but still no action was taken.

2. The Indigenous Peoples Fund (IPF)[1]

The Fund for the Development of the Indigenous Peoples of Latin America and the Caribbean

Amerindian people have resisted assimilation for five centuries. Although they have adapted, they remain separate and different. Growing in adversity, they have taken advantage of the few opportunities offered to them, and have consolidated their customs and ways of life. Now they are demanding alternative modes of development that accept their cultural diversity.

Introduction

At the second Ibero-American Summit in July 1992, the Heads of State of Latin America, Spain and Portugal established the *Fund for the Development of the Indigenous Peoples of Latin America and the Caribbean*. Old patterns of paternalism and assimilation are being cast off and mechanisms for the transfer of resources to Indigenous Peoples to stimulate the development of their potential are being created. Inspired by an initiative of the Government of Bolivia, the agreement to establish the Fund was achieved through a broad consultative process supported by the Inter-American Development Bank and other international agencies. Indigenous Peoples, regional governments and donor agencies participated in the preparation of the proposal for the creation of the Fund.

How is the IPF organised?

The Fund ensures the *direct participation of beneficiaries in all decision making bodies*. It is governed by a *tripartite General Assembly* that includes representatives of Indigenous Peoples of each member state of the region, representatives of each of the Governments of the region, and representatives of extra-regional governments. A Board of Directors, mirroring the tripartite nature of the General Assembly, functions as the Fund's chief executive organ. The day-to-day management of the Fund is in the hands of a small Technical Secretariat, located in La Paz, Bolivia. Indigenous professionals are among the staff of this Secretariat. Also national and international experts for short- and medium term consultancies will be hired by the Secretariat as the need arises.

The Fund is unique in several aspects. First, poverty alleviation is subsidiary to its mandate to create the conditions for native peoples to design their own development programmes. Second, it is regional rather than national in character. Third, it will place a significant amount of emphasis on capacity-building activities. And finally, the IPF is distinguished by the direct participation of the beneficiaries in its direction and administration.

What is the purpose of the IPF?

The general objective of the Indigenous Peoples Fund is to create the conditions for self-development among indigenous groups; to assist in the creation of the legal, political, technical and financial conditions necessary for the development of the indigenous peoples of Latin America and the Caribbean. The fund will ensure that indigenous groups can gain access to the tools and resources necessary to develop their own strategies for development, and to determine their own relationships with national development processes. More importantly, the Fund aims to enhance the State's ability to respond adequately to initiatives of indigenous peoples. It responds to proposals prepared by indigenous peoples, increasing the efficiency and transparency of development programmes and promoting investment in projects that benefit these groups.

The purpose, structure and operation of the Indigenous Peoples Fund is based on the following *guiding principles*:

- Indigenous Peoples exist as Peoples within the National States and as such are entitled to rights as original inhabitants, including the preservation and defense of their lands, as the basis of their physical and cultural existence.
- Indigenous Peoples have the right to control and manage their resources, institutions, identities and ways of life.
- Indigenous Peoples are entitled to improve their living conditions in accordance with their own initiatives and to define their priorities for development.
- the contribution of Indigenous Peoples to the defense and maintenance of biological diversity and sustainable management and conservation of ecological systems has been continuous and beneficial to all.

What type of projects will the IPF support?

Through its secretariat and consultants, the IPF identifies potential projects that are eligible for financing. During the identification process, the IPF will work closely with the beneficiaries and also assist government institutions to facilitate negotiation. IPF supported projects will provide indigenous solutions to indigenous problems and address four critical areas:

- *Resources for sustainable development:* The IPF will support projects that entail the protection, restoration, sustainable management, and appropriate use of indigenous land and natural resources (legal registration and titling of indigenous land, land demarcation, dissemination of indigenous technologies, rehabilitation of indigenous lands or study of indigenous medicine).
- *Indigenous rights:* The IPF will support legislative and regulatory reform initiatives to foster and protect indigenous rights and make society aware of the rights of indigenous peoples. In this area, the Fund might support projects that inform sectoral legislation compatible with indigenous legislation, legislative reform to promote indigenous rights or broaden existing rights, case studies in the application of laws in situations of conflict, etc.
- *Organisational strengthening and training:* The Fund will support activities to strengthen the institutional structure and management of indigenous organisations and foster their ability to organise. It will support projects that

enhance the capacity of indigenous peoples in organisational methods, management and administration etc. to find common ground and negotiating positions vis-a-vis the national government.
- *Identity and culture:* The Fund will support activities that protect, conserve and promote indigenous identity, culture and technologies, and further societies' awareness of the cultural heritage and contributions of native populations. The Fund will support projects that lead to the development of bilingual education programmes, including projects to design curricula and programmes to train indigenous teachers carries out with the full participation of indigenous experts. It will also support projects that disseminate and strengthen indigenous culture among the target populations as well as society at large; projects that aim to regain or preserve the customs, languages and practices of indigenous groups; and projects that promote cultural exchanges among different indigenous groups.

Ad-hoc Secretariat
Casilla 6326
La Paz, Bolivia.
Tel. (5912) 351221
Fax. (5912) 391089

Environment Protection Division, Inter American Development Bank
1300 New York Avenue, N.W.
Washington, D.C. 20577
Tel. 1.202.6231254
Fax. 1.202.6231315

References
1. This chapter is based on the leaflet: *Indigenous Peoples Fund*, the fund for the Development of the Indigenous Peoples of Latin America and the Caribbean and: the booklet, *What is the indigenous peoples fund?*, March 1993.

Part 2

Non-Governmental Organisations

Indigenous Peoples and Protected Areas
I. WWF and IUCH: A New Approach
by Elizabeth Kemf

"Life trees" are revered, whether in North or South America, in Asia or the Pacific, Europe or in Africa. They are often part of what are universally recognised as "sacred groves". The Kuna Indians of Panama call these forests kalu, while the Mijikenda, the tribal peoples of Kenya's coast, refer to their "sacred groves" as kayas. In West Africa, the Sefwi people of Ghana engage in an annual yam-festival, celebrating for three days, visiting magical rainforest gardens where they honour the souls of their dead ancestors.[1]

In northern California — where remnants of some of the Americas' last old growth forest remain — the Hupa Indians still live, dance, fish, raise their young and bury their dead with great ceremony on the land where their ancestors have lived for thousands of years. In former times and occasionally today, when a Hupa child is born, the baby's umbilical cord is saved in a small buckskin bag. When the child is around two years old, one of the men in the family walks to a point high above the valley and searches for a pine or a Douglas fir tree. He splits the top of the tree and ties the bag inside the opening, then prays that the tree and the child will grow healthy and strong together. The family guards over the tree because its survival symbolizes the strength of the child.[2]

Far away on another continent, in Thailand and in Burma, the father of a Karen hilltribe child takes a newborn's placenta and walks deep into the forest until he finds a large tree. He places the placenta in the crook of a branch. This then becomes the "life tree" of the child. The health and well being of the child depend on the tree, which is nurtured and protected throughout the child's lifetime.[3]

Many of these sacred forests now overlap with officially-declared protected areas and are encompassed inside the boundaries of national parks or nature reserves. Indigenous Peoples are the traditional keepers of such woodlands and other sacred habitats. Compared with protected area managers, who control about five percent of the world's land mass, indigenous peoples are the stewards of a much greater proportion of the earth's remaining wild lands.

Initially, protected areas were generally modeled after the world's first national park, Yellowstone, established on Crow, Blackfeet and Shoshone-Bannock territory in 1872. A sub-tribe of the Shoshone lived year round in the present bounds of the park while the other tribes used the area for hunting and fishing on a seasonal basis. Burial grounds accidentally uncovered in 1941 revealed that Native Americans were resident — at least 800 years earlier — on Fishing Bridge, one of the Yellowstone's most popular campgrounds.[4] When the park was created in the 1870s, the Native Americans did not leave willingly as some historical accounts imply. In the summer of 1877, 300 people were killed in a series of pitched battles between tribal groups and civilian superintendents. In 1886, administration of the park was turned over to the US Army who managed it until 1916.[5]

In conformity with the *"Yellowstone model"*, many national parks around the globe were developed as wilderness preserves — for public recreation — without permanent human habitation or extractive use. Yellowstone's outstanding beauty and natural features — the largest mountain lake in North America, its geysers, breathtaking waterfalls, snow-covered peaks and abundance of wildlife — spawned the birth of thousands of parks around the world. For years, park managers strived to create parks based on the Yellowstone model and moved people, sometimes forcibly, from the land where they had lived for centuries. Recognising the limitations of a global application of the Yellowstone model, which was adopted in good faith with the best intentions at the time, park managers today are developing new approaches, methods and guidelines for establishing protected areas with the assistance of IUCN's Commission on National Parks and Protected Areas (CNPPA). These Guidelines, which have been under serious review by the CNPPA since 1984, were the subject of an intensive workshop convened at IUCN — the World Conservation Union's — IV World Parks Congress in Caracas in 1992. By the time of publication of this book, a new set of guidelines should be published. These guidelines will reflect the need for more flexible interpretations to meet the varying conditions around the world.

WWF, nature conservation with indigenous peoples

Regrettably, over the years many protected areas were created without consultation with the communities which lived in or near them, whether they were by definition indigenous or other long term residents. Ironically, it was indigenous peoples who were for millennia the custodians of the earth. Often, but not always, they cared for their habitat so well that it maintained its natural ecosystems in a relatively unspoiled state. Frequently, when protected areas were established, indigenous and local residents were moved out, often to the detriment of the land itself.

In order to acknowledge this critically important relationship between local communities and to explore and better understand this link, WWF-World Wide Fund For Nature organised a six-day workshop at IUCN's Fourth World Congress on National Parks and Protected Areas, in Caracas, Venezuela in 1992.

WWF, known in the USA and Canada as the World Wildlife Fund, and outside of North America as the World Wide Fund For Nature, is the world's largest private international conservation organisation, with 28 Affiliate and Associate National Organisations around the world and over 5.2 million regular supporters. WWF works closely with other organisations such as IUCN, the World Conservation Union, which was founded in 1948 in order to bring together states, government agencies, and a diverse range of NGOs in a unique world partnership: some 720 members in all, spread across 118 countries.

When WWF's recently-elected Director General, Dr. Claude Martin, opened the WWF workshop on People and Protected Areas at IUCN's IV World Parks Congress, he found that almost 300 people had convened for discussions on the most topical issues at the Congress: the dramatically changing relationship between people and protected areas, and the need for a new understanding and definition of protected areas, which involves multiple and harmonious use of these habitats by people as well as wildlife.

"In the past, it was generally believed that protected areas were places where boundaries of protection were established and people were either kept out or removed. Today, as population pressure increases and the rights of indigenous people and local communities gain recognition and respect, an expanded approach to protected areas is emerging. Wilderness areas are shrinking and human activity is spreading", says Dr Martin, who has lived and worked with rural and indigenous peoples in West Africa and India.[6]

In order to illustrate the benefits and disadvantages of people living in or near or using protected areas, and to offer examples of how to involve resident people in planning, creating and managing protected areas, WWF and IUCN have compiled a book based mainly on presentations made during the Workshop on People and Protected Areas in Caracas in 1992: *The Law of the Mother: protecting indigenous Peoples in Protected Areas*.[7] Dr Martin says in the introduction: "Traditions and rituals upheld by tribal chiefs and village elders mystified early explorers, captured the imagination and interest of anthropologists and angered colonial governments who were trying to centralise forest management, and later, create protected areas. Original forest inhabitants and pastoralists had never heard of conservation. But the survival of their culture and way of life depended on it, embodied it. Their life meant conservation".[8]

It was evident from the large number of participants at the People and Protected Areas Workshop, particularly in the group dealing with Indigenous Views, which was chaired by Chief Bill Erasmus of the Dene Nation of Canada, that the voices of indigenous peoples were being heard. "Listening to their voices and paying lip service to their needs and rights is not enough," says Dr Martin. "Action must be taken now, during the United Nations Year for the Worlds' Indigenous Peoples, to insure their survival and long term involvement in caring for the earth".[9]

Since its founding, WWF has steadily recognised the need to work with local people in carrying out its conservation policy. WWF opened the 1980s with the publication of the World Conservation Strategy in collaboration with IUCN and the United Nations Environment Programme (UNEP), which was launched simultaneously in 34 world capitals. Over the years, the organization evolved and grew away from concentrating on problems of endangered species and habitat destruction, and began focusing on broader conservation issues. WWF began the 1990s with the launch of a revised mission and strategy with one of its specific aims being decentralization of decision-making and increased cooperation with local communities. In Irian Jaya, Indonesia, for example, WWF has worked with local NGOs and government officials in helping create two protected areas, Wasur National Park and Arfak Mountains Strict Nature Reserve. Over 2,500 Kanum, Marind, Marori and Yei tribal people inhabit 13 villages inside the

Wasur National Park. "Most of them live in a delicate balance with nature and manage its resources well," report Ian Craven and Wahyudi Wardoyo in *The Law of the Mother*. According to the authors, each clan and family has traditional sacred sites called *dusuns*, predefined by past generations for hunting, gardening and spiritual events. Over the entire 413,810 ha of the park, WWF and YAPSEL, a local NGO, discovered hundreds of *dusun* sites. It was not unclaimed land. Tribal people owned it and used it. At first there was confusion over whether the tribal peoples should be allowed to stay in the Wasur National Park or have access to its resources. But one of the tribal elders said: "To restrict our access to these sites would be the same as barring the door of your church, mosque or shop".[10]

The ideas of the elders are contained in the management plans for the park, drawn up with help of WWF at the request of the PHPA (Indonesia's Directorate General of Forest Protection and Nature Conservation). Until 1991, the PHPA's understanding of the tribal peoples of Wasur was limited, but according to Craven that is changing. Mr. Sutisno, PHPA's Director Genral, who is the highest authority over protected areas in Indonesia says: "The cultural aspects of Wasur National Park must be considered and supported during planning and management, the people must continue to use their *dusuns* in a traditional manner".[11]

Categories of protected areas

A Biosphere Reserve is an internationally designated site that includes the presence and involvement of local people in research, education and training. It integrates resident peoples, employs their traditional knowledge, and conserves natural areas through the establishment of various use or non-use zones. These zones include buffer areas surrounding the strictly protected interior where limited human activity is permitted or even encouraged, strict protection zones in the core area where all disturbance is prohibited, and multi-use zones, where traditional human activities are permitted. A Biosphere Reserve usually encompasses national parks or other types of protected areas.

The concept of *Man and Biosphere Programme* was initiated in 1971 under the auspices of UNESCO, the United Nations Educational, Scientific and Cultural Organisation. Together with World Heritage and Ramsar sites (wetlands of international importance), it compliments or embraces one of eight official international systems of categories classified (by IUCN's CNPPA) according to management objectives. The most well-known of these Categories, is the widely-used term of national park in Category II. This category is the most commonly used definition, and the most commonly misused, according to the strict definition of the CNNPA. The first three categories include: (i) Strict Nature Reserve/Scientific Reserve, (ii) National Park, and (iii) Natural Monument/Natural Landmark, established with the objective of maintaining biological diversity and natural formations.

These categories prohibit human activity or extractive use and "protect nature in an undisturbed state". The other Categories that allow some degree of regulated human use and activity are: (iv) Nature Conservation Reserve/Managed Nature

Reserve/ Wildlife Sanctuary, (v) Protected landscape, (vi) Resource Reserve, (vii) Natural Biotic Area/Anthropological Reserve, and (viii) Multiple Use Management Area/Managed Resource Area.[12]

Although this system is widely used, particularly in accordance with national legislation, it does not always reflect the locally used terms. For example, in Britain 250,000 people live in what the British call national parks. According to the CNPPA classification, they fall under Category v, Protected landscapes, an area where "traditional land uses are maintained". Gerhard Heiss, a consultant to EC, estimates that in western and northern Europe, 80 to 90% of the national parks and protected areas are used seasonally, mainly by pastoral people grazing their flocks. 30% are permanently inhabited, and this is having devastating effects.

Yet in many other areas in the world, such as in Colombia in the Sierra Nevada de Santa Marta National Park, where the Kogi, Arhuaco and Arsario people live, their presence has had mainly a positive effect. Similarly in Indonesia the Arfak Mountains Strict Nature Reserve is also inhabited. By definition this should be under Category I, but villagers are allowed to live in the Reserve. According to CNPPA definitions, the protected area should really be classified as a Protected landscape. But Indonesia, like many countries, exercises the right to call its protected areas what it deems most appropriate. The CNPPA has proposed a universal definition for all protected areas: "An Area of land and/or sea especially dedicated to the protection and maintenance of biological diversity, and of natural and associated cultural resources, and managed through legal or other effective means".[13]

The Site which is probably the most faithful to definition is the World Heritage Site. Since the World Heritage Convention came into force in 1975, 127 countries have become party to the Convention. Less than 100 areas, however, have become inscribed. World Heritage Sites including Mount Everest (Sagarmatha) in Nepal, the Banc d'Arguin in Mauritania, Kakadu and Uluru in Australia, and Manas National Park in India, were inscribed in the Convention in order "to protect the natural features for which the area is considered to be of universal international value".[14]

The role of indigenous peoples

An IUCN survey carried out in 1991 shows that 86% of the National Parks in Latin America are inhabited either permanently or temporarily by indigenous or rural peoples. The survey, carried our by Drs Stephen and Thora Amend, with the assistance of the German Technical Cooperation Agency, also reveals that the greatest problems facing parks managers in Latin America is extraction of natural resources including timber and gold, agricultural encroachment by landless peasants as well as ranchers, illegal grazing, occupation, mining and oil exploration, fires, drug trafficking and terrorist activities. The second biggest problem after extraction of natural resources is the lack of qualified staff to deal with these threats. Invasion of the 184 surveyed national parks is not by the indigenous people, most of whom "live in remote areas, almost unnoticed and unseen within their own country", but by newcomers.[15]

Fortunately, some governments recognised early on the need to respect the rights of indigenous peoples in protected areas. For example, the Government of Mauritania ensured the rights of the Imraguen people to continue living within the boundaries of the Banc d'Arguin National Park right from the time of its creation in 1976.

Although a modicum of recognition has been given to the rights of indigenous people over their homelands, much more needs to be done. From polar regions to the tropics, people are beginning to call for the setting up and management of their own protected areas in which they live. The Miskito Indians of Nicaragua and the Kuna people of Central America, for example, have created protected areas which they manage themselves. Some conservationists are worried that the Kuna are beginning to over-exploit their natural resources, and the same concern has been expressed about the Kayapo of Brazil. WWF and IUCN are working with these and other indigenous groups to develop sustainable methods of management, combining modern and traditional techniques. However, conservationists are divided into several schools of thought: those who think resident people should be able to fish, hunt, and forage in national parks, those who don't, and those who think there should be a compromise between the camps. *But it is also becoming increasingly apparent that the human factor in creating and managing national parks and protected areas has long been overlooked and misunderstood.* Meanwhile, the rights and demands of indigenous people to continue living in and use parks and reserves on a sustainable basis is gaining acceptance. Commenting on the evolution of Australia's national park system, David Foster of the Phillip Institute of Technology, and an IUCN Consultant, says: "Park managers have had to come to terms with a whole new set of issues, concepts and ideas as well as to learn to communicate with a group of people with a different language, culture and world view. Of particular concern to many has been the challenge to their fundamental beliefs about the very nature of national parks themselves".[16] The Secretary General of IUCN's IV World Congress on Parks and Protected Areas has proposed 10 principles that he believes could help governments to mobilise the resources — human, financial, cultural and moral — to ensure integration of economic principles with economic development. (i) Build on the Foundation of the local culture, (ii) Give responsibility to local peole, (iii) Consider returning ownership of at least some protected areas to indigenous people, (iv) Hire local people, (v) Link government development programmes with protected areas, (vi) Give priority to small-scale local development plans, (vii) Involve local people in preparing management plans, (viii) Have the courage to enforce restrictions, (ix) Build Conservation into the evolving new national cultures, (x) Support diversity as a value.[17]

A growing number of rural communities are approaching WWF for help in setting up, develop management plans for protected areas or their own land. They are exploring ways in which they can participate in planning and land management from the outset. These include the Hoopa Tribe (Hupa) of northern California, the Inuit of Isabella Bay in Canada, the Zoque Indians of Mexico, the Karen of Thailand and the Imagruen of Mauritania. These groups are with increasing frequency asking WWF, IUCN and other NGOs to assist them in developing management and land use plans for buffer zones of national parks or multi-use zones of protected areas. Speaking at a joint press conference with WWF and Pacific Gas and Electric Co. in April of 1993, in San Francisco, California, Vice Chairman of the Hoopa Valley Tribe explained that the first time the Hoopa Tribe has ever reached outside its own group was to the WWF in 1991.

"Indians in general are very proud people, but we reached a point where we needed that outside help", Sherman said. So far, WWF, in cooperation with the Hoopa Tribe and with support from Pacific Gas and Electric Co. have planted 30,000 trees along streams on the Hoopa's 89,000 acre (222,000 ha) reservation in an attempt to stem the effect of logging on the salmon fisheries. This tree-planting effort was one of the first steps of the Hoopa Valley Tribe Integrated Resource Management Plan that defines four closely interrelated goals: (i) tribal self-governance, (ii) economic sustainability, (iii) protection of biological diversity (iv) preservation of the Hoopa Tribe's culture and traditions. The Henry M. Jackson Foundation provided early encouragement and financial support for this phase of the project, according to WWF-US. It is believed that the partnership between WWF and the Hoopa Tribe marks the first time a Native American tribe and a US national conservation organization have worked together to develop a long-range management plan for tribal natural resources.[18]

Other indigenous groups, such as the Bisnoi people of Rajasthan, India, have chosen to work somewhat more independently, and are trying to manage their land, combining modern and traditional methods, better than most trained park managers have managed officially declared nature reserves or national parks. The Bisnoi people of Rajasthan, who have inhabited the Great Indian Desert known as the Thar, have conserved the land as it was for centuries — covered by trees and bushes, inhabited by wildlife that lives unafraid of and in close proximity to one of the most remarkable communities in the world. Kailash Sankala, a renowned Indian environmentalist whose firm hand held India's Project Tiger in place for the first five of its now 20 years — has often described the 500 year history of the Bisnoi in the area and how their presence in the Thar desert has ensured its survival. During WWF's workshop on People and Protected areas he revealed the new threats that this culture and the land are facing today, and explained his recommendation for establishing the Thar Desert as an international Biosphere Reserve.

The example of Mexico

Today, an increasing number of biosphere reserves are being established in response to the request of indigenous and rural peoples. WWF and other non-governmental organisations are helping them to establish these. For example, in Mexico, WWF, together with a Mexican NGO *(Maderas de Pueblo Sureste)* based in the region of Chimalapas in the southern state of Oaxaca, are working with indigenous and rural peoples in the hope of creating the country's first Campesino (rural poor) Biosphere Reserve. Located inland on the Isthmus of Tehuantepec, the Chimalapas is comprised of some 600,000 ha of woodland including, tropical moist and dry forest, cloud forest, elfin, and pine-oak forest.

Around 300,000 ha of the mountainous terrain is uninhabited primary forest, owned by the Zoque Indian communities of Santa Maria Chimalapa and San Miguel Chimalapa. According to WWF's former field representative, Alejandro de Avila, "Title to part of the communal lands have been encroached by loggers and cattle ranchers, a situation precipitate and aggravated by a state boundary conflict between Oaxaca and Chiapas. In order to control illegal logging, grazing, and drug cultivation, the local communities are seeking to protect their natural resources by creating a community-managed reserve." This would lead to more sustainable management practices as well as give protection to watersheds that feed critical river systems and coastal lagoons on which thousands of people depend for their livelihoods. WWF expects that the biosphere reserve will be demarcated and declared officially in 1993.

A variety of conservation activities have been spawned as a part of the people-centred conservation and development project that has been funded by WWF in Chimalapas since 1989. Project workers have established improved methods of maize production and propagation of valuable timer and fruit species including mahogany, cedar, and orange trees in six settlements within the Zoque communal lands. In Santiago Comaltepec in the Sierra Juarez of Oaxaca the Chinantec indigenous municipal and communal authorities approached WWF and requested advice and support to develop their municipal legislation, including a land use plan. WWF hopes this bottom-up approach, originating at the grassroots, can be replicated throughout Mexico.

In 1990, WWF offered technical and financial assistance to help draft legislation for land use, not yet approved by the communal assembly or state government. The second phase of the project will involve a study of the natural resources of the community and mapping vegetation types and land use patterns. Alejandro de Avila hopes it will lead to a communal definition of the activities allowed in different ecological zones. Despite internal conflicts regarding the management of the communal forestry enterprise, WWF is trying to work with the different factions in the area, which is considered to be one of the most biologically diverse municipalities in Mexico.[19]

To date, WWF has invested over US$330 million in more than 10,000 projects in 130 countries, many of which involve rural and indigenous communities similar to the Zoque villages in Mexico. For example, in Oaxaca, Mexico WWF has also been supporting ethno-botanical research — since 1985 — in cooperation mainly with the Chinantec, Mixtec and Mixe people. In one village alone six local women interviewed members of some 150 households to help document the classification of 1,000 species of plants. Likewise, in North America, WWF-Canada has worked with the Inuit community of Clyde River, Baffin Island, to devise a conservation plan to protect critical habitat for endangered bowhead whales at Isabella Bay. *Igalirtuuq*, the community's proposal for a Marine National Wildlife Area and Biosphere Reserve, is moving forward through the approvals process for the new territory of Nunavut. In the African country of Mauritania, WWF is supporting development of sustainable fisheries practices and a fisheries co-operative run by the Imraguen people who live inside the park.

Presently, WWF is collaborating with indigenous and rural communities on every continent. According to WWF's Director General, Claude Martin, "Traditional and modern park management methods are at a crossroads. If they can meet on the same road, they have great potential for creating protected areas that conserve and enrich cultural and biological diversity".

ELIZABETH KEMF, photo-journalist and a Senior Conservation Editor at WWF International since 1981, was editor of the organisation's international newspaper, the WWF News *for 10 years. In 1985-1986 she carried out a WWF research project in Vietnam, and is author of the book,* Month of Pure Light: the regreening of Vietnam, *on which several television films have been based. She is the editor of the WWF/IUCN book entitled* The Law of the Mother: Protecting Indigenous Peoples in Protected Areas.

> WWF, World Wide Fund For Nature
> CH-1196 Gland
> Switzerland
> Tel: 41.22.3649111.
> Fax: 41.22.3644238.
> IUCN; The World Conservation Union
> Rue Mauverney 28
> CH-1196 Gland
> Tel: 41.22.999001.
> Fax: 41.22.999002.

References
1. Martin, Claude, *The Rainforests of West Africa*, Basel, Switzerland, Birkhäuser, 1991.
2. Nelson, Byron Jr., *Our Home Forever: the Hupa Indians of Northern California*, Howe Brothers, Salt Lake City, Utah, 1988.
3. Hulse, David L and Thongmak, Seri, "The winds of Change", chapter from *The Law of the Mother: protecting indigenous peoples in protected areas*, edited by Elizabeth Kemf, Sierra Club Books, San Francisco, 1993.
4. Scharff, Robert, *Yellowstone and Grand Teton National Parks*, David Mckay Co. New York, 1966.
5. Haines, Aubrey L., *Yellowstone National park: its exploration and establishment*, US Department of the Interior, National Park Service, Washington, 1974.
6. Martin, Claude, *Introduction to The Law of the Mother*: protecting indigenous peoples in protected areas, edited by E. Kemf, Sierra Club Books, San Francisco, 1993.
7. The 320 page volume, whose introduction was written by Sir Edmund Hillary, is published by Sierra Club Books, distributed by Random House in the USA and Canada, and published by Earthscan under the title, *Indigenous Peoples and Protected Areas: the Law of Mother Earth* in the UK and other Commonwealth countries. Publication of the book was in part made possible by a grant to IUCN by the European Commission and was published as a contribution to the UN International Year of the World's Indigenous People.
8. Ibid.
9. Ibid.
10. Craven, Ian and Wardoyo, Wahyudi, "Gardens of the Forest", *The law of the Mother: protecting indigenous peoples in protected areas*, edited by Elizabeth Kemf, Sierra Club Books, San Francisco, 1993. Ian Craven, who worked in Irian Jaya for WWF since 1985, died in a plane crash in August 1993, while surveying Wasur National Park's deer population. He was survived by his wife who worked closely with him.

11. *Ibid.*
12. *1990 United Nations List of National Parks and Protected Areas*, Gland, Switzerland and Cambridge, England, IUCN and UNEP, pp.10-14.
13. *Ibid.*
14. *Ibid.*
15. Amend, Stephen and Thora, "Human occupation in the National Parks of South America: a fundamental problem": Parks magazine, IUCN, Gland, Switzerland, January, 1992.
16. Foster, David, "Applying the Yellowstone Model in America's Backyard: Alaska", *Aboriginal involvement in Parks and Protected Areas*, edited by Jim Birckhead, Terry de Lacey, and Laura Jane Smith, Panther publishing and printing, Canberra, 1992.
17. McNelly, Jeffrey, Afterword to *The Law of the Mother, protecting indigenous peoples in protected areas*, edited by Elizabeth Kemf; Sierra Club Book; S.F., 1993.
18. *Hoopa Valley Tribe Ingetrated Resource Management Plan* (IRMP) Needs Assessment Report, World Wildlife Fund & the Hoopa Valley IRMP Task Force, November, 1992, unpublished.
19. Avila de, Alejandro B., *WWF's Conservation program in Oaxaca, Mexico*, September, 1992, unpublished.

II. Amnesty International
by Tracy Ulltveit-Moe

During 1992, the 500th anniversary of the arrival of Europeans to the region now known as the Americas, the eyes of the world were on the area. It's original inhabitants used this increased interest in the region to call attention to the abuses they continue to suffer and the steps they are taking to reclaim their rights. Many non-governmental organisations throughout the world responded to these initiatives with their own efforts to protect indigenous rights. This article reviews the special indigenous peoples of the Americas programme undertaken by Amnesty International in 1992. It also looks to the new partnership urged by the United Nations between indigenous peoples and others in 1993, the UN's International Year for the World's Indigenous Peoples.

The story of Amnesty International's founding by a British lawyer in 1961, as a one year campaign to work for the freedom of "prisoners of conscience" — people detained for their beliefs, colour, sex, ethnic, language or religion who have not used or advocated violence — is already known to many. Today, *Amnesty International is the world's largest human rights organisation with more than 1,100,100 members*, subscribers, and regular donors in over 150 countries and territories, and more than 6,000 local groups in over 70 countries in Africa, the Americas, Asia, Europe and the Middle East. Amnesty International also enjoys formal relations with the UN Economic and Social Council (ECOSOC); the UN Educational, Scientific and Cultural Organization (UNESCO); the Council of Europe, Organisation of American States, Organisation of African Unity; and the Inter-Parliamentary Union.

Amnesty International's mandate has also broadened over the years since the organisation's foundation: it now works against violations of certain other civil and political rights as well — extrajudicial executions, "disappearances," arbitrary arrests, torture and ill-treatment, unfair trials of political prisoners and the judicial death penalty.

Amnesty International and Indigenous Peoples

Since colonisation, indigenous peoples have been persecuted, victimised, and murdered, often for nothing more than who they are, what they believe in or for the very land they live on. Today, in many parts of the world they continue to suffer the abuses Amnesty International works to end. Over the years, Amnesty International has campaigned to stop abuses against indigenous peoples, both in the course of its normal work to end such violations whenever and wherever they occur, and in special actions focusing on indigenous peoples. It has, for example, repeatedly called for inquiries into killings of tribal people in the Chittagong Hill Tracts by members of the Bangladeshi security forces and has pressed for action against violations inflicted on non-combatant indigenous people in Myanmar by government counter-insurgency forces. It has also denounced political killings of members of Cordillera tribal communities in the Philippines, murdered in circumstances strongly suggesting official involvement, apparently because of their work for tribal peoples' rights. In India, the organisation has campaigned world-wide against torture, rape and deaths in custody: many victims have been tribal people. In Australia, Amnesty International has called on the government to fully investigate the high incidence of Aboriginal deaths in custody and bring any officials implicated to justice. It has also raised concern at aspects of Australia's criminal justice system which make Aboriginals distinctly vulnerable to highly disproportionate incarceration rates, in conditions sometimes amounting to cruel, inhuman or degrading treatment.

Amnesty International's "500 Years On" Campaign
For many years, Amnesty International has also campaigned against the abuses suffered by indigenous peoples of the region now known as the "Americas." However, the organisation considered 1992, the 500th anniversary of the arrival of Europeans there, an appropriate moment to increase its efforts to help raise the level of international consciousness regarding continuing violations against the region's original inhabitants.

Amnesty International therefore launched a special programme of activities — 500 Years On — the organisation's first ever world-wide campaign to focus especially on indigenous peoples. *The campaign aimed to join Amnesty International to efforts to those of the many indigenous organisations already working to protect indigenous rights.* Specific objectives were to: (i) harness heightened media and public interest in the Americas and its indigenous peoples during 1992 to publicise the violations that indigenous peoples there continue to suffer and by so doing, (ii) press governments to take effective measures to protect and promote their rights and thereby (iii) bring about a reduction in the level of rights violations. Additional aims were to: (iv) support and protect human rights activists working on behalf of indigenous rights, and finally, (v) to highlight the discrimination, land disputes and other factors which contribute to violations against the region's indigenous peoples.

First, Amnesty International sought to inform itself, both staff and membership, more thoroughly about America's indigenous peoples: their locations, problems and concerns. It also undertook increased outreach to indigenous peoples to identify ways it could best work alongside them to end the abuses they continued to suffer throughout the region. Special visits were undertaken to research human rights violations against indigenous peoples in Mexico, the USA and Canada. A six months special project in Brazil investigated the situation of especially vulnerable remote indigenous groups, some of them only recently in contact with the surrounding society. Other research missions to Panama, Bolivia and Argentina included contacts with indigenous peoples amongst their objectives. To further broaden its understanding of the objectives and aims of indigenous peoples and establish contact with the many new indigenous organisations which have come into being in recent years to defend their rights, Amnesty International followed the UN Working Group on Indigenous Populations (WGIP) with special interest at its 1991 and 1992 sessions in Geneva, and sent delegates to several indigenous gatherings in the Americas at which initiatives to call attention in 1992 to the plight of indigenous peoples in the region were planned. Many Amnesty International membership structures undertook their own special actions to build bridges to indigenous organizations in their own countries.

The "Mobilization of Shame": Urgent action for indigenous peoples

Amnesty International depends on the power of people acting together to change the behaviour of governments, to stop them perpetrating abuses and to stimulate them to take pro-active steps to protect the human rights of threatened individuals or sectors. One of the strongest weapons in its human rights campaigning arsenal is the "mobilisation of shame" — arousing the power of public opinion against offending governments.

Amnesty International's urgent action technique was also adapted to give special prominence to indigenous cases and issues in 1992. Well over 50,000 people in 77 countries stand ready to act immediately to try and save the lives or protect the physical integrity of persons in imminent danger of abuses such as torture, "disappearance," extrajudicial execution or the judicial death penalty. In a special innovation during Amnesty International's 1992 programme, urgent appeals concerning indigenous victims were also sent by air-mail, telex, fax and electronic mail to new indigenous peoples' action networks forming in several Amnesty International Sections. Another new step was to specifically target indigenous organisations throughout the world, calling on them to join their voices to those already insisting that the governments concerned ensure the lives and security of indigenous people feared to be in danger of abuses, and bring any officials found responsible to justice. In all, in the course of 1992, 22 urgent appeals were issued on behalf of 74 Indigenous Americans. Although it is often not possible to assess the amount of action generated by each appeal or their effect, Amnesty International knows that Urgent Actions have generated as many as 10,000 appeals from all over the world; a recent examination of past appeals suggested that improvement occurred in 40% of cases surveyed. With respect to one such situation on which Amnesty International appealed, concerning abuses against the Yanomami of Brazil, a leader of the group, David Yanomami, told London human rights activists in 1992 that "You put a lot of pressure on the President. You wrote many letters — and used the news and newspapers and telephone calls — and he couldn't stand the pressure . . . You really helped our lives. We need this help . . . DON'T FORGET US!"

Special 1992 Appeals

Special campaign appeal cases represented adaptation of another Amnesty

International technique for the organisation's 1992 campaign. The individuals featured were chosen not because their cases were more important than others, but to illustrate the sorts of abuses suffered by indigenous peoples in the Americas and the contexts which give rise to them. Amnesty International members, special interest groups and others world-wide called for inquiries into the specific abuses, and pressed the responsible authorities to make known what they had done to prevent any future violations.

Appeal participants called for example on the Guatemalan government to clarify the fate of one-month-old Quiché Indian María Josefa, who "disappeared" along with her mother María Tiu Tojín in 1990 in the context of that country's long-term internal conflict. The two were seized by the army along with 85 others, accused by the government of supporting the armed opposition. The rest of the group was eventually transferred to a displaced persons' reception centre, but although lists prepared by both the army and the centre clearly listed mother and baby, neither reached the centre. Instead, they were taken to a nearby military base. Although soldiers told relatives that the two were held there, and it is known that soldiers at the base had a baby in their possession at the time of María Josefa's "disappearance," neither mother or baby has ever been seen again.

Campaign participants also appealed on behalf of Lakota Sioux Leonard Peltier, a leader of the American Indian Movement (AIM), imprisoned for more than 16 years for the murder of two FBI agents in 1975 on a reservation in South Dakota. His conviction came at a time when the FBI was involved in a "dirty tricks" campaign apparently intended to crush ethnically-based activist political organizations such as the Black Panthers and AIM. Peltier's extradition from Canada was granted in part on the basis of affidavits which the FBI itself later admitted it knew were false, and his trial fraught with irregularities. In the interests of justice, Amnesty International urged the American government to grant Leonard Peltier a re-trial. Amnesty International also called on the US authorities to take into account the special circumstances and needs of indigenous prisoners, citing a number of stipulations of the UN's Standard Minimum Rules for the Treatment of Prisoners which were often breached with respect to indigenous prisoners, including, for example, those governing religious rights. Amnesty International also expressed concern that minority groups including Native Americans are victims of racially-related disparities in death penalty sentencing throughout the US. The organization called for abolition of this cruel, inhuman and degrading punishment both in the US and elsewhere in the Americas where it remains on the statute books.

In Canada as well, Aboriginal people are arrested and imprisoned in disproportionate numbers, and are more likely to be incarcerated if convicted. It has also been found that the rigour with which the Canadian police investigate crimes may depend on the victim's race. The 1991 report of an Aboriginal Justice Inquiry carried out by Manitoba province looked in depth at two cases — the rape and murder of 16-year-old Cree Betty Helen Osborne, and the fatal shooting by the Winnipeg police of Wasagmack leader J.J. Harper. The Inquiry found that racism had been an important factor in both deaths and in the flawed police inquiries into them. It took 16 years to convict one of the four youths responsible for the abduction, rape and murder of Betty Helen Osborne even though everyone in the small community where she died knew who had been responsible. The inquiry found that the Winnipeg police department did not search actively or aggressively for the truth about J.J. Harper's death, and suggested that the police investigation's primary motivation appeared to have been to exonerate the officer responsible and vindicate the Winnipeg police department. Amnesty International called on the Manitoba authorities to implement the inquiry's recommendations, including proper and more independent investigations of officer-involved shootings.

Other 500 Years On appeal cases dealt with arbitrary detentions, torture, "disappearance," and extrajudicial executions of indigenous people from Brazil, Chile, Colombia, Ecuador, Honduras, Mexico and Peru. Many victims were leaders in efforts to protect their peoples' lands from incursions or seizure by government or private interests for mining, lumbering, drug cultivation or processing, energy or tourism projects. In some cases, government agents were directly responsible or complicit; in others, those responsible benefitted from impunity.

October 1992: A world-wide call to action

In October, Amnesty International's campaign accelerated with publication of a special brochure, poster display and electronic news release and the launch in Mexico City of a major 114 page report detailing violations against America's original inhabitants. Indigenous representatives joined Amnesty International on the platform to call on governments throughout the Americas to stop turning their backs on the rights of indigenous peoples and end the hundreds of years of violations they have suffered.

Meanwhile, throughout the world, from the arctic north to Tierra del Fuego, Amnesty International's membership mobilised support to end abuses against indigenous peoples. In Norway and Switzerland, a day of mourning was declared to commemorate indigenous victims since colonization. Candles burned in windows the length and breadth of Norway in their memory and black-clad mourners led torch-light parades from Trondheim and Tromso to Bergen, Stavanger, Oslo, Geneva, Zurich and Berne. In Bergen, after the first performance of a new ballet dedicated to Amnesty International and America's indigenous peoples, the theatre stayed open for an all-night vigil commemorating indigenous victims.

In Ireland, inmates in six different prisons constructed sections of a totem pole which was then displayed country-wide in solidarity with indigenous prisoners in the Americas. UK Amnesty International groups and indigenous representatives made their way on their hands and knees in an "Embassy crawl" to North and South American embassies to plead for respect for indigenous peoples' rights.

Ceremonies greeted the dawn of 12 October across the US, to commemorate indigenous victims of the Americas, but also to celebrate their survival, and declare commitment to their future. The campaign elicited a remarkable degree of participation from Amnesty International USA's membership; virtually all Section youth and campus groups lent their support. To the north, Amnesty

International Canada's English-speaking branch approached indigenous organizations and media outlets throughout the country, including over 180 indigenous radio stations, to invite participation in branch campaign activities.

Amnesty International Chile and Venezuela translated human rights materials into indigenous languages, while in Uruguay, a message from world-famous writer Eduardo Galeano to all radio stations supported campaign aims. In Ecuador, 500 Years On activities were launched in the National Congress by indigenous leader José María Cabascango, featured as one of the campaign's special 1992 appeals after his torture by a special police intelligence division following his arrest by the army during a 1991 indigenous protest march.

Meanwhile, Amnesty International Japan took the message of Amnesty International's 500 Years On campaign to the *Ainu people*, while Amnesty International Austria brought American diplomatic representatives to Austria together with Austrian parliamentarians for a discussion on the situation of America's indigenous peoples.

Governmental responsibility

Amnesty International also appealed directly to governments of the region to urgently tackle key indigenous human rights issues by inter alia carrying out effective investigations into abuses against indigenous peoples and bringing perpetrators to justice; justly and speedily resolving land disputes that all too often lead to abuses; and, as a specific gesture to the UN's 1993 International Year for the World's Indigenous Peoples, establishing special commissions to review their country's record in implementing all international human rights standards for indigenous people. Amnesty International called the attention of governments to the contribution which ratification and implementation of the new International Labour Organization Convention 169 (1989) on Indigenous and Tribal Peoples Convention could make to protecting indigenous peoples' rights. It considers Convention 169 the most substantive international instrument affirming and providing specificity to indigenous peoples' rights: Provisions relating specifically to rights within Amnesty International's mandate include those on protection of physical integrity; enjoyment of human rights and fundamental freedoms without hindrance or discrimination; penalties before the law in accordance with internationally recognised human rights; specific safeguards against abuse of indigenous peoples' rights; and rights to freedom of association and lawful trade union activities.

Mindful of the useful forum which WGIP has provided for indigenous peoples to draw attention to abuses and suggest preventative measures, Amnesty International urged governments to respond to its requests for information and on-site visits, take full account of its conclusions, recommendations and proposals, and support its efforts to promote better protection of indigenous peoples' fundamental rights.

Inter-governmental initiatives

At inter-governmental level Amnesty International made special statements to WGIP's 1991 and 1992 sessions, documenting its concern that discrimination meant indigenous people were more likely to have their rights trampled on in the first place and then be let down by the judicial system.

In 1992, Amnesty International also took its concerns to the ILO, the OAS and the EC Institutions while national Governors of the World Bank were pressed by Amnesty International sections to ensure that the Bank was implementing its announced concern for the wider implications of Bank-supported development projects affecting indigenous peoples. Amnesty International asked the Bank for examples of specific applications of the Operational Directive 4.2.

Human rights complementarity: Amnesty International and social and economic rights

Some advocates of indigenous rights have difficulty understanding why Amnesty International's mandate focuses on particular individual civil and political rights, and not on collective social and economic rights such as treaty obligations, religious freedom, land rights, cultural integrity and group survival. To address such concerns Amnesty International made clear in all of its 1992 materials that *its focus on protecting certain civil and political rights should not be interpreted to suggest that the organisation ignores the importance of others.* Amnesty International's work on behalf of individuals is clearly centred in the context of other rights and their violation and the organisation is fully aware of the close relationship between these rights and the social and economic rights which indigenous organisations struggle to attain: Amnesty International campaigns for example for governments to ratify the International Covenant on Economic, Social and Cultural Rights, and protection of these rights is implicit in the organisation's advocacy of the principles of the Universal Declaration of Human Rights. Amnesty International believes, however, that *it can best contribute to protection of indigenous rights by concentrating on those within its strictly defined mandate, whilst making clear the social and economic conditions and contexts which give rise to abuses.*

Accordingly, the organisation's 1992 campaign materials emphasized the contexts which gave rise to violations against indigenous peoples and those who work with them in the Americas — land and resource disputes, repression of indigenous activists, discrimination and deprivation, the so-called "war against drugs" and internal conflicts such as faced by Peru and Guatemala, when indigenous peoples can be "caught between two fires" and subjected to violations from both sides. Amnesty International materials stressed that although the manifestations of the abuses directed at America's indigenous peoples differ — discrimination in the judicial process in Canada and the US, torture in Mexico, massive extrajudicial executions in Peru — the root causes are the same throughout the region, lying in the discrimination, deprivation and marginalisation to which indigenous peoples have been subjected since Europeans first arrived in the region.

The recommendations which concluded Amnesty International's report also took careful cognizance of the relationship between social and economic rights and protections and the violations against which Amnesty International fights. For example, Amnesty International called on governments to take into account several factors when resolving land disputes, including Article 18 of ILO convention No.169, which requires that adequate penalties be established by law against unauthorized intrusion upon or use of indigenous peoples' lands, and that only authorized evictions in accordance with fundamental principles of justice be permitted. Amnesty International also called on governments to ensure that bilateral and multilateral lending and development projects, including debt for nature swaps, were carried out in consultation with indigenous peoples, taking due consideration for their welfare and protection of their fundamental rights.

1993 and Beyond: A Continuing Partnership

Amnesty International's special 1992 campaign has now officially ended, but new Amnesty International actions have been launched to help protect the rights of indigenous peoples in Brazil, the US and Australia, and others are planned. Amnesty International continued to work alongside indigenous organisations during 1993, the UN's International Year for the World's Indigenous Peoples, and beyond, to help protect indigenous peoples from imprisonment as prisoners of conscience, unfair trials, torture and ill-treatment, "disappearances," extrajudicial executions and the judicial death penalty as they struggle to retain their lands, their identities and even their lives. There is already much common ground. As a Guatemalan indigenous leader wrote to Amnesty International at the height of the army counter-insurgency campaign which claimed so many indigenous victims there in the early 1980's:

> "Your work has supported and renewed our conviction that no matter how poor or ill-treated we are, we have the right to life and to respect, that to kill a new-born baby or an old person bowed down by the persecution of the army constitutes the gravest of crimes that deserves the most energetic condemnation. I believe it is on this point that your work and our own as a peasant organization converge: the defence of the right to life in all its aspects: the right to physical integrity, to security . . . to a simple but fully human life, the end to all of the threats that have weighed so heavily on all our people, both Indian and non-Indian for so many centuries."

TRACY ULLTVEIT-MOE is a senior researcher in Amnesty International's Americas Research Department. She was responsible for coordinating Amnesty International's indigenous peoples of the Americas 1992 campaign, and prepared the documents for it, including the: Human Rights Violations against Indigenous Peoples of the Americas *report (AMR 01/08/92).*

Amnesty International, International Secretariat
1 Easton Street, London WC1X 8DJ, UK
Tel: 44.71.4135690
Fax: 44.71.9561157

Annexes

ANNEX I

Resolutions on Indigenous Peoples Adopted by the European Parliament

a. **Resolution on the** *catastrophic environmental impact of large scale deforestation in Sarawak*, **(based on Committee report Doc. A2-92/88, OJ C235)**[1]
The European Parliament, (relevant recitals and paragraphs),
B. whereas the Community imports a significant proportion of the felled timber from Malaysia and from Sarawak, in particular sawn timber and substantial amounts of poles and split poles,
C. whereas the present large scale logging in Sarawak constitutes a serious threat to the environment and to the indigenous people who live in and from the tropical rain forest, whereas when logging concessions are granted insufficient attention is paid to such threats and the traditional land rights of the indigenous peoples are ignored,
F. whereas the way of life of the local indigenous people in Sarawak is generally in keeping with the possibilities and constraints of the ecological situation and whereas they, more than anyone else, have the knowledge and skills to exploit these forests in a manner which does not cause damage,
G. sympathetic to the steps taken by the *Penan, Kelabit and Kayan* with a view to combating the further destruction of their surroundings,
1. Calls on the Community and its Member States to suspend imports of timber from Sarawak until it can be established that these imports are from concessions which do not cause unacceptable ecological damage and do not threaten the way of life of the Indigenous People;
3. Calls on the Community to comply with the bilateral timber agreement with Malaysia and to provide in this agreement for the setting up of an independent committee, including ecologists, anthropologists and representatives of indigenous people of Sarawak, to be established and coordinated under the auspices of the ITTO.[2]

b. **Resolution on** *the negative effects of financing from the European Community and various international organisations on the environment of the Amazon region* **(Doc.A2-124/89, OJ C158, June 26)**
C. concerned that the deforestation activities including the building of roads, burning forests for large-scale stock breeding and other agricultural activities, wood-cutting and building dams, continue to cause the genocide of the Indian population in the Amazon region, which has fallen from 10 million in about the year 1600 to roughly 650,000 today, of whom fewer than 200,000 live in the Brazilian part of the Amazon region, and who are subject to every sore of violence and also to diseases previously unknown to them,
With regard to the Amazon region:
2. To make the conservation of the Amazon region a major priority in Community cooperation with Latin America and not to cooperate in projects which are a threat to the Indians and the natural environment,
With regard to Carajas:
6. To declare a moratorium on imports of pig iron from Carajas, pending modifications to the iron production plans and the related enegy supplies so that they are not to the detriment of the Indians, the natural forests, the environment or local population.

c. **Resolution** *on the position of the world's Indians* **(Doc.A2 44/89, OJ C120, April 14, 1989)**;
3. Urges the governments of countries concerned to ensure that indians are not deprived of their way of life and are protected against the harmful consequences of industrial and agro-industrial development;
4. Calls upon the European Commission to make its involvement in areas containing Indian communities contingent upon the fulfilment of demanding conditions, as regards observing the

rights of indigenous peoples, and to conduct ongoing checks as to whether these conditions are being met;
5. Asks the Commission to devise support programmes designed to provide Indian communities with all legal assistance they require to uphold their rights;

d. Resolution *on the situation of the Yanomami Indians in Brazil* **(Doc. B3 — 0119/90, OJ No C38/80, January 1990).**
A. whereas the continued existence of the Yanomami Indians in the Brazilian Amazon region is threatened because of on-going conflicts with gold miners,
4. Calls on western governments, the IMF, the World Bank and private banks to take rapid measures to reduce the Third World debts, which are one of the basic causes for the destruction of the tropical rainforests and the genocide practised against the Indigenous People.

e. Resolution *on the situation of the indigenous peoples in Canada* **(Doc. B3-1659/90, OJ C260, September 13, 1990).**
1. Urges the parties concerned to cease hostilities and commit themselves to the use of judicious and prudent measures to secure a peaceful and just resolution to the current situation;
2. Acknowledges the Mohawk Nation's demands, as expressed in numerous treaties and agreements;
3. Urges the development and implementation of an agreement between Canada/Quebec and the Six Nations Confederacy about the fundamental freedoms and human rights of the Mohawk Nation;
4. Asks the Council to express to the Canadian government its concern about developments with regard indigenous peoples;
5. Calls on its delegation for relations with Canada to send observers to Quebec and to enter the Mohawk question on the agenda for the next interparliamentary meeting.

f. Resolution *on the Tuareg People in Mali and Niger* **(Doc.B3-1627/90, September 13, 1990, OJ C260);**
The European Parliament expresses alarm about reports of massacres and inhuman treatment of Tuaregs in Mali and Niger (Rec.A). The Tuaregs in detention are treated as prisoners of conscience, persecuted on account of their ethnic origins (Rec.B). The Parliament recognises that the nomadic life followed by the Tuareg people for centuries leads them to ignore national frontiers and that this can lead to conflict with the forces of national states in the Sahara (Rec.E). If the killing, uprisings and bloody repressions continue, an entire people will be threatened with annihilation (Rec.F).
1. Expects the government of Niger to meet in full the promises of reintegration it has made to the Tuaregs returning from Libya;
2. Calls for the release of imprisoned Tuaregs and an end to torture.
3. Proposes the setting up of an international committee of inquiry into the rumours and reports of massacres said to have taken place in the two countries in question and which are apparently still continuing in Mali.
4. Calls on the Commission to take account of these violations of human rights in implementing the Lome IV Convention, pursuant to Article 5 thereof,
5. Demands that the governments of Mali, Niger and Algeria, which are members of the commission monitoring the movement of the Tuaregs, allow the Tuaregs freedom of movement of goods and persons in accordance with the same article.

g. Resolution on the *environmental problems in the Amazon region* **(Doc.A3-0182/90, OJ C295).**
3. Regrets the role played by the World Bank in promoting and financing the Carajas iron mining project without taking adequate account of the consequences for the indigenous peoples and the natural environment;
5. Urges the Commission to support Brazil in its use of alternatives charcoal for the production of pig iron which are acceptable in social and environmental terms and from the point of view of the indigenous community and to obtain funds to this end through the ECSC;
10. Urges the Commission to put together a clear package of instruments and procedures and to publicise them with a view to preventing undesirable consequences for the environment and the indigenous and local people from EC aided projects located outside the Community;

h. Resolution on *measures to protect the ecology of the tropical forests* **(A3-0181/90, OJ C295).**

i. Resolution on the *Conservation of tropical forests* **(A3-0231/90, OJ C295).**

C. whereas the Indigenous Peoples living in tropical forests have assumed the mantle of genuine 'guardians of the earth' in that they safeguard and appreciate the value of its produce;

D. whereas if these 'guardians of the earth' and the forests themselves are to survive, the right of these ethnic groups to their territory, that is, their land rights, must be recognised;

1. Stresses that the issue of the conservation and long-term management of the tropical forests must be considered within the global context of the long-term management of the natural resources of the planet, which are under threat from the expansion of the productionist model, and considers that it is essential to create structures for dialogue between the sovereign countries in which the forests are located, indigenous peoples' organisations, NGOs, the governments of the countries which import tropical products and the major international organisations;

2. Urges the Commission, the Council and the Member States to view the conservation and sustained management of the tropical forests, respect for the indigenous peoples, forest dwellers and rural populations as a paramount consideration in the Community's cooperation and environmental policy;

3. Urges the Commission, the Council and the Member States to use every means to their disposal to promote a genuine Community policy to combat the breaking up of indigenous communities, genocide and the destruction of the cultural values of the peoples of the forests;

6. Urges the Commission to set up a Unit within Commission Directorate General VIII for the sole purpose of dealing with this question, staffed by specialists in ecology and anthropology;

8. Urges the Commission to refuse, therefore, all financial or technical assistance to any project which endangers the environment or the indigenous population or adversely affects the cultural freedom of the forest people;

9. Urges the Commission to mandate the unit to implement an assessment and action programme to research possible ways of diversifying the use and marketing of tropical forest products by the forest peoples themselves as a means of supporting them within and overall framework for the sustained management of these products that does not jeopardise their traditional uses;

10. Urges the Commission, the Council and the Member States to establish a diplomatic mission of the indigenous peoples to the Community, with a view to systematic consultation of the indigenous peoples concerning each and every Community action involving tropical forests;

16. Urges the Commission, the Council and the Member States to make efforts to alter how the TFAP operates in practice, so that it focuses on protecting and managing tropical forests and on the rights of indigenous peoples, forest dwellers and rural population, and to make assistance for the TFAP conditional thereon;

19. Urges the Commission, the Council and the Member States to make efforts to induce the World Bank and the International Monetary Fund to take such account of the burning need for tropical forest protection and sustained management and respect for indigenous peoples, forest dwellers and rural populations that they carry out a thorough review of the structural adjustment programmes which place these priority considerations under such threat;

21. Urges the Commission, the Council and the Member States to increase budgetary allocations for tropical forest protection purposes within the framework of cooperation programmes with ACP States and countries in Asia and Latin America, so as to encourage sustained management and the conservation of these forests, giving priority to:
    a) programmes for the restitution of their property rights to the indigenous people;

25. Urges the Commission, the Council and the Member State to make the activities of Community-Based firms, particularly large multinationals, in any tropical forest areas subject to a binding code of conduct which ensures sustained forest management and conservation and respect the cultures and way of life of local communities.

j. Resolution on *the right of nations to information concerning their history and the return of national archives* **(Doc.A3-0258/90, March 1990, OJ C48)**

demands (Art. 8) that Member States, acting in a spirit of mutual understanding and solidarity, should grant all requests from the ACP countries for the return of cultural artefacts and archives, where these are, within the criteria established by UNESCO of fundamental spiritual and cultural value. It further;

9. Believes that in principle developing countries have a legitimate right to the return of their archives, but considers there is a need for appropriate guarantees of the conservation of archives and cultural artefacts, *including those of minority groups*;
12. Recommends, by analogy with article 146 of the Fourth ACP-EEC Convention, that a data bank be established for the storage of all archives currently scattered amongst Members States which concern the ACP countries, particularly those archives which are of importance for reconstructing the history of the ACP nations;
13. Regrets that some Member States still have in their possession scientific, historical, political and cultural information concerning the colonial and pre-colonial period in the developing countries, which is not available to these countries but is of major importance both for their cultural identity and their economic development;
15. Calls on the Commission, in the framework of the Lome Conventions, and if asked to do so by the ACP States, to support projects likely to help developing countries to acquire and/or inspect archive data relevant to them.

k. Resolution on *the human and ecological disaster in the Pastaza region in Ecuador* (Doc.B3 1150/91, OJ C240, July 1991).

D. whereas deforestation and contamination of the hydrological system with oil as a result of petrol exploitation, is becoming a threat to the very survival of indigenous cultures of the region of North Oriente (the land of the Siona, Secoya, Cofan, Quiscuah and Huaorani) and will soon also affect the South, (the province of the Pastaza where the Quischua, Shiwiar and Achuar nations live) if the oil companies receive consent from the Ecuadorian government to commence exploitation and if the World Bank goes ahead with a 100 million dollar loan to develop oil infrastructure.

E. recalling the Sarayacu Agreement of 7 May 1990 between the government of Ecuador and Indigenous Federations which settles legalisation of indigenous territory and compensation of damage suffered by Indian communities,

F. recalling also the statement of the Organisation of the Huaorani People (ONHAE) whose territories are already suffering from the effects of oil exploitation and therefore have denounced the contamination caused by oil companies which destroys the ecological balance,

I. having regard to its position that no financial aid be granted for development projects which may damage the situation of the indigenous populations or the environment,

1. Requests the Ecuadorian authorities and the Indigenous Federations to resume negotiations, implement the Sarayacu agreements and resolve the conflicts by peaceful means;
2. Requests the Ecuadorian government to recognise the inherited rights of their Indigenous Peoples to land they have lived on for centuries and to impose a moratorium on oil prospecting and exploitation until this has been achieved;
3. Requests the World Bank also to consult the local population in their planning procedures and conduct a study in the Pastaza region on the effect of oil exploitation on the local people and the environment before any financial support is granted to develop the necessary infrastructure;
4. Requests the Interparliamentary Delegation for Relations with South America to study further the situation in the Pastaza region during its next visit to South America;
5. Instructs the Commission to investigate whether, also in view of 1992, special projects could be sponsored for indigenous peoples in Latin America and in particular in Ecuador.

l. Resolution on the *disastrous consequences of the Narmada project in India*. (B3-1181/91, OJ C240, July, 1991)

notes that resettlement arrangements, necessary for the construction of the Sardar Sarovar Dam, have been unsatisfactory and that the resettled people complain about poor quality land, poor irrigation and lack of employment opportunities (Rec.D) in their new homes.

4. Calls for the Members States to refuse approval for any further applications to the World Bank for loans for individual sub-projects forming part of the Sardar-Sarovar project or for the next major Narmada dam project, until comprehensive resettlement programmes have been submitted, sufficient fertile land has been designated for this purpose and every farmer receives adequate compensation in the shape of at least an equivalent number of hectares of comparable quality;
7. Calls on the Indian authorities and government, the World Bank and the Members States to take

particular care to involve the affected populations when examining and drawing up alternatives to the planned dams.

m. Resolution on *1992, Indigenous peoples and the Quincentenary*, (B3-0334/92, March 1992, OJ C94).

1. Welcomes the progress made by the governments of Brazil (land for the Yanomami people); Argentina (land for the Guarani people), Canada (land for the Innuit called Nunavut) and Colombia (the establishment of 'resguardos') in granting indigenous people large territories for autonomy;
3. Calls upon governments of countries with Indigenous Peoples to settle disputes over land before engaging in economic activities in those areas where indigenous people claim to have titles to the land and where the activities are not supported by the majority of the Indigenous population;
5. Requests the European Community Institutions to comply with the wish of this Parliament and allocate funding for special projects with indigenous peoples, developed by and for native communities.
6. Calls on international organisations and governments to consult indigenous peoples on any economic exploitation, any planning project and any other project and any other project concerning them.
8. Requests the European Commission, the World Bank and the IMF to include in their criteria for financing development programmes, both environmental impact assessments and indigenous impact analyses.
11. Instructs its human rights unit to provide a background document on the situation of indigenous peoples, and its competent committee to appoint a rapporteur to analyse the human, territorial and cultural rights of the indigenous peoples of the Americas.

n. Resolution on *the need to take international action against the SLORC, Myanmar*, (Doc.B3-0486/92, April 9, 1992, OJ C125)

expresses shock by evidence that the Burmese Army seems to have been given licence to kill, torture and rape (Rec. C), considers that the time has come when the gross abuse of human rights and the defiance of international opinion by the SLORC requires the EC to take the lead in imposing sanctions (Par. 2) and calls for the immediate release of Aung San Suu Kyi and all other political prisoners (Par. 10).

A. appalled by the reports of the persecution of minorities in Burma which has driven tens of thousands of Rohingyas to seek refuge in Bangladesh and several hundreds of *Nagas* to flee to India, and by the massive military attack on the *Karen* Minority near the Thai border,
8. Calls on European Political Cooperation to seek the cooperation of ASEAN, its Member States and Japan in ending the import of Burmese tropical woods which, by adding to the destruction of the rain forest, has potentially devastating effects on the global environment and which provides the SLORC with the means of purchasing weapons.

o. May 14, 1992, Resolution (Doc.A3 0023/92, OJ C150) *On the Community's policy in relation to the developing countries;*

14. Calls on the Commission to give an undertaking by 1995 that the *import of tropical hardwoods* that are not produced using sustainable methods will be prohibited, and to prohibit it for itself and press in the appropriate fora for a worldwide strategy on this matter, considers that the import of non sustainable tropical hardwood from Sarawak must be prohibited immediately, until sustainable production methods are used;
38. Calls on the Community, in collaboration with the UNEP, IUCN and WWF, to give maximum support to the developing countries in framing good environmental legislation.

p. Resolution *on human rights in Colombia* (Doc.B3 0850/92, June 9, 1992, OJ C241)

voices a strong protest against the massacre of Paez Indians in Coloto on 16 December 1991 (par.1), following a pattern of harassment and abuse against the indigenous people by gunmen employed by landowners and drug traffickers.
2. Calls on the Colombian government to punish those gulty of violation of human rights.

3. Calls on the Colombian government and the guerilla movement to adhere strictly to international human rights legislation.

q. Resolution on the *Narmada dam in India*, (Doc.B3-1012/92, July 1992, OJ C241)

5. Calls upon all Member States to draw the appropriate conclusions from the report of the Morse Committee and to urge their executive directors to vote against further World Bank support for the project.
6. Points out to the Commission that the human rights of the people in the region in question are at stake and requests that it questions this aspect of the dam project in the context of development cooperation relations with India.
7. Recommends that the World Bank withdraws from the project, pays compensation to those who have suffered as a result of the Sardar Sarovar projects and writes off the US$250 million spent on building the dam if it is not completed.

r. Resolution on *the situation of the Tuareg People* (Doc.B3-0967/92, July 9, 1992), strongly condemns the arrests and executions of Tuaregs and calls for administrative autonomy for the Tuareg people and;

2. Calls on the Malian Government to enforce the agreement with Tuareg organisations by granting bodies set up under its terms the requisite powers and resources;
3. Calls on the authorities Niger to establish genuine dialogue with a view to reconciliation with the Tuareg and to call off the military operations;
4. Calls for an international committee of inquiry to be set up to establish responsibility for the Tchin-Tabaradene, Gao, Timbuktu, Lere, Gossi and Foita massacres;
5. Believes it is essential to grant the regions of northern Niger a degree of administrative autonomy, for which the Tuaregs themselves should be responsible, this being the only sure way restore confidence;
6. Calls on the Malian and Niger authorities to grant the Tuaregs and their goods freedom of movement and to recognise the Tuaregs as full citizens;
7. Believes that it is incumbent on the EC and its Member States to impress on the governments and political forces in Mali and Niger that the treatment of the Tuaregs in the future will have a decisive influence on the aid policies and relations of the EC and its Member States with both countries.

s. Resolution on *human rights in Bangladesh* (Doc.B3-1169, OJ284, September 17, 1992).

The Parliament expressed its alarm at the reported massacre on April 10, 1992 of hundreds of unarmed *Jumma* civilians in Logang, *Chittagong Hill Tracts*, Bangladesh and notes that the Jumma peoples are subject to forcible relocation in large numbers into 'cluster villages' to make way for Bengali occupants of Jumma lands. The Subcommittee on Human Rights is instructed to investigate the situation and if possible sent a mission to the CHT and its President, the EPC and the Commission are requested to bring the matter to the attention of the Government of Bangladesh.

1. Vigorously condemns the massacres in Logang;
2. Calls on the government of Bangladesh to publish the full outcome of the inquiry to be undertaken by Justice Sultan Hussein Khan, to terminate military involvement in the CHT area, to respect human rights and to end its policy of forcible relocation of Indigenous People;
5. Calls on the UN Commission on Human Rights to appoint a special rapporteur to monitor the situation in the CHT;

t. October 29, 1992 Resolution (Doc.B3 1418/92 OJ C305) on *the award of the Nobel Peace Prize to Rigoberta Menchu*.

A. warmly welcoming the award of the 1992 Nobel Peace Prize to the indigenous human rights activist from Guatemala, Rigoberta Menchu,
B. supporting the statement of the Norwegian Nobel Committee that Rigoberta Menchu stands out as a vivid symbol of peace and reconciliation across ethnic, cultural and social dividing lines in her own country, on the American continent and in the world,
C. bearing in mind that the month of October 1992 is exactly 500 years since the arrival of

Columbus, which marked the starting point of the conquest of the Americas, and that Rigoberta Menchu is the co-ordinator of the American Continent's Five Hundred Years of Resistance Campaign,
D. noting the inauguration of the lighthouse in the Dominican Republic on the 12th of October and distressed by the enormous financial and social costs involved in its construction,
H. recognising that assimilationist policies have not only delayed the drafting of an appropriate international instrument on the rights of Indigenous People, but have also deeply affected Indigenous communities,
1. Congratulates Rigoberta Menchu on the Nobel Peace Prize and on her decision to use the money she has received to establish a foundation for the protection of Indigenous Peoples in the Americas;
2. Calls on the Twelve and the member states at the UN, to respond to Rigoberta Menchu's appeal and press for substantially more money to be allocated to the Voluntary Fund for Indigenous Peoples for the UN International Year for the World's Indigenous People;
3. Hopes that awarding the Nobel Peace Prize to Rigoberta Menchu will not only represent a recognition of her efforts but also pave the way for improving the human rights and social, economic and political conditions of Indigenous Peoples and towards advancing the peace process in Guatemala;
5. Calls on the Commission to set up more projects with indigenous communities, also outside tropical forest regions, on the basis of a recognition of their values, traditional knowledge and resource management practice with a view to promoting environmentally sound and sustainable development and calls on the Community automatically to include in its third generation treaties a clause on the rights on Indigenous Peoples;
6. Welcomes and supports the 'Charter of Rights' of the Global Alliance of the Indigenous Tribal Peoples of the Tropical Forests and the Kari-Oca Declaration and Indigenous Peoples Earth Charter;
7. Welcomes the work on the drafting of a Declaration on Indigenous Rights by the Working Group on Indigenous Peoples aimed at protecting and strengthening the collective rights of Indigenous Peoples, including the right to maintain their language, culture, religion, education, land and resources, prevent use of their lands and resources for military purposes or dumping of toxic wastes and develop their territories according to their indigenous traditions;
8. Deplores continuing human rights violations against indigenous peoples, NGOs and lawyers who support them, as has been rigorously documented by many international NGOs;
9. Calls upon all governments of countries with Indigenous People to ratify ILO Convention 169 and, in particular, welcomes the ratification by the Guatemalan Congress on the 8 of October;
10. Instructs its appropriate committee to investigate the possibility of contributing to the setting of standards concerning the rights of Indigenous Peoples at the United Nations;
11. Calls on the World Bank to develop a special fund for grants for projects developed by Indigenous Peoples;
12. Calls for a comprehensive nuclear test ban and a moratorium on British tests, following the French, Russian and American moratoria and requests the International community and national governments to support Indigenous Peoples communities that were affected by these tests;
13. Requests the Interparliamentary Delegations for North, Central and South America and the European Political Cooperation in their relations with their American counterparts, to place the issue of Indigenous Peoples on their agendas;

u. Resolution on *human rights in Sudan* (Doc.B3-1411, October 29, 1992 OJ C305)

expresses great concern (Rec.E.) about the plight of the now remaining population of Juba, which is exposed to hunger and massacres by the army.
1. Condemns the systematic abuses of human rights throughout the country including recently reported persistent human rights violations by government forces in Juba and in the *Nuba Hills*;

v. Resolution *on economic and commercial relations between the EC and Brazil* (Doc.A3-0310/92, Nov 1992 OJ C337)

1. Expresses concern at the fact that, despite Brazil's declared efforts towards democractic development, there are still unacceptable violations of human rights, the characteristics of

Indigenous Peoples are not respected and there is corruption in the institution.

12. Welcomes the fact that in July 1992, Brazil reached an agreement with the credito banks on the reducction of its external debt, in keeping with the Brady plan, leading to a considerable reduction in the debt and a substantial postponement of repayments, welcomes also the agreement reached, in the form of a debt for nature swap, to use the external debt to fund a macro project to preserve the Amazon rainforest.

17. Supports the project for a pilot programme for the Brazilian Amazon basin, co funded by the EC, the Brazilian government and the World Bank, suggests to the Commission that it encourages regional cooperation between all the Amazonian countries with regard to establishing and implementing a strategy for the conservation and rational exploitation of the rainforest.

w. Resolution on *the situation in Sudan*, (Doc. B3-0532/93, OJ. April 22, 1993)

D. Alarmed by the Government's large-scale systematic campaign of forcible relocation of the *Nuba people*, with the apparent aim of the destruction of Nuba identity by violently removing the ethnic Nuba population from their ancestral lands and scattering them in small camps throughout northern Kordofan, where they are exposed to hunger and disease, an exercise accompanied by widespread and numerous human rights abuses, arrests, systematic slavery, killings and extra-judicial executions of Nuba men,

E. Recognising that the main cause of these disasters has been the attempt by successive governments in Khartoum to impose dictatorial rule and Islamic law on the Animist and Christian population of Southern Sudan, but that the rebel leaders in the South have, especially by their internal rivalries, contributed to the disaster,

1. Calls on the Sudanese authorities to put an end to these systematic violations of human rights, which must be regarded as a means of warfare and ethnic cleansing, and to respect the rights of minorities and the freedoms of the population without any distinction as to race, religion or language;

2. Calls on the Community and the Member States to organise massive aid for the Sudanese population and do everything possible to ensure that this aid actually reaches the population by channelling it through the NGOs.

x. Resolution on *the escape of the murderers of Chico Mendes in Brazil* (Doc.B3-0372/93, March 11, 1993, OJ C115)

B. recalling with great respect the work of the trade unionist and grassroots environmentalist, Chico Mendes, who worked with rubber tappers to preserve the Amazon rainforest,

C. recalling his brutal murder on 22 December 1988 and the quick investigation of this crime, which led to the arrest, conviction and sentence to 19 years imprisonment of Darci and Darli Alves da Siva,

D. noting that, according to Amnesty International, this fact marked the first time that a Brazilian court had convicted a landowner for ordering the murder of a rural trade unionist,

H. whereas the forest lands for which Chico Mendes gave his life, like those of the Yanomami people, have once again been invaded by gold prospectors, Awa forest land continues to be destroyed by illegal settlers, loggers and farmers and there is a serious delay in the implementation of Article 231 of the Brazilian Constitution, which requires all indigenous lands to be demarcated by October 1993,

4. Welcomes the Brazilian Government's Operacao Selva Livre to remove the gold prospectors from Yanomami Reserve to Boa Vista;

5. Appeals to the Brazilian Government to provide education and employment for the ex-miners in Boa Vista and also demarcate, protect and ratify Awa Guaja land and other indigenous territories further to Article 231 of the Constitution by October 1993.

y. Resolution B3-0694, on the *United Nations World Conference in Vienna in June 1993* (Doc.B3-0694, May 1993, OJ C176)

10. Calls on the Twelve and the Member States at the UN to press for a strengthening of the mandate of the Working Group on Indigenous Peoples, even after the adoption of the Declaration on Indigenous Peoples;

11. Reiterates its appeal to the Commission and the Member States to allocate funds to the UN

Voluntary Fund for the International Year to assist with the programmes and activities;
12. Calls upon the World Conference on Human Rights to take into account the work of the UNWGIP and the text of the Universal Draft Declaration of the Rights of Indigenous Peoples, in particular with regard to the question of self-determination, in the adoption of the final declaration of principles;
13. Calls upon the UN to facilitate the participation of indigenous peoples' representatives, particularly from the developing world, in its meetings where matters affecting them are being discussed, and at the World Conference on Human Rights in Vienna.

z. Resolution on the *human rights situation in Sarawak and the moratorium on imports of tropical hardwoods and wood products from Sarawak, Malaysia* (Doc.B3-1696, May 1993, OJ C176)

B. Recalling that, in its resolution of 8 July 1988, on the catastrophic environmental impact of large-scale deforestation in Sarawak, it called for a moratorium on the imports of tropical hardwoods from this Malaysian State and subsequently repeated this in later resolutions on the rain forests,
C. Aware that the EC Council and Commission have never agreed to implement its call,
D. Stressing that the way of life of the indigenous people of Sarawak continues to be destroyed by logging,
E. Noting that the Dutch government wants an import ban on non sustainable exploited hardwood from 1995,
1. Calls on the Council and the Commission to consider urgently imposing this moratorium notwithstanding the economic interests of firms from the Community established in Malaysia;
2. Calls on these two EC institutions to implement quickly eco-labelling on all forest woods and products whether of tropical, boreal or temperate origins;
3. Urges the Council and Commission to make representations to the Malaysian Government on the need to respect its obligations to ITTO and the natural rights of the indigenous peoples to the safe possession of their land;
4. Calls on the Japanese Government to discourage Japanese companies, as the largest consumers of Sarawakian forests, from further imports of tropical woods which are a major cause of deforestation;
5. Calls on the Commission to implement an import ban of non-sustainable exploited hardwood at the beginning of 1995,

aa. Resolution on *the violation of human rights in Brazil* (Doc. B3-1265, September 1993)

D. Shocked and dismayed by the brutal murder of at least 18 Yanomami, men, women and children from the community of Haximu, probably by gold prospectors working illegally on the borders of Venezuela and Brazil in July 1993, declared by the UN to be the Year of the World's Indigenous People,
5. Forcefully condemns the massacre of Yanomami Indians and welcomes the strong words of the Attorney-General of Brazil in condemning the massacre, calling it 'genocide';
6. Calls on the Brazilian authorities to ensure the removal of all gold prospectors from indigenous land and repeats its appeal for the demarcation, protection and ratification of indigenous land, which, under the 1988 Constitution should be completed by October 1993.

ab. Resolution (B3-0057, January 1994) *on the peasant uprising in Chiapas (Mexico)*

B. recognizing that the causes of these events included the exploitation, hunger, poverty, injustice and humiliation suffered by the indigenous population,
D. whereas the framework agreement signed in April 1991 between the European Community and the United States of Mexico (OJ L340, 11.12.1991, p.2) stresses that human beings should be the principal beneficiaries of cooperation and that respect for human rights should therefore be promoted,
1. Condemns unreservedly the use of armed force in a state subject to the rule of law, even when it is allegedly prompted by political, social, ethnic or cultural conflicts, as well as the excesses committed by the army during the repression;
2. Welcomes the swift reaction of the President of Mexico in his effort to bring to an end the hostilities and establish a dialogue;

3. Hopes that this dialogue between the Government and the rebels will lead as soon as possible to a definitive ceasefire and help remedy the injustices and discrimination suffered by the poorest sectors of the Mexican people;
4. Stresses the need for progress in the democratisation process in Mexico;
5. Calls on the joint committee established under the EEC-Mexico Agreement to increase the planned cooperation in the public health, rural and agricultural sectors, emphasizing above all the need to protect tropical forests in common agreement with their indigenous populations.

ac. **Resolution (A3-0059/93, 9 February 1994)** *on action required internationally to provide effective protection for indigenous peoples*

1. Adopts the definition of indigenous peoples given by the ILO in its Convention No.169 and believes that this convention together with the Kari Oca Declaration (Rio, June 1992) and the declaration of the UN conference in Vienna on the rights of indigenous peoples (June 1993) are the benchmark texts in this regard;
2. Declares that pursuant to UN provisions, and in the context of a non-violent and fully democratic procedure with due regard for the rights of other citizens, indigenous peoples have the right to determine their own destiny by choosing their institutions, their political status and that of their territory;
3. Takes the view that the UN must take advantage of its 50th anniversary to make its bodies more democratic and more effective by enabling peoples without a state, in particular indigenous peoples, to be better represented, especially by involving them in the work of the General Assembly;
4. Solemnly reaffirms that those belonging to indigenous peoples have, just as any other human being has, the right to life, to respect, the right to freedom of thought and action, to physical security, to health, to justice and to equality concerning the right to work, to housing, to education and to culture; this right to a separate culture must involve the right to use and disseminate their mother tongue and to have the tangible and intangible features of their culture protected and disseminated and to have their religious rights and their sacred land respected;
5. Calls for censuses to be taken of indigenous peoples in the states in which they are established;
6. Calls for indigenous peoples to be given help in marketing the craft products made by indigenous peoples, with verification of origin;
7. Declares that indigenous peoples have the right to the common ownership of their traditional land sufficient in terms of area and quality for the preservation and development of their particular ways of life, such land to be placed at their disposal free of charge; it will therefore be indivisible, non-transferable, imprescriptible and cannot be rented;
8. Takes the view that, with regard to legal matters, those belonging to indigenous peoples have the right to a qualified defence lawyer and to full information about their rights, with the assistance of an interpreter if necessary, and that, as far as is compatible with the Universal Declaration of Human Rights, preference should be given to the use of customary law to judge their offences;
9. Declares that indigenous peoples who have been robbed of their rights must be able to obtain fair compensation; if deprivation involves the loss of land, this will be made good, first and foremost, by returning the land in question or, alternatively, by providing land at least equal in terms of quality and size to that which has been lost;
10. Calls in the strongest possible terms on states which in the past have signed treaties with indigenous peoples to honour their undertakings, which remain imprescriptible, and in this connection gives its firm backing to the UN special rapporteur responsible for studying and resolving this problem;
11. Reaffirms the positive contribution of indigenous peoples' civilizations to mankind's common heritage and the essential role which they have played and which they must continue to play in the conservation of their natural environment;
12. Considers that the European Union, but also the United Nations, should take all possible steps to ensure that international treaties, policies and the activities of commercial undertakings do not, either directly or indirectly, adversely affect the rights of indigenous peoples; calls in this connection for the Council and the Commission to make a precise political statement on indigenous peoples;
13. Calls on the Commission and the Council to make a tangible contribution to the International

Year of Indigenous Peoples and to this end calls for:
— criteria to be drawn up for the financing of Community projects in the light of the rights of indigenous peoples,
— indigenous peoples to be directly involved, as part of development and cooperation policy, in projects concerning them,
— European officials to be given special training and assigned for following-up questions concerning indigenous peoples,
— the technical and legal information intended for indigenous peoples' representatives to be enhanced,
— appropriate budget lines to be clearly allocated for the defence of the rights of these peoples;
14. Undertakes to set up, at the beginning of the next parliamentary term, an interparliamentary delegation composed of Members of this Parliament and representatives of indigenous peoples and instructs its Subcommittee on Human Rights to monitor questions concerning their rights very closely;
15. Calls on the Member States of the European Union to show their determination to provide tangible protection for indigenous peoples by acceding to ILO Convention No.169 and by calling on other states to do the same.

References

1. OJ stands for *Official Journal* of the European Communities. *A-documents* are reports of a Parliamentary committee prepared by a rapporteur appointed by the committee further to a motion for a resolution. *B-documents* are motions for resolutions tabled in the European Parliament by members or groups of members, e.g. under rule 64 (urgency debates) of the rules of procedure. An urgency resolution is not debated and prepared by a committee before being submitted to a vote at the plenary session and there is no report attached to it. *A2 and B2* documents are reports and resolutions adopted by the European Parliament during its second electoral period (1984-1989), *A3 and B3* documents are those that are adopted during the third and present mandate of the Parliament (1989-1994).
2. The last paragraph of each European Parliament resolution is always a request to its President to forward the resolution to the relevant European Institutions, the governments of the countries that are treated in the resolution and sometimes to intergovernmental and UN bodies.

ANNEX II

European Commission Involvement in Indigenous Peoples' Projects

DG I, External Relations, supports a number of tropical forest projects in Central and South America with an important Indigenous Peoples component.

	Amount (ECU)	Duration	Date
RFT — Brazil	11.9m	3 yrs	1992
COAMA — Colombia	2.5m	3 yrs	1989
NCI — Brazil	450.000	2 yrs	1991
Amazon Pact-Demarcation	550.000	2 yrs	1992

A first priority focus on Brazil was considered justified by the scale and importance of Brazil's forest and by the progress made in correcting past errors and adopting positive policies favouring conservation and sustainable development. An initial EC contribution was made to the Rain Forest Trust Fund (RFT), the core fund of the Pilot Programme for the conservation of Tropical Forests in Brazil. This programme contributes to an important project for Indigenous reserves. The *COAMA programme* aims to consolidate indigenous reserves ("resguardos") and adapt government health and education programmes for Indigenous Peoples in collaboration with NGOs. The purpose of COAMA is to develop a project for conservation and a strategy for reinforcing the traditional indigenous model of use and management of their territories. It was implemented in the context of the recognition of land rights over 18 million hectares, as collective property belonging to some 70.000 people from 50 different indigenous communities. COAMA is based on the premise that conservation is the result of decisions taken at social and cultural levels and that to stimulate local processes is much more important than to implement a project. According to COAMA philosophy, "supporting the indigenous communities, with regard to their identity, culture and decision making ability, can make it possible to help them retain that traditional wisdom which forms the basis for their management of the tropical forest". The programme emerged as "a response to the requirements and priorities of the indigenous people of the Amazon, and has developed as a process of long term accompaniment". All COAMA projects are organised on the basis of indigenous participation and could lead to the "exploration of alternative paths to traditional development theories". COAMA calls itself a programme of support to the initiatives arising within the community, especially those designed to put into practice the rights recognised by State policy.[1]

The *NCI project*, based in Golania, Brazil, is aimed at preservation of and research into Indigenous culture and knowledge, in collaboration with 'Nucleo de Cultura Indigena', a local Brazilian NGO.

The *Amazon Pact Programme* includes an indigenous lands consolidation project to demarcate territory in Bolivia, Peru, Ecuador. The Commission has developed contacts with the Amazon Pact's Pro-Tempore Secretariat in Quito. Programmes are initiated of institutional strengthening for the Pact, together with regional projects for the planning and management of protected areas across the region, and for consolidation of indigenous areas. The Amazon Pact Project for demarcation of indigenous territory in the eight member countries of the Amazon Pact is part of a wider programme of cooperation. The governments of the "Cuenca Amazonica" established the Special Commission of Indigenous Affairs of the Amazon Pact, CEAIA. At its meeting in Lima, April 1991, the members of the Pact unanimously adopted as one of its principle priorities, the legal recognition of indigenous territories. It was agreed to (i) support indigenous communities in the Amazon in the legalisation and demarcation of their territories, and (ii) create conditions for the management, conservation and ecological and sustainable exploitation of the natural resources by the communities. More specifically, the project aims at designing a plan for legalisation of indigenous territory in the Cuenca Amazonica, supporting the governments and indigenous organisations in the demarcation of the indigenous territories and promoting the exchange of experiences with legalisation and demarcation between the eight countries. The project is administered by a local director specialised in indigenous affairs and an indigenous co-director who is a representative of the COICA. Both are working in the offices of the seat of the Amazon Pact in Quito. The pilot projects of legalisation and demarcation in Bolivia, Ecuador and Peru will be finalised through a written treaty between the indigenous organisation on the one hand and the government institution responsible for indigenous territory on the other.

Other projects in Central and South America[2]

Central America — (i) In mid 1993, the Commission sent a mission of experts to Central America to identify pluri-annual indigenous peoples programmes that could be financed by the Community in the context of development cooperation. These programmes will include local, grass-root actions concerning land rights and the social, cultural and productive situation of indigenous communities. The purpose is to develop projects of a more political nature, to promote the recognition of the rights and aspirations of indigenous peoples at the level of national authorities, and to contribute to institution building. The programmes aim at supporting indigenous peoples initiatives, guide governmental policies, help improve the dialogue between both parties and stimulate dynamics at sub-regional level in order to contribute to strengthening the position and recognition of the indigenous peoples as a group. 7.5 MECU has been allocated.

(ii) Regional seminar on "Indigenous Peoples in Central America and International Cooperation" — 20.000 ECU. (iii) Support for regional coordination of indigenous organisations in Central America — 20.000 ECU.

Brazil — (i) Emergency aid for Yanomami indigenous people in the province of Roraima in the North of Brazil. This aid, 280.000 ECU was transmitted to Medecins sans Frontieres in March 1991 for the purpose of financing a medical-nutricial programme; (ii) Non Predatory Management and Environmental Protection of Indigenous Areas in Brazilian Amazon involving the Nambiquara, Kritaki, Kraho and Waiapi. The project receives a total of 339.058 ECU and is implemented by the Brazilian 'Centro de Trabalho Indigenista' (CTI). (iii) Geographical Information System for Monitoring Indigenous Lands, CEDI — Sao Paulo, 437.796 ECU; (iv) Primary health care for Indigenous Communities in Acre State, August 1989, ECU 115 551; (v) Support for the development of indigenous communities in the federal territory of Roraima, June 1989, ECU 299 102; (vi) Various small operations financed through block grants to European NGOs. Project under consideration: Mercury Contamination in the Brazilian Rainforest, Fundacao Esperanca Bresil, 1.334335 ECU.

Bolivia — Rural education programme for Guarani Indigenous Peoples in Santa Cruz, Mani Tese (It) — 406.633 ECU.

Chile — (i) The European Community financed a project of 10 MECU for integrated development of the Northern Regions of Chile. These regions have no industrial fabric, agriculture is nigh non-existent, water supply precarious and the environment is deteriorating. The programme is aimed at improving the production activities of the Indigenous populations and to help small scale fishermen. (ii) Support for the improvement of the productive system and commercialisation in two Mapuche communities in the region of d'Araucania and Los Lagos, Intermon (E) — 201.525 ECU. (iii) Construction of a primary school in the Community of Pehuenche, Valle of Quinquen, IBIS (DK) — 2.749 ECU.

Colombia — (i) 1992, Amazon Fund for Sustainable Development, Government of Colombia — 5 MECU. The aim of the project is to promote sustainable development in 6 "Departments" in the Colombian Amazon including forest conservation, improvement of the level and quality of life in the indigenous and colonist communities and protection of their traditions and cultural identity. (ii) Project for the support of indigenous communities of the Cauca (1992). Training of indigenous communities in the field of the workings of State institutions in order to increase indigenous participation at municipality and departmental level and also identification, design and implementation of development plans and conservation of the environment. The beneficiaries are 25 indigenous resguardos, Paez, Totoro and Guambiano — 305.000 ECU, (iii) ONIC, the National Organisation of Colombian Indigenous Peoples for a project of consolidation of land for indigenous communities — 910.235 ECU.

Projects under consideration: (i) Development of alternatives for the sustainable conservation and utilisation of the forest of the Serrania de Abibe, Organizacion Indigena de Antiquia Corporacion Penca de Sabila — 463.338 ECU. (ii) Development of a map of the indigenous territories and large projects, Gesamthochschule Kassel —396.132 ECU.

Costa Rica — Training of representatives of seven indigenous peoples in the field of human rights, CODEHU (1992) — 73.000 ECU.

Ecuador — In recent years, three projects have been co-financed to help Amazonian Indians in the Ecuadorean provinces of Napo and Pastaza. The special feature of this aid is that it is channelled directly to the recipients without going through government bodies and is based on the direct contacts which the European non governmental organisations have with their counterparts in the country. This provides a special channel of aid to deal with the particular problem of the Indigenous communities. Technical and financial aid is channelled through the government. (ii) support for the production of text books on the impact of oil exploitation on the environment of the Ecuadorian Amazon, Terra Nuova — 5.520 ECU. (It). Projects under consideration: (i) Support for COICA, the regional organisation of indigenous peoples in the Amazon region, 1 MECU. (ii) Study on the impact of the effects of oil exploitation in the Amazon region, Ministerio de Energia y Minas, Subsecretaria de Medio Ambiente, Ecuador — 265.000 ECU. (iii) Project for indigenous integrated self-development, legal aspects of the territorial programmes of the OPIP, Pastaza, IBIS (Dk) — 1.583.195 ECU.

Guatemala — (i) Seminar on indigenous peoples of the Americas — 41.000 ECU. (ii) Support for democratisation through radio programmes on education and training for indigenous peoples, Fondation Alfons Gopper, Munich, in cooperation with IGER in Guatemala — 1 MECU. (iii) Support for the Maya Documentation and Research Centre, Terra Nuova (It) — 6.974 ECU. Substantial assistance was given in the last few years under Article B7-302 (refugees) for indigenous Guatemalans in Mexico (10 projects totalling 12 MECU) and Guatemala (13 projects totalling 8.7 MECU), for indigenous Nicaraguans (10 projects totalling 8.7 MECU) and for various indigenous refugee groups in Honduras. (iv) Integral Rural Development Programme, Quiché — 17.5 MECU.

Honduras — (i) Project Nog. NA/SO-23/011, the development of indigenous communities, an integrated agricultural development project covering wood-felling, restructuring of agriculture, the building of roads, housing, schools and social centres for the Jicaque;[3] (ii) Support to CAHDEA to provide free judicial assistance and training in the field of human rights and promotion of the rights of indigenous peoples — 130.000 ECU.

Mexico — Support the work of CEPROJUSDAC on human rights in the indigenous communities of the Sierra Zangolica, Broederlijk Delen (B) — 8.419 ECU.

Nicaragua — (i) Support for the process of consultation and discussion on the rights of indigenous peoples, 100.000 ECU. (ii) Regional seminar on the topic of indigenous peoples in Central America and international cooperation — 20.000 ECU, Consejo Mundial de los Pueblos Indigenas. Project under consideration: Conservation of the Tropical Forest and Ecoturism in the Cuenca de los Rios San Juan, Nicaragua and Costa Rica — 398.474 ECU;

Panama — (i) Training, promotion and defense of human rights of indigenous peoples in Panama and the establishment of a unit of legal defense, CONAPIP — 53.000 ECU. (ii) Celebration of the National Indigenous Congress (1993), National Coordinator of indigenous peoples in Panama — 57.000 ECU. (iii) Promotion of indigenous peoples rights in Panama, General Congress GUAYAMI — 80.000 ECU. (iv) Sustainable development of Indigenous Kuna communities — 560.000 ECU.

Peru — (i) Communities in the Amazon and Sustainable Production Pilot Phase (CASPI) — 372.832 ECU. (ii) Conservation and Ecologically Sustainable development in the Manu Biosphere Reserve (Machiguengas and Quechuas), WWF UK — 676.440 ECU; (iii) Support for a health project for the Indigenous people of Alto Amazonas province, Oct. 1990 — 98070 ECU. (iv) Civil and electoral registration of indigenous peoples in the Peruvian Amazon — 245.000 ECU.

Venezuela — Under consideration: Biosphere Reserve Alto Orinoco Casiquiare, SADA-Amazonas/ IUCN — 3.700.000 ECU.

Indigenous Peoples and the Quincentenary

The following is a list of European Community activities/events funded by the Commission in connection with the Quincentenary. 1992 has been marked by a great number of events, many of which have taken place with the support of the Community; (i) Seminar on economic cooperation and development in Washington, by: Sociedad Estatal 5' Centenario (Madrid) — 60.000 ECU. (ii) Seminar on Europe-Latin America and 1992, by: Sociedad Estatal 5' Centenario (Madrid) — 65.000 ECU. (iii) Grant for publication of a book "Notre Amerique Métisse", by: Edition La Decouverte (Paris) — 20.000 ECU. (iv) Publication of a book "Historia y Sociedad en Centro America"; by: Sociedad Estatal 5' Centenario — ECU 300 000. (v) Rio Group-EC meeting of businessmen, by: Confederacion de Empresarios de Andalucia — 209.000 ECU. (vi) Euro-America 92 (a) Meeting of Chambers of Commerce, (b) Industrial cooperation, by: Consejo superior de Camaras de Comercio de Espania — 500.000 ECU. (vii) EUR-LA Inter-university meeting in Granada, by: Coimbra Group (Brussels) — 115.000 ECU. (viii) Desarrollo cultural de la region Guaranitica, by: Provincia de Corrientes (Argentina) — 50.000 ECU. (ix) Production of a video-disc on EUR-LA relations, by: Sociedad Estatal 5' Centenario — 100.000 ECU. (x) Exhibition on the history of maize, by: Coimbra Group (Brussels) — 100.000 ECU (xi) Exhibition of Contemporary Andean ceramics, by: Circulos Europeos en AL — 150.000 ECU.

ACP Countries

On the 28th of September 1990, the Commission decided to earmark *24 million ECU for a programme aimed at the Conservation and Rational Utilisation of Africa's Forest Resources*. This is the largest amount of financial assistance accorded by the Commission for environmental projects outside its own territory. The regional allocation of the Third Lomé Convention covers seven countries at the heart of the African Tropical Rainforest, Cameroon, Central African Republic, Congo, Equatorial Guinea, Gabon, Sao Tome e Principe and Zaire. The grant follows both the resolution adopted by the Development Council on 29 May 1990 stressing the importance of the protection of tropical rainforests, and the meeting between the Ministers of the Central African region and the Commission on the tropical forests in Brazzaville on 31 May/1 June 1990. The programme approved by the Commission covers a set of specific projects carried out in each of the seven countries and implemented in a defined protected area. The necessary surveillance and management of these areas will be strengthened and activities by the existing population will be developed in a way compatible with the maintenance and strengthening of the forest ecosystems. The programme will help establish a regional network of protected areas, which will serve as sites on which to test a series of projects, intended to reconcile a viable forest ecosystem with the exploitation of these resources by the local population.[5]

Kenya — (i) In October 1992, after receiving a favourable opinion from the EDF Committee, the European Commission approved a scheme of 4.200,000 ECU for technical assistance to the Kenyan Directorate General for forests for the implementation of programmes for the management and conservation of natural forests. (ii) Health programme for the semi-nomadic peoples of the district of Kajiado, Masaai Health Care (Irl), 184.800 ECU.

Nigeria — Conservation of the Southern part of Cross River National Park, funded by the National Indicative Programme. Also for the conservation of the Northern part of the Park, a financing agreement was reached. The two parts of Cross River National Park at the Southeastern border of Nigeria form, with the Korup National Park at the Western border of Cameroon, one unit of remaining natural forest with unique ecological systems. In 1992, funding for ongoing activities was increased.

Niger and Mali — The Commission, recognising the seriousness of the conflict between *Tuareg* returnees from Algeria and Libya and the Niger and Malian authorities in the period from May to August 1990, played an active part in seeking a settlement and in September of that year, made representations to the governments concerned. The Community over the years, has provided both Mali and Niger with food aid measures. Niger received "Aid for returnees" (2 MECU) under article 104 and resources of its national indicative programme for Lome IV were also used with a view to improving the living conditions of the nomadic and semi-nomadic people by means of an integrated stock-rearing development approach, setting up and running schools and providing basic access roads. In Niger tension has mounted since the arbitrary arrest of members of the Tuareg community (particularly in Agadez) in late August/early September 1992. Representations were made to the national authorities in Niamey by the Community and its Member States in an effort to obtain information about the situation of those arrested and encourage gestures of reconciliation. As in the past, the Commission is willing to support any initiative to promote negotiation. At the same time, the Commission will make every effort to ensure the respect for human rights in Niger, in accordance with the letter and the spirit of Article 5 of the Fourth Lomé Convention.

Mali's national indicative programme for Lomé IV, at the specific request of the Malian authorities, provided for the continuation of operations to protect the environment, ensure food security and open up areas where the Tuaregs have resettled. The signatories to these two programmes have agreed that in accordance with Article 5 of Lomé IV (the human rights clause), cooperation must entail respect for and promotion of all human rights and participation by the population in the development process. The Commission has taken preparatory measures to contribute to the implementation of the National Pact that the Malinese government signed with Tuareg organisations; providing alternative resources as a substitute for food aid, aid to the health sector, redeployment of microprojects and programmes, relaunching projects suspended because of the security situation.

Uganda — Natural Forest Management and Conservation Project. The EC contributes 8,5 MECU of the total 38 MECU (the World Bank, Danida and Norad). The objective of the project is to improve environmental management and to arrest uncontrolled cutting of natural forests.[6]

Asia

In South East Asia, technical and financial cooperation is defined by the Commision as a specific investment in favour of poor segments of the society in order to improve income. EC Projects are thus concentrated in neglected rural areas where ethnic minorities [indigenous peoples] live. Community development experts and anthropologists often conduct prelemÌnary research to involve local communities and avoid popssible negative development impacts.

Following a mission in April 1992, an initial action in forest monitoring is to be implemented for peninsular *Malaysia*. The Commission has also shown concern over the situation in Sarawak and, following the State's December 1991 ITTO commitment to reduce logging, **the Commission made an offer of assistance. So far there has been no uptake from the Sarawak side**.

In the context of the tropical forestry action plan, donors have been submitted a list of potential projects for tropical forest conservation, called IFAP. A workshop took place on the plan in February 1992, which was attended by the Commission's services. In this context, forest sector support actions financed under financial and technical assistance (radio communications, forest monitoring) are being complemented with a fire prevention and control project focused on Sumatra.[7]

Recently two new forest programmes involving indigenous peoples entered into a preliminary study stage in *Indonesia*: (i) Development of Bentuang Karimun Reserve as a National Park and development of the Lanjak-Entimau Wildlife Sanctuary as a totally Protected Area (Malaysia and Indonesia, 2 MECU). The objectives of this project are to develop a national park by conserving the biodiversity value of the area and by developing and using its research, educational, recreational and tourism potential, to contribute to socio-economic development with the involvement of the local and regional communities, and to establish cooperation in conservation activities between Indonesia and Malaysia through the development of transfrontier joint management reserve. Bentuang Karimun is closely linked to local and regional communities both in Indonesia and Malaysia. (ii) Gunung Leuser National Park. The objectives of this project are: to safeguard ecological life-supporting functions of the Park involving all relevant provincial and local levels of society, to guide sustainable development of the communities in the immediate surroundings of the Park, and to strengthen institutions in applied ecological research and development. The Commission approach is to start both projects with workshops inviting local peoples, local and national government representatives etc. and to work into the project with a 1 year preparatory period, so the local situation is properly understood and the interests of those concerned properly taken into account. (iii) The WWF administers another Community funded project in Indonesia for Conservation Management in the Kayan Mentarang Nature Reserve in East Kalimantan (342.330 ECU). The Lun Dayet and Kanyah (Dayaks) are involved in the project.

In *Laos* the Commission funds the (i) Luang-Prabang Micro Projects (Lao PDR), 6 MECU. The project key assumption is the participation/involvement of local communities in project areas and the appropriate definition of a bottom-up approach. In following local community development oriented objectives, the project will ensure that natural resources (water, soil, forest) which are endangered by on-going practises are appropriately preserved, maintained and improved. The project will address the needs of local communities in: development of agricultural production and marketing of agri-products; improvement of rural infrastructure; improvement of irrigation systems and networks; improvement of local community public services. The target population are the rural peoples of of Luang-Prabang province belonging to the three ethnic origins represented in the province (*Lao Louma, Lao Theung and Lao Soung*). (ii) Luang Namiha Area Development Project (a World Bank project). The immediate objectives are to achieve food security, establish a new balance in the supply and demand for rice and shift upland populations (e.g. Hmong people) away from unproductive cultivation into sustainable, cash-generating endeavours (8 MECU). DG I currently discusses with the Lao PDR a possible intervention (iii) in the field of reinstallation and reintegration of Laotian refugees of Hmong origin. (iv) It also evaluates the possibility of supporting a project for forest conservation and local development in the provinces of Phong Saly for 300.000 ECU.

Currently, the European Commission is financing a 5 MECU project aiming at the sustainable utilisation of non-timber forest products in the island of Palawan, *Philippines*. This project directly benefits members of the Batak and Tagbanua indigenous communities. In the Philippines, the Commission finances three other projects that have an impact on indigenous communities. In these cases, however, indigenous peoples do not appear in the project description; (i) the Aurora Integrated Area Development Project (10.8 MECU), 1986. This project provides financial and technical assistance for the implementation of an integrated area development project serving the province of Aurora, in Eastern Luzon. The project in particular helps to strengthen agricultural support services and to develop both lowland and upland agricultural production, rehabilitate and upgrade irrigation and feeder-road infrastructure, prepare and commence implementation of an overall programme of watershed protection, and undertake a number a small activities in the field of social development, health and sanitation. (ii) Central Cordillera Agricultural Programme, CECAP, (18,5 MECU), 1987. This project provides financial and technical assistance for the implementation of a programme of rural micro-projects in five provinces of the Cordillera area in northern Luzon. It is intended to raise rural incomes and living standards in the project area, to support ecologically stable and diversified farming systems, to strengthen local capabilities in planning and implementation, operating, maintaining, monitoring and evaluating development efforts. The project will help reduce disparities between upland and lowland areas of the country. It will give priority to actions which address problems of depressed incomes and low productivity among the poorer segments of the farming population, and which encourage self-reliant and self-sustaining development among farming communities. Particular emphasis is given to implementing a quick-acting programme of small actions with immediate and visible impact, and *to ensuring the maximum participation of local communities in the preparation and implementation of individual project actions*. (iii) Southern Mindanao Agricultural Programme (SMAP), 16,5 MECU, 1989. The project is intended to improve living conditions and revenue of upland farming communities, and to protect the long-term development potential of the area through safeguarding its resource base, by means of a programme aimed at the intensification and diversification of upland agriculture, the strengthening of local farmers' organisations, the upgrading of the basic rural infrastructure, and an expansion of the use of environmentally sound upland agricultural technology.

In *Thailand*, a health project is funded for *Karen people*, 750.000 ECU.

Finally, the Commission, under the supervision of DG 11, Environment, Consumer Protection and Nuclear safety, sponsored a study on the situation of Indigenous Peoples living in tropical forests.[8] The purpose of this study was to make an assessment of their situation in order to better integrate their human and cultural elements in the framework of environmental protection and/or EC sustainable management programmes that could be envisaged for the forest areas concerned. It should help integrate the indigenous peoples component more effectively into EC programmes and projects relating to tropical forests in Africa (particularly Zaire, Gabon and the Congo), Asia (Indonesia, Malaysia, the Philippines and Papua New Guinea) and Latin America (Brazil, Bolivia and Peru).

Any additional information regarding these Community projects can be obtained from the Commission Desks responsible for the countries concerned.

References
1. Source: COAMA. Since December 1989, the EC has provided 1 million ECU in support of this programme. A new project proposal for 2 million ECU is currently under consideration by the European Commission. The director of the programme is anthropologist Martin von Hildebrand, former presidential adviser for Indigenous Peoples in Colombia. The programme is administered by the GAIA Foundation in the UK.
2. In view of the fact that some of the projects have not yet been approved, the exactness of the figures quoted in this text can not be guaranteed.
3. When she visited Brussels in 1992, Mauricia Castro Garmendia, Jicaque from Honduras, submitted a full report to the European Parliament and the Desk Officer for Honduras of the Commission regarding this project and the failure to secure the land rights of the indigenous peoples in spite of the provisions made in the project design in the beginning of the eighties.
4. Document IP/90/787, Commission grants funds towards Central African Rainforest, 90/10/01.
5. In August 1992, Oxfam UK/Ireland was requested to assist the Ugandan Ministry of Labour and Social Affairs to resettle some 30,000 people. The majority belonged to the Bakiga people who

had been evicted earlier that year from the Kibale Forest Reserve and Game Corridor. Oxfam took up the matter with DG VIII pointing out that forced evictions without a proper resettlement plan are in violation of the OECD Guidelines on Involutary Displacement and Resettlement (OCDE/GD (91)201). It considers that international financial institutions and donors should take the necessary measures to inform and obtain the participation of people affected by their programmes and to ensure that these programmes and policies do not adversely affect economic, social and cultural rights.
6. Working document of the Commission Services on Tropical Forests Cooperation in 1992 under Budget Line B7-5041.
7. *Situation des populations indigenes des forets denses humides*, Lacito, ULB, Juin 1993, Rapport redige sous la direction de Serge Bahuchet et Pierre Maret.

ANNEX III

UNCED Declarations

1a. The Kari-Oca Conference in Rio[1]
by Marcos Terena

"Many, many years ago, when man conquered new worlds, our forefathers were more in harmony with nature, deciphering the tokens of time and living a cycle of life never understood and even considered unreal and utopic by the coloniser. That is why they were violently silenced, treated as savages, denied freedom and culture to make room for a new civilisation called the Americas. Now, however, as we are approaching the 21st century, modern man with all his technology discovers that indigenous peoples were right: modern civilisation is killing Mother Earth. The water and the air are polluted and the forests devastated. The United Nations, in line with this, decided to invite its Member States, its ecologists and scientists, to discuss and propose solutions for environmental preservation and development. At our first PREPCOM meetings, we observed that various governments were not prepared to listen to the voice of the Indigenous Peoples, but rather were lobbying to get financing in the name of 'transfer of technology', in the name of 'biodiversity' and of 'intellectual property'.

When we therefore consulted our spiritual leaders, they asked us 'how come that white man is concerned with Mother Earth only now?' Could it be that he is beginning to understand that nature is the dwelling place of the Great Creator? What is the meaning of indigenous participation in this Conference?. For folklore or simply to attract tourists?. If we want to participate with dignity, we have to build our own way, we have to create a platform from which the Earth itself can have the floor".

That is how KARI-OCA was born, a temple of indigenous wisdom, constructed for a science and know-how that cannot be learned in an ordinary school. 700 indigenous representatives from Asia, Africa, Europe, the Pacific, Australia and the Americas, needed to find a place to meet as the first ecologists of the planet. For five days they were to meet each other despite their different languages to talk not only of their problems such as self-determination, but also of the greater concern of the survival of humanity, poverty and hunger that dominate the white man's world. It was then decided to use the same language as in UNCED and draft a CHARTER OF THE EARTH inspired by indigenous philosophy. When it was completed, we were afraid that it would be transformed into just another historic document only to lie in the archives of the UN.

The relation of the Indigenous Peoples to nature is not only ecological or preservationist, it is particularly a relation of spiritual strength and of physical survival. Nature stands for hope for a better future for the coming generations.

Today, KARI-OCA no longer exists. The village was destroyed by arson. It was, however, not able to destroy the dreams of the Indigenous Peoples about the Earth and about the survival of the Peoples of the Earth. KARI-OCA was a symbol of indigenous resistance and has contributed its wisdom towards universal knowledge. It was for the first time that so many Indigenous Peoples had come together to help white man save the Earth: Could it be that after 500 years, white man and his modern society are now capable of listening to us? In the future, relations between white and indigenous peoples should be reconstructed. The great ecological resources are concentrated in areas where our peoples live, are also a concentration of great material wealth that fuels the ambition of white man. We were never an obstacle to progress when he wanted to realise some kind of development in indigenous territory, so accordingly white man should have respected indigenous thinking. The future of the Indians will be the future of the white man and will be the future of Mother Earth. We believe in this and we want the great leaders of the Earth such as the United Nations and the European Community to help us to continue to protect nature and guarantee a common future.

MARCOS TERENA was one of the principle organisers of the KARI-OCA Conference. He is a Terena Indigenous from Pantanal. He is a professional pilot, the spokesperson of the Indigenous Peoples at UNCED, Rio 1992, the President of the Intertribal Committee in Brazil. the organiser of the International Year of the World's Indigenous Peoples of Brazil and of the Second World Conference of Indigenous Peoples in 1994. Tel/Fax: 55.61.2432096.

1b. Kari-Oca Declaration

PREAMBLE:

The indigenous peoples of the Americas. Asia. Africa. Australia, Europe and the Pacific, united in one voice at KARI-OCA village express our collective gratitude to the indigenous peoples of Brazil.

Inspired by this historical meeting. We celebrate the spiritual unity of the indigenous peoples with the land and ourselves.

We continue building and formulating our united commitment to save our Mother the Earth.

We, the indigenous peoples, endorse the following declaration as our collective responsibility to carry our indigenous minds and voices into the future.

DECLARATION

WE THE INDIGENOUS PEOPLES, walk to the future in the footprints of our ancestors.

From the smallest to the largest living being, from the four directions, from the air, the land and the mountains, the creator has placed us, the indigenous peoples upon our Mother the Earth,

the footprints of our ancestors are permanently etched upon the lands of our peoples.

We, the indigenous peoples, maintain our inherent rights to self-determination, we have always had the right to decide our own forms of government, to use our own laws, to raise and educate our children, to our own cultural identity without interferance.

We continue to maintain our rights as peoples despite centuries of deprivation, assimilation and genocide.

We maintain our inalienable rights to our lands and territories. To all our resources — above and below — and to our waters. We assert our ongoing responsibility to pass these onto the future generations.

We cannot be removed from our lands. We, the indigenous peoples, are connected by the circle of life to our lands and environments.

We, the indigenous peoples, walk to the future in the footprints of our ancestors.

INDIGENOUS PEOPLES EARTH CHARTER

Human rights and international law

1. We demand the right to life.

2. International law must deal with the collective human rights of indigenous peoples.

3. There are many international instruments which deal with the rights of individuals but there are no declarations to recognise collective human rights. Therefore, we urge governments to support the United Nations Working Group on Indigenous Populations (UNWGIP) Universal Declaration of indigenous rights, which is presently in draft form.

4. There exist many examples of genocide against indigenous peoples. Therefore, the Convention against Genocide must be changed to include the genocide of indigenous peoples.

5. The United Nations should be able to send indigenous peoples' representatives, in a peace keeping capacity into indigenous territories where conflicts arise. This would be done at the request and consent of the indigenous peoples concerned.

6. The concept of *terra nullus* must be eliminated from international law usage. Many state governments have used internal domestic laws to deny us ownership of our own lands. These illegal acts should be condemned by the world.

7. Where small numbers of indigenous peoples are residing within state boundaries, so-called democratic countries have denied indigenous peoples the right of consent about their future, using the notion of majority rules to decide the future of indigenous peoples. Indigenous peoples right of consent to projects in their areas must be recognised.

8. We must promote the term "indigenous peoples" at all fora. The use of the term "indigenous peoples" must be without qualifications. (For the purposes of the declaration and this statement any use of the term indigenous peoples also includes tribal peoples).

9. We urge governments to ratify International Labour Organisation (ILO) Convention 169 to guarantee an international legal instrument for indigenous peoples.

10. Indigenous peoples' distinct and separate rights within their own territories must be recognised.

11. We assert our right to free passage through state imposed political boundaries dividing our traditional territories. Adequate mechanisms must be established to secure this right.

12. The colonial systems have tried to dominate and assimilate our peoples. However, our peoples remain distinct despite this pressure.

13. Our indigenous governments and legal systems must be recognised by the united nations, state governments and international legal instruments.

14. Our right to self-determination must be recognised.

15. We must be free from population transfer.

16. We maintain our right to our traditional way of life.

17. We maintain our right to our spiritual way of life.

18. We maintain the right to be free from pressures from multinational (transnational) corporations upon our lives and lands. All multinational corporations which are encroaching upon indigenous lands should be reported to the united nations transnational office.

19. We must be free from racism.

20. We maintain the right to decide the direction of our communities.

21. The united nations should have a special procedure to deal with issues arising from violations of indigenous treaties.

22. Treaties signed between indigenous peoples and non-indigenous peoples must be accepted as treaties under international law.

23. The united nations must exercise the right to impose sanction against governments that violate the rights of indigenous peoples.

24. We urge the united nations to include the issue of indigenous peoples in the agenda of the world conference of human rights to be held in 1993. The work done so far by the United Nations Inter-American Commission on Human Rights and the Inter-American Institute of Human Rights should be taken into consideration;

25. Indigenous peoples should have the right to their own knowledge, language, and culturally appropriate education, including bi-cultural and bi-lingual education. Through recognising both formal and informal ways, the participation of family and community is guaranteed.

26. Our health rights must include the recognition and respect of traditional knowledge held by indigenous healers. This knowledge, including our traditional medicines and their preventive and spiritual healing power must be recognized and protected against exploitation.

27. The World Court must extend its powers to include complaints by indigenous peoples.

28. There must be a monitoring system from this conference to oversee the return of delegates to their territories. The delegates should be free to attend and participate in international indigenous conferences.

29. Indigenous women's rights must be respected. Women must be included in. All local, national, regional and international organisations.

30. The above mentioned historical rights of indigenous peoples must be guaranteed in national legislations.

Lands and territories

31. Indigenous peoples were placed upon our mother, the earth by the creator. We belong to the land. We cannot be separated from our lands and territories.

32. Our territories are living totalities in permanent vital relation between human beings and nature. Their possession produce the development of our culture. Our territorial property should be inalienable, unceasable and not denied title. Legal economic and technical back up are needed to guarantee this.

33. Indigenous peoples inalienable rights to land and resources confirm that we have always had ownership and stewardship over our traditional territories. We demand that this be respected.

34. We assert our rights to demarcate our traditional territories. The definition of territory includes space (air), land, and sea. We must promote a traditional analysis of traditional land rights in all our territories.

35. Where indigenous territories have been degraded, resources must be made available to restore them. The recuperation of those affected territories is the duty of the respective jurisdiction in all nation states which can not be delayed. Within this process of recuperation the compensation for the historical ecological debt must be taken into account. Nation states must revise in depth the agrarian, mining and forestry policies.

36. Indigenous peoples reject the assertion of non-indigenous laws onto our lands. States cannot unilaterally extend their jurisdiction over our lands and territories. The concept of terra nullius should be forever erased from the law books of states.

37. We, as indigenous peoples, must never alienate our lands. We must always maintain control over the land for future generations.

38. If a non-indigenous government. Individual or corporation wants to use our lands. Then there must be a formal agreement which sets out the terms and conditions. Indigenous peoples maintain the right to be compensated for the use of their lands and resources.

39. Traditional indigenous territorial boundaries, including the waters, must be respected.

40. There must be some control placed upon environmental groups who are lobbying to protect our territories and the species within those territories. In many instances, environmental groups are more concerned about animals than human beings. We call for indigenous peoples to determine guidelines prior to allowing environmental groups into their territories.

41. Parks must not be created at the expense of indigenous peoples. There is no way to separate indigenous peoples from their lands.

42. Indigenous peoples must not be removed from their lands in order to make it available to settlers or other forms of economic activity on their lands.

43. In many instances, the numbers of indigenous peoples have been decreasing due to encroachment by non-indigenous peoples.

44. Indigenous peoples should encourage their peoples to cultivate their own traditional forms of products rather than to use imported exotic crops which do not benefit local peoples.

45. Toxic wastes must not be deposited in our areas. Indigenous peoples must realise that chemicals, pesticides and hazardous wastes do not benefit the peoples.
46. Traditional areas must be protected against present and future forms of environmental degradation.
47. There must be a cessation of all uses of nuclear material.
48. Mining of products for nuclear production must cease.
49. Indigenous lands must not be used for the testing or dumping of nuclear products.
50. Population transfer policies by state governments in our territories are causing hardship. Traditional lands are lost and traditional livelihoods are being destroyed.
51. Our lands are being used by state governments to obtain funds from the world bank, the international monetary fund, the asian-pacific development bank and other institutions which have led to a loss of our lands and territories
52. In many countries our lands are being used for military purposes. This is an unacceptable use of the lands.
53. The coloniser governments have changed the names of our traditional and sacred areas. Our children learn these foreign names and start to lose their identity, in addition, the changing of the name of a place diminishes respect for the spirits which reside in those areas.
54. Our forests are not being used for their intended purposes. The forests are being used to make money.
55. Traditional activities such as making pottery, are being destroyed by the importation of industrial goods. This impoverishes the local peoples.

Biodiversity and conservation

56. The vital circles are in a continuous interrelation in such way that the change of one of its elements affects the whole.
57. Climatic changes affect indigenous peoples and all humanity. In addition ecological systems and their rhythms are affected which contribute to the deterioration of our quality of life and increase our dependency.
58. The forests are being destroyed in the name of development and economical gains without considering the destruction of ecological balance. These activities do not benefit human beings, animals, birds and fish. The logging concessions and incentives to the timber, cattle and mining industries affecting the ecosystems and the natural resources should be cancelled.
59. We value the efforts of protection of the biodiversity but we reject to be included as part of an inert diversity which pretend to be maintained for scientific and folkloric purposes.
60. The indigenous peoples strategies should be kept in a reference framework for the formulation and application of national policies on environment and biodiversity.

Development strategies

61. indigenous peoples must consent for all projects in our territories. Prior to consent being obtained the people must be fully and entirely involved in any decisions. They must be given all the information about the project and its effects. Failure to do so should be considered a crime against the indigenous peoples. The person or persons who violate this should be tried in a world tribunal within the control of indigenous peoples set for such a purpose. This could be similar to the trials held after world war II.
62. We have the right to our own development strategies based on our cultural practices and with a transparent, efficient and viable management and with economical and ecological viability.
63. Our development and life strategies are obstructed by the interests of the governments and big companies and by the neo-liberal policies our strategies have, as fundamental condition, the existence of international relationship based on justice, equity and solidarity between the human beings and the nations.
64. Any development strategy should prioritise the elimination of poverty, the climatic guarantee. The sustainable manageability of natural resources, the continuity of democratic societies and the respect of cultural differences.
65. The global environmental facility should assign at best 20% for indigenous peoples' strategies and programmes of environmental emergency, improvement of life quality, protection of natural resources and rehabilitation of ecosystems. This proposal in the case of South America and the

Caribbean should be concrete in the indigenous development fund as a pilot experience in order to be extended to the indigenous peoples of other regions and continents.

66. The concept of development has meant the destruction of our lands. We reject the current definition of development as being useful to our peoples. Our cultures are not static and we keep our identity through a permanent recreation of our life conditions, but all of this is obstructed in the name of so called developments.

67. Recognising indigenous peoples harmonious relationship with nature, indigenous sustainable development models, development strategies and cultural values must be respected as distinct and vital sources of knowledge.

68. Indigenous peoples have been here since the time before time began. We have come directly from the creator. We have lived and kept the earth as it was on the first day. Peoples who do not belong to the land must go out from the lands because those things (so called "development" on the land) are against the laws of creator.

69.(a) In order for indigenous peoples to assume control, management and adminstration of their resources and territories, development projects must be based on the principles of self-determination and self-management.

(b) Indigenous peoples must be self-reliant.

70. If we are going to grow crops, these crops must feed the people. It is not appropriate that the lands be used to grow crops which do not benefit the local peoples.

71.(a) Regarding indigenous policies, state governments must cease attempts of assimilation and integration.

(b) We must never use the term "land claims". It is the non-indigenous people which do not have any land. All the land is our land. It is non-indigenous peoples who are making claims to our lands. We are not making claims to our lands.

72. There should be a monitoring body within the united nations to monitor all the land disputes around the world prior to development.

73. There should be a united nations' conference on the topic of "indigenous lands and development".

74. Non-indigenous peoples have come to our lands for the purpose of exploiting these lands and resources to benefit themselves, and to the impoverishment of our peoples. Indigenous peoples are victims of development. In many cases indigenous peoples are exterminated in the name of a development programme. There are numerous examples of such occurrences.

75. Development that occurs on indigenous lands, without the consent of indigenous peoples, must be stopped.

76. Development which is occurring on indigenous lands is usually decided without local consultation by those who are unfamiliar with local conditions and needs.

77. The Euro-centric notion of ownership is destroying our peoples. We must return to our own view of the world, of the land and of development . The issue cannot be separated from indigenous peoples' rights.

78. There are many different types of so-called development: road construction, communication facilities such as electricity, telephones. These allow developers easier access to the areas, but the effects of such industrialisation destroy the lands.

79. There is a world wide move to remove indigenous peoples from their lands and place them in villages. The relocation from the traditional territories is done to facilitate development.

80. It is not appropriate for governments or agencies to move into our territories and to tell our people what is needed.

81. In many instances, the state-governments have created artificial entities such as "district council" in the name of the state-government in order to deceive the international community. These artificial entities then are consulted about development in the area. The state-governments, then, claim that indigenous peoples were consulted about the project. These lies must be exposed to the international community.

82. There must be an effective network to disseminate material and information between indigenous peoples. This is necessary in order to keep informed about the problems of other indigenous peoples

83. Indigenous peoples should form and direct their own environmental network.

Culture. Science and intellectual property
84. We feel the earth as if we are within our mother. When the earth is sick and polluted, human health is impossible. To heal ourselves. We must heal the planet and to heal the planet we must heal ourselves.
85. We must begin to heal from the grass roots level and work towards the international level.
86. The destruction of the culture has always been considered an internal, domestic problem within national states. The united nations must set up a tribunal to review the cultural destruction of the indigenous peoples.
87. We need to have foreign observers come into our indigenous territories to oversee national state elections to prevent corruption.
88. The human remains and artifacts of indigenous peoples must be returned to their original peoples.
89. Our sacred and ceremonial sites should be protected and considered as the patrimony of indigenous peoples and humanity. The establishment of a set of legal and operational instruments at both national and international levels would guarantee this.
90. The use of existing indigenous languages is our right. These languages must be protected.
91. States that have outlawed indigenous languages and their alphabets should be censored by the United Nations.
92. We must not allow tourism to be used to diminish our culture. Tourists come into the communities and view the people as if indigenous peoples were part of a zoo. Indigenous peoples have the right to allow or to disallow tourism within their areas.
93. Indigenous peoples must have the necessary resources and control over their own education systems.
94. Elders must be recognised and respected as teachers of the young people.
95. Indigenous wisdom must be recognised and encouraged.
96. The traditional knowledge of herbs and plants must be protected and passed onto future generations.
97. Traditions cannot be separated from land, territory or science.
98. Traditional knowledge has enabled indigenous peoples to survive.
99. The usurping of traditional medicines and knowledge from indigenous peoples should be considered a crime against peoples.
100. Material culture is being used by the non-indigenous to gain access to our lands and resources, thus destroying our cultures.
101. Most of the media at this conference were only interested in the pictures which will be sold for profit. This is another case of exploitation of indigenous peoples. This does not advance the cause of indigenous peoples.
102. As creators and carriers of civilisations which have given and continue to share knowledge, experience and values with humanity, we require that our right to intellectual and cultural properties be guaranteed and that the mechanism for each implementation be in favour of our peoples and studied in depth and implemented. This respect must include the right over genetic resources, gene banks, biotechnology and knowledge of biodiversity programmes.
103. We should list the suspect museums and institutions that have misused our cultural and intellectual properties.
104. The protection norms and mechanisms of artistic and artisan creation of our peoples must be established and implemented in order to avoid plunder, plagiarism, undue exposure and use.
105. When indigenous peoples leave their communities, they should make every effort to return to the community.
106. In many instances, our songs, dances and ceremonies have been viewed as the only aspects of our lives. In some instances, we have been asked to change a ceremony or a song to suit the occasion. This is racism.
107. At local, national, international levels, governments must commit funds to new and existing resources to education and training for indigenous peoples, to achieve their sustainable development, to contribute and to participate in sustainable and equitable development at all levels. Particular attention should be given to indigenous women, children and youth.
108. All kinds of folkloric discrimination must be stopped and forbidden.
109. The united nations should promote research into indigenous knowledge and develop a network of indigenous sciences.

2. Non-legally binding authoritative statement of principles for a global consensus on the management, conservation and sustainable development of all types of forests[2]

2.(d) Governments should promote and provide opportunities for the participation of interested parties, including local communities and indigenous people, industries, labour, NGOs and individuals, forest dwellers and women, in the development, implementation and planning of national forest policies.

5.(a) National forest policies should recognise and duly support the identity, culture and the rights of indigenous people, their communities and other communities of forest dwellers. Appropriate conditions should be promoted for these groups to enable them to have an economic stake in forest use, perform economic activities and maintain cultural identity and social organisation, as well as adequate levels of livelihood and well being, through inter alia, those land tenure arrangements which serve as incentives for the sustainable management of forests.

6.(d) The role of planted forests and permanent agricultural crops as sustainable and environmentally sound sources of renewable energy and industrial raw material should be recognised, enhanced and promoted. Their contribution to the maintenance of ecological processes, to offsetting pressure on primary/old-growth forest and to providing regional employment and development with the adequate involvement of local inhabitants should be recognised and enhanced.

8.(f) National policies and/or legislation aimed at management conservation and sustainable development of forests should include the protection of ecologically viable representative or unique examples of forests, including the protection of ecologically viable representative or unique examples of forests, including primary/old forests, cultural, spiritual, historical, religious and other unique and valued forests of national importance.

12(d) Appropriate indigenous capacity and local knowledge regarding the conservation and sustainable development of forests should, through institutional and financial support, and in collaboration with the people in local communities concerned, be recognised, respected, recorded, developed and as appropriate, introduced in the implementation of programmes. Benefits arising from the utilisation of indigenous knowledge should therefore be equitably shared with such people.

3. Convention on Biological Diversity[3]

5 June, 1992.
Preamble

Recognising the close and traditional dependence of many indigenous and local communities embodying traditional lifestyles on biological resources, and the desirability of sharing equitably benefits arising from the use of traditional knowledge, innovations and practices relevant to the conservation of biological diversity and the sustainable use of its components,

Article 8, In-situ Conservation
Each Contracting Party shall, as far as possible and as appropriate:
(j) Subject to its national legislation, respect, preserve and maintain knowledge, innovations and practices of indigenous and local communities embodying traditional lifestyles relevant for the conservation and sustainable use of biological diversity and promote their wider application with the

approval and involvement of the holders of such knowledge, innovations and practices and encourage the equitable sharing of the benefits arising from the utilization of such knowledge, innovations and practices;

Article 9, Ex-situ Conservation
Each Contracting Party shall, as far as possible and as appropriate:
(d) Support local populations to develop and implement remedial action in degraded areas where biological diversity has been reduced;

Article 14, Impact Assessment and Minimising Adverse Impact
Each contracting Party, as far as possible and as appropriate, shall:
(a) Introduce appropriate procedures requiring environmental impact assessment of its proposed projects that are likely to have significant adverse effects on biological diversity with ta view to avoiding or minimising such effects, and, where appropriate, allow for public participation in such procedures;

Article 17, Exchange of information
2. Such exchange [of information from all publicly available sources, relevant to the conservation and sustainable use of biological diversity, taking into account the special needs of developing countries] shall include exchange of results of technical, scientific and socio-economic research, as well as information on training and surveying programmes, specialised knowledge, indigenous and traditional knowledge as such and in combination with the technologies referred to in Article 16, par. 1 (technologies relevant to the conservation and sustainable use of biological diversity). It shall also, where feasible, include repatriation of information.

Article 18, Technical and Scientific Cooperation
4. The Contracting Parties shall, in accordance with national legislation and policies, encourage and develop methods of cooperation for the development and use of technologies, including indigenous and traditional technologies, in pursuance of the objectives of this Convention. For this purpose, the Contracting Parties shall also promote cooperation in the training of personnel and exchange of experts.

4. Rio Declaration on Environment and Development

Having met at Rio de Janeiro from 3 to 14 June 1992
Reaffirming the Declaration of the UN Conference on the Human Environment, adopted at Stockholm on 16 June 1972, and seeking to build upon it,
With a goal of establishing a new and equitable global partnership through the creation of new levels of cooperation among States, key sectors of societies and people,
Working towards international agreements which respect the interests of all and protect the integrity of the global environmental and developmental system,
Recognising the integral and interdependent nature of the Earth, our home,
Proclaims that:

Principle 13
States shall develop national law regarding liability and compensation for the victims of pollution and other environmental damage. States shall also cooperate in an expeditious and more determined manner to develop further international law regarding liability and compensation for adverse effects of environmental damage caused by activities within their jurisdiction or control to areas beyond their jurisdiction.

Principle 22
Indigenous people and their communities, and other local communities, have a vital role in environmental management and development because of their knowledge and traditional practices. States should recognise and duly support their identity, culture and interests and enable their effective participation in the achievement of sustainable development.

AGENDA 21
CHAPTER 11
Combatting deforestation
A. Sustaining the multiple roles and functions of all types of forests, forest lands and woodlands.
Basis for action
11.1 There are major weaknesses in the policies, methods and mechanisms adopted to support and develop the multiple ecological, economic, social and cultural roles of trees, forests and forest land... More effective measures and approaches are often required at the national level to improve and harmonise policy formulation, planning and programming;...participation of the general public, especially women and indigenous people...

(a) Management related activities

(b) Promoting participation of the private sector, labour unions, rural cooperatives, local communities, indigenous people, youth, women, user groups and non-governmental organisations in forest-related activities, and access to information and training programmes within the national context;

(g) Establishing and strengthening capabilities for research related to the different aspects of forests and forest products, for example, on the sustainable management of forests, research on biodiversity, on the effects of air-borne pollutants, on traditional uses of forest resources by local populations and indigenous people, and on improving market returns and other non-market values from the management of forests;

(b) Data and information
(a) Collecting, compiling and regularly updating and distributing information on land classification and land use, including data on forest cover, areas suitable for afforestation, endangered species, ecological values, traditional/indigenous land use values, biomass and productivity, correlating demographic, socio-economic and forest resources information at the micro- and macro-levels, and undertaking periodic analyses of forest programmes;

B. Enhancing the protection, sustainable management and conservation of all forests, and the greening of degraded areas, through forest rehabilitation, afforestation, reforestation and other rehabilitative means.

(a) Management-related activities
11.13. Governments should recognise the importance of categorising forests, within the framework of long-term forest conservation and management policies, into different forest types and setting up sustainable units in every region/watershed with a view to securing the conservation of forests. Governments, with the participation of the private sector, NGOs, local community groups, indigenous people, women, local government units and the public at large, should act to maintain and expand the exiting vegetative cover wherever ecologically, socially and economically feasible, through technical cooperation and other forms of support. Major activities to be considered include:

(b) Establishing, expanding and managing, as appropriate to each national context, protected area systems, which includes systems of conservation units for their environmental, social and spiritual functions and values, including conservation of forests in representative ecological systems and landscapes, primary old-growth forest, conservation and management of wildlife, nomination of World Heritage Sites under the World Heritage Convention, as appropriate, conservation of genetic resources, involving in situ and ex situ measures and undertaking supportive measures to ensure sustainable utilisation of biological resources and conservation of biological diversity and the traditional forest habitats of indigenous people, forest dwellers and local communities;

(i) Launching or improving opportunities for participation of all people, including youth, women, indigenous people and local communities in the formulation, development and implementation of forest-related programmes and other activities, taking due account of the local needs and cultural values;

(b) Data and information
11.14 Management-related activities should involve collection, compilation and analysis of data/information, including baseline surveys. Some of the specific activities include;
(d) Carrying out surveys and research on local/indigenous knowledge of trees and forests and their uses to improve the planning and implementation of sustainable forest management;

(c) International and regional cooperation and coordination
(c) Human resource development
(c) Supporting local organisations, communities, NGOs and private land owners, in particular women, youth, farmers and indigenous people/shifting cultivators, through extension and provision of inputs and training.

(d) Capacity building
11.19. National governments, the private sector, local organisations/communities, indigenous people, labour unions and NGOs should develop capacities, duly supported by relevant international organisations, to implement the programme activities. Such capacities should be developed and strengthened in harmony with the programme activities. Capacity-building activities include policy and legal frameworks, national institution building, human resource development, development of research and technology, development of infrastructure, enhancement of public awareness etc.

C. Promoting efficient utilisation and assessment to recover the full valuation of the goods and services provided by forests, forest lands and woodlands.

(a) Management-related activities
11.22 Governments, with the support of the private sector, scientific institutions, indigenous people, NGOs, cooperatives and entrepreneurs, where appropriate, should undertake the following activities, properly coordinated at the national level, with financial and technical cooperation from international organisations:
(a) carrying our detailed investment studies, supply-demand harmonisation and environmental impact analysis...
(b) Formulating scientifically sound criteria and guidelines for the management, conservation and sustainable development of all types of forests;
(c) Improving environmentally sound methods and practices of forest harvesting...
(h) Promoting and supporting the management of wildlife, as well as eco-tourism, including farming, and encouraging and supporting the husbandry and cultivation of wild species, for improved rural income and employment, ensuring economic and social benefits without harmful ecological impacts (etc.);

CHAPTER 26
Recognising and strengthening the role of indigenous people and their communities

PROGRAMME AREA

Basis for action
26.1. Indigenous people and their communities have an historical relationship with their lands and are generally descendants of the original inhabitants of such lands. In the context of this chapter the term 'lands' is understood to include the environment of the areas which the people concerned traditionally occupy. Indigenous people and their communities represent a significant percentage of the global population. They have developed over many generations a holistic traditional scientific

knowledge of their lands, natural resources and environment. Indigenous people and their communities shall enjoy the full measure of human rights and fundamental freedoms without hindrance or discrimination. Their ability to participate fully in sustainable development practices on their lands has tended to be limited as a result of factors of an economic, social and historical nature. In view of the interrelationship between the natural environment and its sustainable development and the cultural, social, economic and physical well-being of indigenous people, national and international efforts to implement environmentally sound and sustainable development should recognize, accommodate, promote and strengthen the role of indigenous people and their communities.

26.2. Some of the goals inherent in the objectives and activities of this programme area are already contained in such international legal instruments as the ILO Indigenous and Tribal Peoples Convention (No. 169) and are being incorporated into the draft universal declaration on indigenous rights, being prepared by the United Nations working group on indigenous populations. The International Year for the World's Indigenous People (1993), proclaimed by the General Assembly in its resolution 45/1640f18 December 1990, presents a timely opportunity to mobilise further international technical and financial cooperation.

Objectives

26.3. In full partnership with indigenous people and their communities, Governments and, where appropriate, intergovernmental organisations should aim at fulfilling the following objectives:
(a) Establishment of a process to empower indigenous people and their communities through measures that include:
 (i) Adoption or strengthening of appropriate policies and/or legal instruments at the national level;
 (ii) Recognition that the lands of indigenous people and their communities should be protected from activities that are environmentally unsound or that the indigenous people concerned consider to be socially and culturally inappropriate;
 (iii) Recognition of their values, traditional knowledge and resource management practices with a view to promoting environmentally sound and sustainable development;
 (iv) Recognition that traditional and direct dependence on renewable resources and ecosystems, including sustainable harvesting, continues to be essential to the cultural, economic and physical well-being of indigenous people and their communities;
 (v) Development and strengthening of national dispute resolution arrangements in relation to settlement of land and resource-management concerns;
 (vi) Support for alterative environmentally sound means of production to ensure a range of choices on how to improve their quality of life so that they effectively participate in sustainable development;
 (vii) Enhancement of capacity-building for indigenous communities, based on the adaptation and exchange of traditional experience, knowledge and resource management practices, to ensure their sustainable development;
(b) Establishment, where appropriate, of arrangements to strengthen the active participation of indigenous people and their communities in the national formulation of policies, laws and programmes relating to resource management and other development processes that may affect them, and their initiation of proposals for such policies and programmes;
(c) Involvement of indigenous people and their communities at the national and local levels in resource management and conservation strategies and other relevant programmes established to support and review sustainable development strategies, such as those suggested in other programme areas of Agenda 21.

Activities

26.4. Some indigenous people and their communities may require, in accordance with national legislation, greater control over their lands, self-management of their resources, participation in development decisions affecting them, including, where appropriate, participation in the establishment or management of protected areas. The following are some of the specific measures which Governments could take:
(a) Consider the ratification and application of existing international conventions relevant to

indigenous people and their communities (where not yet done) and provide support for the adoption by the General Assembly of a declaration on indigenous rights;
(b) Adopt or strengthen appropriate policies and/or legal instruments that will protect indigenous intellectual and cultural property and the right to preserve customary and administrative systems and practices.

26.5. United Nations organisations and other international development and finance organisations and Governments should, drawing on the active participation of indigenous people and their communities, as appropriate, take the following measures, *inter alia,* to incorporate their values, views and knowledge, including the unique contribution of indigenous women, in resource management and other policies and programmes that may affect them:
(a) Appoint a special focal point within each international organisation, and organise annual inter-organisational coordination meetings in consultation with Governments and indigenous organisations, as appropriate, and develop a procedure within and between operational agencies for assisting Governments in ensuring the coherent and coordinated incorporation of the views of indigenous people in the design and implementation of policies and programmes. Under this procedure, indigenous people and their communities should be informed and consulted and allowed to participate in national decision-making, in particular regarding regional and international cooperative efforts. In addition, these policies and programmes should take fully into account strategies based on local indigenous initiatives;
(b) Provide technical and financial assistance for capacity building programmes to support the sustainable self-development of indigenous people and their communities;
(c) Strengthen research and education programmes aimed at:
(i) Achieving a better understanding of indigenous people's knowledge and management experience related to the environment, and applying this to contemporary development challenges;
(ii) Increasing the efficiency of indigenous people's resource management systems, for example, by promoting the adaptation and dissemination of suitable technological innovations;
(d) Contribute to the endeavours of indigenous people and their communities in resource management and conservation strategies (such as those that may be developed under appropriate projects funded through the Global Environmental Facility and Tropical Forestry Action Plan) and other programme areas of Agenda 21, including programmes to collect, analyze and use data and other information in support of sustainable development projects.

26.6. Governments, in full partnership with indigenous people and their communities should, where appropriate:
(a) Develop or strengthen national arrangements to consult with indigenous people and their communities with a view to reflecting their needs and incorporating their values and traditional and other knowledge and practices in national policies and programmes in the field of natural resource management and conservation and other development programmes affecting them;
(b) Cooperate at the regional level where appropriate, to address common indigenous issues with a view to recognising and strengthening their participation in sustainable development.

References
1. This introduction was originally written in Portuguese by Marcos Terena.
2. The principles apply to all types of forest in all geographic regions and the preamble reads that forestry issues and opportunities should be examined in a holistic and balanced manner within the overall context of environment and development, taking into consideration the multiple functions and uses of forests, including traditional ones, and the likely economic and social stress when these uses are constrained or restricted, as well as the potential for development that sustainable forest management can offer. The paragraphs quoted above refer to the rights of Indigenous Peoples.
3. Articles of particular relevance to Indigenous Peoples are quoted in full.

ANNEX IV

B'okob' Declaration
(Chimaltenango)

In B'okob' (Chimaltenango), territory of the Maya-Kaqchikeles in the martyred and heroic land of Guatemala, today in a state of Emergency, we held the First World Summit of Indigenous Peoples from May 24 to 28 with representatives from the four corners of the universe responding to the invitation of our sister Rigoberta Menchú Tum, Nobel Peace Prize and Good Will Ambassador of the International Year of Indigenous Peoples representing the Secretary General of the United Nations.

This first Summit was carried out as one of the satellite meeting of the World Conference on Human Rights scheduled for June 14 through 26, 1993 in Vienna, Austria, it created a space for us to bring together our words, our wisdom, our projects and our work for life and peace in the world.

In analyzing the current situation, we agreed that we live in constant danger of death as demonstrated in various ways: the increase in the most perverse and irrational of human activity; the rise of racism; the environmental destruction that threatens the future of the planet; the obscene opulence existing next to extreme misery and poverty; the voracious search for easy money that stops at nothing and tramples the weakest members of our societies as we can see in the trade of children etc. To summarise: we face world-wide disorder that is creating an unprecedented global crisis.

As we approach the twenty-first century, we, the indigenous peoples of the world are deeply concerned about the systematic violation of the rights of indigenous peoples, the increase in violence against indigenous women and children, the marginalisation that we suffer in decision-making, the increasing discrimination we face, and the various forms of exploitation carried out by Nation-States and transnational corporations against our peoples.

Before this disturbing situation, the ancient cultures which our peoples embody are emerging with a message of hope for a more equal and just future. We are living examples that such a future is possible, as we have demonstrated throughout our histories, with our efforts, our values, our worldview. We hope for a future in which our mother earth becomes healthy again, in which we enjoy equal relationships, mutual respect, and solidarity among individuals, peoples and the different nations of the world.

Despite the advances of the past years in spreading the voices and demands of the indigenous peoples, we still suffer notable inequalities in how our problems are responded to at the national and international levels. As a result of our efforts, the United Nations has created several instruments meant to protect the specific rights of the indigenous peoples. However, there are many States which have still not ratified these instruments and others which have responded only in a formal manner, without incorporating these instruments into their practices. Despite our efforts the marginalisation of the indigenous peoples continues.

While the declaration of the International Year of the Indigenous Peoples constituted an important step forward, in practice we have found that one year is not enough to effectively develop the "new relationships" that we are proposing.

Taking this situation into consideration, the First Summit of the Indigenous Peoples resolves:
1) to establish the Decade of Indigenous Peoples from 1994 to 1004, and to urge the United Nations to endorse this decade.
2) To reaffirm the rights of Indigenous Peoples to political, economic, social and cultural development based on full participation in the decision making process and self-determination.
3) To urge all governments to ratify all international instruments that promote respect for indigenous peoples' rights.
4) To support the convening of summits of indigenous peoples at the national level to encourage unity and the struggles of indigenous peoples.
5) To create the High Commission on Indigenous Peoples meant to ensure respect for indigenous peoples' rights.
6) To declare December 10th of every year International Day of the Indigenous Peoples of the World.

We also call on the United Nations to ratify, endorse and support this Declaration.

We propose the following goals for the International Decade of Indigenous Peoples:
1) To sensitise the world's peoples to the reality and the perspectives of the indigenous peoples through the development of educational campaigns directed towards the entire society, as well as education among indigenous peoples directed towards affirming their identities and their rights.
2) To demand that the United Nations approve the Universal Declaration of the Rights of Indigenous Peoples and the respective ratifications and implementations on the part of the various States.
3) To demand that the United Nations continue and strengthen the Working Group on Indigenous Peoples as a permanent institution working to monitor and ensure the fulfilment of the rights stated in the declaration.
4) Urge the United Nations, governments and multilateral agencies to guarantee and ensure the access and participation of the indigenous peoples' delegations to the decision making bodies.
5) To support a world-wide campaign against racism.
6) To encourage the building of strong linkages and exchange networks among indigenous peoples.
7) To develop more effective communication systems for the exchange of information among indigenous peoples.
8) To foster the human development of the indigenous peoples.
9) To create, approve and subsequently ratify an international convention for the elimination of discrimination against indigenous peoples.

This Decade is not meant to benefit only indigenous peoples, but instead represents an effort to find creative alternatives to the problems face by all people who are politically marginalised, economically exploited and culturally discriminated against.

Our contribution to the creation of a new model of society must be accompanied by the support and solidarity of the entire society, of the Nation-States, and the different international organisations so that we can establish new relations within a pluri-linguistic and multi-cultural framework.

Indigenous brothers and sisters: from the land of the Mayan chiefs Kahib'Imox and B'elejeb'K'at, drawing on the strength, heroism, and wisdom of our ancestors, we call on you to continue to work with us to consolidate our unity. Our struggle and our energy must go from now on to the creation and implementation of activities that will ensure the development and the future of our peoples.

B'okob' (Chimaltenango) May 27, 1993.

ANNEX V

Final outcome of the World Conference on Human Rights Vienna, 14-25 June 1993[1]

PART I — Preamble
Preambular 10
Welcoming the International Year of the World's Indigenous People in 1993 as a reaffirmation of the commitment of the international community to ensure their enjoyment of all human rights and fundamental freedoms and to respect the value and diversity of their cultures and identities;

PART II — Declaration of Principles
Paragraph 11
The World Conference recognises the inherent dignity and the unique contribution of indigenous people to the development and plurality of society and strongly reaffirms the commitment of the international community to their economic, social and cultural well-being and their enjoyment of the fruits of sustainable development. States should ensure the full and free participation of indigenous people in all aspects of society, in particular in matters of concern to them. Considering the importance of the promotion and protection of the rights of indigenous people, and the contribution of such promotion and protection to the political and social stability of the States in which such people live, States should, in accordance with international law, take concerted positive steps to ensure respect for all human rights and fundamental freedoms of indigenous people, on the basis of equality and non-discrimination and recognise the value and diversity of their distinct identities, cultures and social organisation.

PART III — Action Programme
II.B Indigenous People

1. The World Conference calls on the Working Group on Indigenous Populations of the Sub-Commission on Prevention of Discrimination and Protection of Minorities to complete the drafting of a declaration on the rights of indigenous people, at its eleventh session.

2. The World Conference recommends that the Commission on Human Rights consider the renewal and updating of the mandate of the Working Group on Indigenous Populations upon completion of the drafting of a declaration on indigenous people.

3. The World Conference also recommends that advisory services and technical assistance programmes within the United Nations system respond positively to requests by States for assistance which would be of direct benefit to indigenous people. The World Conference further recommends that adequate human and financial resources be made available to the Centre for Human Rights within the overall framework of strengthening the Centre's activities as envisaged by this document.

4. The World Conference urges States to ensure the full and free participation of indigenous people in all aspects of society, in particular in matters of concern to them.

5. The World Conference recommends that the General Assembly proclaim an International Decade of the World's Indigenous People, to begin from January 1994, including action-oriented programmes, to be decided upon in partnership with indigenous people. An appropriate Voluntary Trust Fund should be set up for this purpose. In the framework of such a Decade, the establishment of a permanent forum for indigenous people in the United Nations system should be considered.

References
1. The European Community, being aware of the important role of NGOs with respect to the worldwide promotion of human rights, has made available funds amounting to more than 1 MECU in order to support the participation of NGOs (also indigenous peoples organisations) in the regional conferences held during the preparatory process and in the World Conference itself.

ANNEX VI

List of International and Interregional Indigenous Peoples Organisations and Support Groups[1]

International Indigenous Organisations[2]

Indigenous Survival International, 105/298 Elgin St, Ottawa ON K1N 9K1, Canada. Tel: 1.613.2303616.

World Council of Indigenous Peoples, (WCIP), 555 King Edward Avenue, Ottawa, Ontario K1N 6N5, Canada. Tel: 613.2309030. Fax: 613.2309340.

International Indian Treaty Council, IITC, 710 Clayton St. 2, San Francisco CA 94117, USA. Tel: 415.5660251. Fax: 415.5660442.

Assembly of First Nations, 47 Clarence St. Suite 300, Ottawa ON K1N 9K1, Canada. Tel: 1.613.2360673. Fax: 2385780.

Samiraddi, Saami Council, FIN-99980 Ohcejohka/Utsjoki, Finland, Tel: 358.69771351. Fax: 358.69771353.

Information Network of Indigenous Peoples of the Americas, INIPA, 54 Lochearne Street, Hamilton, Ontario LFR 1W1, Canada. Tel: 4165237356.

COICA, Coordinadora de Organisaciones Indigenas de la Cuenca Amazonica. Calle Alemania 832 y Av. Mariana de Jesus, Quito; Casilla Postal 17-21753, Quito, Ecuador. Tel: 553297. Fax: ibid. and; U.S. Address: 1011 Orleans St. New Orleans LA 70116. Tel: 504.5227185. Fax: 504.5227185.

SAIIC. South & Meso American Indian Information Centre, PO Box 28703, Oakland, CA 94604. Tel: 510.8344263. Fax: 510.8344264.

Inuit Circumpolar Conference, 429 O Street Suit 211, Anchorage AK 99501, Alaska. And, Address in Canada; 650 32nd Avenue, Lachine Quebec H8T 3K4, Canada. Tel: 514.6373771. Fax: 514.6373146.

Instituto Indigenista Interamericano, J. Matos Mar, Avda. Nubes 232, Col. Pedregal de San Angel, Delegacion Alvaro Obregon, Mexico City, Mexico, Tel: 52.5.6521133. Fax: 52.5.6521274.

Indigenous Women's Network, National Office, PO Box 174, Lake Elmo MN, 55042, USA. Tel: 512.2583880.

Encuentro de Mujeres Indigenas de Centro y Sud America, ACIMA, Casilla 9775, La Paz, Bolivia. Tel: 591.2.330478.

Asia Indigenous Peoples Pact, 80/138 Soi Ram Town House, Ramkhamhaeng SOI 24, BKK 10240, Thailand. Tel: and Fax: 66.2.3189034.

Nuclear Free and Independent Pacific Movement, Pacific Concerns Resource Center, General Coordination Office, C.P.O. Box 3148, Auckland, New Zealand. Tel: 09.3075.862. Fax: 09.3777651.

The Coordinating Committee of the *World International Alliance of the Indigenous-Tribal peoples of the Tropical Forests*[3]
AMAZONIA
COICA, Coordinadora de las Organizaciones, Indigenas de la Cuenca Amazonica, Calle Alemania 832 y Mariana de Jesus, Quito, Ecuador. Casilla Postal 17-21-753. Tel and Fax: 593.2.553297.
CENTRAL AMERICA AND CARIBBEAN
Associacion Cultural Sejecto, 400 Mts. Este Municipalidad de Moravia, San Jose, Costa Rica. Tel: (606) 361 427. Fax: (506) 402 276.

SOUTHERN CONE
Centro Mocovi 'lalek Lav'a, Casilla de Correo 36, 2728 Melincue (Santa Fe), Ariel Aruajo, Argentina. Tel: 54 (465) 99 015.

AFRICA
Association for the promotion of the BATWA, BP 2472 Kigali, Rwanda. Tel: 250.75619 (COSNV). Tel: 250.74074 (OXFAM)

CONTINENTAL ASIA
Naga Peoples Movement for Human Rights, c/o CEC Office F-20 Ground Floor, Jangpura Extn. New Delhi 14, India.

BAHASA REGION
Sahabat Alam Malaysia (Sarawak), SAM Office Marudi, PO Box 216, 9858 Baram, Sarawak, East Malaysia. Tel: (085) 755 501.

MARITIME ASIA AND PACIFIC
KAMP, National Federation of the Indigenous Peoples of the Philippines, Kalipunan ng mga Katutubong Mamamayan ng Pilipinas Webjet Bldg., Room 701, No. 64 Quezon Avenue, Cor BMA St., Quezon City, Philippines or: P.O. Box No 10125, Main, Quezon City, Philippines. Tel: 63.2.7120951.

Regional indigenous organisations

ASIA
CONTO, Center for the Coordination of Non Governmental Tribal Development Organisations, P.O. Box 113, Amphur Muang, Chiang Mai 50000, Thailand.

Karen National Union (KNU), Department of Foreign Affairs of the National Coalition Government of the Union of Myanmar, Dr. Em Marta, PO Box 11-792, Phrakhanong PO, Bangkok 10110, Thailand.

Ainu Association of Hokkaido, Hishi 7, Kita 3, Chuo-ku, Sapporo, Hokkaido, 060 Japan.

Cordillera Peoples Alliance, (mailing address): Lock Box 596, GARCOM-Baguio, P.O. Box 7691, DAPO 1300, Pasay City, Philippines. (Office address: c/o Room 314 Laperal Building, Session Road, Baguio City, 2600 Philippines.

Indigenous Peoples Research Centre, Mindanao, PO Box 332, 8000 Davao City, Philippines, Tel: 79947.

Chittagong Hill Tracts Hill Peoples Council, Suboth Bikash Chakma, 98 Tejkuni Para (G Floor), Farm Gate, Dhaka 1275, Bangladesh.

West Papuan Peoples Front, P.O. Box 40066, 1009BB, Amsterdam, The Netherlands. Tel: 31.15.619308, Fax: 31.15.566071.

AUSTRALASIA AND THE PACIFIC
La Ligue Polynesienne Independante des Droits de l'Hommes Te Hui Tiamu, Faone, P.K. 54.200 Tairapu-est, Tahiti, Polynesie francaise, B.P. 4611 Papeete Tahiti, Gabriel Tetiarahi, Coordinateur national, Tel: 689.521371. Fax: 689.572880.

NCDBR, National Coalition to defend Black Rights, P.O. Box 498, Broadway 2007, N.S.W. Australia. Tel: 61.2.6989826. Fax: 6126989166.

National Maori Congress, PO Box 2799 Wellington, Aotearoa, New Zealand. Tel: 61.4.4992429. Fax: 61.4.4992422.

RUSSIA
Association of Small Peoples of the Soviet North. Sanghi Wladimir Michailowitsch, Nebereshnara, T. Schewtschenko 3, Korpus 3, Quartira 119, 121248 Moscow, Russia. Tel: 0952434159.

AFRICA
Ethnic Minority Rights Organisation of Africa, 63 Tejuosho Street, PO Box 696, Swrulere, Lagos,

Nigeria. Tel: 01.832218, 837955. Fax: 2341.832218.

Survie Touaregue — Temoust, 252 bis rue Paul Bert, 69003 Lyon, France. Tel: 33.72335187. Fax: 33.72120797.

Nyae Development Foundation, (Bushmen) P.O. Box 9026, Eros, Windhoek, Namibia. Tel:061.36327, Fax: 061.225997.

Centre for Human Rights, Private Bag 00416, Gaborone, Botswana. Tel: 267.306998. Fax: 267307778.

Inyuat e Maa, Maa Pastoralist Development Organisation, P.O. Box 2720, Arusha, Tanzania. Fax: 8289.8690.8220.

Korongoro Integrated Peoples oriented to conservation, PO Box 94, Loliondo, Tanzania.

Maa Development Welfare Association, P.O. Box 75303, Nairobi, Kenia.

SOUTH AND CENTRAL AMERICA
COIAB, Cordinacao das Organizacoes Indigenas da Amazonia Brasileira, Av. Ayrao 235, Matinha, Cxa Postal 3264, 69025290 Manaus, AM Brasil. Tel: 092.2330548, Fax: 0922330209.

COIP, Caribbean Organisation of Indigenous Peoples, PO Box 229, Belize City, Belize. Tel: 501.44100. Fax: 50132136.

CORPI, Coordinadora Regional de Pueblos Indigenas de Centro America, Mexico y Panama, Apartado 2720, San Jose 1000, Costa Rica.

COI, Congreso de Organizaciones Indias de Centro America, Mexico y Panama, Apartado Postal 536, Panama 1, Panama.

SUPPORT GROUPS
Survival International, 310 Edgware Rd. London W2 1DY, UK, Tel: 44.71.7235535. Fax: 44.71.7234059.

European Alliance with Indigenous Peoples, Keltenlaan 20, 1040 Brussels, Belgium. Tel: 32.2.7333653. Fax: 32.2.7368054.
Member Organisations;
IWGIA, International Work Group for Indigenous Affairs, Fiolstraede 10, DK 1171, Copenhagen, Denmark. Tel: 45.33.124724. Fax: 45.33.147749.
KWIA, Support Group for Indigenous Peoples, Breughelstraat 31-33, B-2018 Antwerp, Belgium, Tel: 32.3.2188488. Fax: 32.3.2304540.
NCIV, Netherlands Centre for Indigenous Peoples, PO Box 4098, Amsterdam 1009 AB, The Netherlands. Tel: 31.20.6938625. Fax: 31;206652818.
Anti Slavery International, 180 Brixton Rd, London SW9 6AT, UK. Tel: 44.71.5824040. Fax: 44.71.5870573.[4]

Minority Rights Group, 379 Brixton Road, London SW9 7DE, UK. Tel: 44.71.7386265. Fax: 44.71.9789498.

UNPO, Unrepresented Nations and Peoples Organisation, M. Walt van Praag, Office of the General Secretary, 40A Javastraat, 2585 AP The Hague, The Netherlands, Tel: 31.70.3603318, Fax: 31.70.3603346.

Gaia Foundation, 18 Well Walk, Hampstead, London NW3 1LD, UK. Tel: 44.71.4355000. Fax: 44.71.4310551.

Amigos de los Indios, Apartado de Correos 20-174, Madrid 28080, Spain. Tel: 34.1.205032. Fax: 34.1.205032.

Incomindios, Switzerland, Jupiter Strasse 4, Zurich CH-8032, Tel: 41.1.3832131. Tel: 41.61.2727249. Fax: 41.61.2727181.

Gesellschaft Fur Bedrohte Volker, Deutschland, Dustere Strasse 20a, Goettingen D-340. Tel: 49.551.499060. Fax: 49.551.58028.

Gesellschaft für Bedrohte Völker - Osterreich, Mariahilfer Strasse 105/11/13, A-1060, Vienna, Austria, Tel: 43.1.5972276. Fax: 43.1.5973743.

Cultural Survival, 53 A Church St. Cambridge MA 02138, USA, Tel: 617.4952562. Fax: 617.4951396.

Tribal Act, BP 134, 75675, Paris, Cedex 14, France.

ICRA, International Commission for the Rights of ethnic minorities and Aboriginal people, B.P 1-498, Route du Lac, 88400 Xonrupt-Longemer, France. Tel: 3329600819. Fax: 3329630559.

CASNP, Canadian Alliance in Solidarity with the Native Peoples, PO Box 574, Stn P Toronto, Ontario, M55 2T1. Tel: 416.9721573.

European Committee for Human Rights in Malaysia, Dr. Paul Lim, c/o Av. Demolder, 92, Limelette, Belgium. Tel: 32.2.7367645.

World Rainforest Movement, 8 Chapel Row, Chatlington, OX73NA, UK, Tel: 44.60876691. Fax: 44.60876743.

OTHER RESOURCES

Office of Rigoberta Menchú Tum, Nobel Prize 1992, Patricio Sanz Num. 449, Col. Del Valle, C.P. 03100 México D.F., Telefax: 52.5.5230492/6827624.

doCip, Indigenous Peoples Centre for Documentation Research and Information, 14, Av. Trembley, CH-120g Geneva, Switzerland. Tel: 41.22.7403433. Fax: 41.22.7403454.

AIPIN, Agencia Internacional de Prensa India Madero 67, Room 611, Col. Centro, México 06000 D.F., México. Fax: 52.5.7618573. Tel: 1031151 AIPIN, UK. Tel/Fax: 44.81.5148546.

CLACPI, Comite Latinoamericano de Cine de Pueblos Indigenas, AP 270031, Lima, Peru. Tel. 51.14.617949. Fax: ibid.

American Indian Film Institute, 333 Valencia Street 322, San Francisco CA 94103, Tel: 415.5540525.

Third Horizon Foundation & CIMR (distribution of indigenous films and films on indigenous peoples), Mijndensedijk 74, NL-3631NS Nieuwersluis, Tel: 31.29433459, Fax: 31.29431877.

Indigenous Knowledge Resource Centres, c/o Nuffic/CIRAN, Centre for International Research and Advisory Networks, PO Box 90734, 2509 LS The Hague, The Netherlands. Tel: 31.70.3510574. Fax: 31.70.3510513.

References
1. I am very grateful to Johan Bosman of the Belgian support group for indigenous peoples, KWIA for providing most of the names and addresses of above indigenous organisations and support groups.
2. Above list is by no means exhaustive. It contains a number of addresses of indigenous and support group organisations that we have met, worked with or that are known to KWIA. For a comprehensive overview of local, national and regional indigenous organisations and support groups in the Americas, please consult the *1992 International Directory & Resource Guide,* 500 years of resistance, published by the South and Meso American Indian Information Centre (SAIIC), PO Box 28703, Oakland, CA 94604, Tel: 510. 8344263; Fax: 5108344264.
3. From 12-15 February 1992 the first Conference of the World Alliance of the Indigenous and Tribal Peoples of the Tropical Forests was held in Penang, Malaysia. At this conference, a **Charter** of the Indigenous-Tribal Peoples of the Tropical Forests and a **resolution** of the Conference of Indigenous-Tribal Peoples of the Tropical Forests were adopted. Also the **World International Allicance** of the Indigenous-Tribal Peoples of the Tropical Forests' was constituted.

4. The European Alliance is producing a practical manual on the European Community and indigenous peoples. This manual wil provide factual information about EC activities affecting indigenous peoples, including an explanation of how the EC works, what are its policies, how organisations should get in touch with the EC and how and who to lobby.

Both the Alliance and its members have been receiving financial support from the European Commission under Budget heading A3030; since 1994 — B7/5240.